From Viracocha to the Virgin of Copacabana

From Viracocha to the Virgin of Copacabana

Representation
of the Sacred
at Lake Titicaca

VERÓNICA SALLES-REESE

University of Texas Press, Austin

Photo credits: Figures 2 and 3 courtesy of Teresa Mesa and Museo Casa Moneda, Potosí; Figure 4 courtesy Museo Casa Moneda, Potosí.

Requests for permission to reproduce material from this work should be sent to Permissions, University of Texas Press, P.O. Box 7819, Austin, TX 78713-7819.

∞ The paper used in this publication meets the minimum requirements of American National Standard for Information Sciences—Permanence of Paper for Printed Library Materials, ANSI Z39.48-1984.

Library of Congress Cataloging-in-Publication Data

Salles-Reese, Verónica, 1950–
    From Viracocha to the Virgin of Copacabana : representation of the sacred at Lake Titicaca / Salles-Reese. — 1st ed.
        p.   cm.
    Includes bibliographical references and index.
    ISBN 0-292-77712-4 (cloth : alk. paper).—ISBN 0-292-77713-2 (pbk. : alk. paper)
    1. Folk literature, Bolivian—Lake Titicaca (Peru and Bolivia)—History and criticism.   2. Colla Indians—Religion.   3. Colla mythology.   4. Incas—Religion.   5. Inca mythology.   6. Mary, Blessed Virgin, Saint—Cults—Bolivia—Copacabana (Manco Kapac)   7. Mary, Blessed Virgin, Saint, in literature—History and criticism.   8. Bolivian literature—Colonial influences—History and criticism.   9. Sacred space—Titicaca Lake (Peru and Bolivia)   10. Titicaca Lake (Peru and Bolivia) in literature—History and criticism.
I. Title.
GR133.T57S35   1997
200'.984'12—dc20   96-21683

Design by Jace Graf

For Bethsy, Alan, Mutzy, Paula, Ximena, and Natasha

Contents

Acknowledgments

During the writing of this project, which began as a doctoral dissertation at Johns Hopkins University, I received invaluable support and encouragement from my professors and fellow graduate students. I want to express my gratitude in particular to Sarah Castro-Klaren, under whose direction I completed the dissertation; to Sabine MacCormack and Rolena Adorno, both of whom provided the inspiration for my research; to John Russell-Wood, who enthusiastically supported my project; and to Nicolás Wey-Gómez, who provided not only constant intellectual dialog, but also constructive readings of my work at every stage of the process.

The evolution of the dissertation into the present book involved a translation from the original Spanish version for which I am deeply indebted to Jorge Olivares, Michael Gerli, Tom Walsh, and John Breslin. Some of the ideas and materials of the present study have appeared as articles in the *Journal of Hispanic Philology;* in *Crítica y Descolonización,* edited by Beatriz González and Lucia Costigan; and in *Etnicidad, Economía y Simbolismo en los Andes,* edited by Silvia Arze, et al. I am grateful to those who have given me permission to reprint. I also wish to thank Teresa Mesa and the Museo Casa Moneda in Potosí for allowing me to reproduce their artwork as part of the illustrations in the book.

Without the understanding and constant support of Alan Reese neither the dissertation nor the book would have ever become a reality. My daughters, from whom I have had to steal innumerable hours, filled me with the love necessary to endure the most trying moments.

Note: The spelling of the toponymy "Tiwanaku" that appears throughout this study has many variants, such as Tiahua nacu or Tiagua nacu. I chose to use "Tiwanaku" in my text.

From Viracocha to the Virgin of Copacabana

Introduction

En los principios del mundo os veo,
oh dioses de los páramos y de las cordilleras.
Dioses que alimentaron
el pavor y las vigilias de mis antepasados,
reinando desde la hosca montaña sin auroras,
el ceño cruzado de centellas,
la mano sobre el trueno.
—Óscar Cerruto

Lake Titicaca has performed a sacred function for all of the cultures which have flourished on its shores. In both ancient and modern times, each culture has marked the lake's sacredness through various modes of representation: through its own material production, its own intellectual constructs, and its own narratives.

The purpose of this study is to offer a history of the discourse of the representation of the sacred in the region of Lake Titicaca by focusing on narratives which relate this geographical space to a transcendent or divine order. My aim is to shed light on the cultural contexts which shape these discursive representations. I interpret the sacred relevance of the lake diachronically, from pre-Hispanic times to the enthronement of the Virgin of Copacabana in 1583, the latest avatar of sacredness at Lake Titicaca.

Numerous chronicles published in the sixteenth and seventeenth centuries that contain narratives and testimonials of the pre-Hispanic and colonial periods constitute the primary sources for this inquiry. Alonso Ramos Gavilán's *Historia del celebre santuario de Nuestra Señora de Copacabana* (1621), which concerns itself with Lake Titicaca's special religious significance, is for this study the most important of these chronicles. Many of the scholars who have studied the surviving chronicles of the region have generally discredited their supposed historical veracity. I intend, however, to analyze their discursive dimensions without delving into their historical referentiality. I propose, for example, that Ramos Gavilán's *Historia*, like many chronicles written during the colonial period, is a remarkable attempt both to understand and

1

to reorganize the religious experience of the Andean world before the Conquest. To be sure, this text implies a reorganization of that experience within religious categories acceptable to the hegemonic order during the colonial period. Ramos Gavilán's text, more than any other chronicle of the period, is an invaluable source for those who would seek to understand the intellectual and cultural history of the region. I show that the originality of Ramos Gavilán's text resides in the paradoxical stance it takes when confronting the issue of evangelization. Apparently subscribing to the official policy on the abolition of idolatry which had been in effect since the middle of the sixteenth century, the Augustinian friar describes and advocates a plan for evangelization which replicates the nonviolent precepts that had been laid out some fifty years before by Fray Bartolomé de Las Casas. In essence, Ramos Gavilán attempts to reconcile the Andean past with the advent of Christianity to the region.

I argue that the history of the sacred in the region of Lake Titicaca may be divided into three narrative cycles: the Kolla, the Inca, and the Christian. Although these narrative cycles correspond to three culturally distinct and chronologically sequential periods (the pre-Inca, Inca, and Christian), they often merge anachronistically in one text. In order to reconfigure each of these narrative cycles, not only do I make use of the existing written narratives, but I also take into account the oral and iconographic traditions. I pay particular attention to the way in which each narrative cycle appropriates and recontextualizes material from previous cycles and to the way they all create links of continuity in the representation of the sacred at Lake Titicaca. The history of the representation of the sacred at Lake Titicaca shows that the discourse of the sacred from the different cultures of the region is a sustained discourse of appropriation and recontextualization that corresponds to changes in the nature of culturally hegemonic structures over time.

In the first chapter, in which I discuss how and why Lake Titicaca must be regarded as a sacred space, I employ the tools of religious phenomenology in order to examine the way in which the constitutive elements of sacred spaces manifest themselves at Lake Titicaca throughout history.

In the second chapter, in which I focus on the narrative cycle of the Kolla, employing the categories that anthropologists and historians have distinguished as exclusively Andean, I outline the history of the different cultures on the lake before the Inca conquest of the area (ca. A.D. 1400). I particularly examine the different versions of the Andean creation myth compiled by the chroniclers, in order to parse out from these myths those elements that pertain exclusively to Western thought. Moreover, offering possible explanations for the multiple versions, I trace their points of convergence in an attempt to retrieve the pristine myths which the Indians sought to communicate to the Spaniards.

In the third chapter, which opens with a description of the historical circumstances at the time the Incas conquered the Kollao region, I analyze those narratives that placed the origin of the Incas in Lake Titicaca. The analysis of these myths allows one to infer the existence of two parallel subcycle narratives which pertain to two distinct social units: the Inca ethnos and the royal *panaca*. I also discuss in this chapter the relationship between the Inca narrative cycle and the Kolla narrative cycle.

In the fourth chapter, in which I briefly discuss the historical events that led to the Christianization of the region of Lake Titicaca, I pay particular attention to the political and religious context within which emerge the controversy concerning the issue of evangelization and the related polemic on the abolition of idolatry. Two Christian narrative subcycles appear at this time: the first describes a pre-Hispanic evangelization which attempts to link the Andean past to contemporary attempts at Christianization in the area; the second centers on the miracles of the Virgin of Copacabana. I also examine Fray Alonso Ramos Gavilán's evangelical and cultural program. The Augustinian friar aspires, as does the Inca narrative cycle, to make a connection between the hegemonic present and the region's historical ethnic past in order to lend continuity and coherence to a world shaken by the conflicts and divisions caused by the Spanish conquest.

My investigation has profited from recent methodologies which have contributed to a deeper understanding of Andean culture. I have specifically availed myself of historical, ethnological, anthropological, and theological studies published in recent years by scholars such as Mircea Eliade in his work on religions and myths, Roger Caillois in his studies on the sacred, Sabine MacCormack in her contribution on Andean religion, Thérése Bouysse Cassagne in her research on Lake Titicaca and Aymara thought, and Teresa Gisbert in her work on pre-Hispanic and colonial art in the Viceroyalty of Peru.

1

The Sacred Dimension of Lake Titicaca

SIGNIFICANT PLACES

There are places in the world that, for obvious or not-so-obvious reasons, are privileged by their inhabitants or by their visitors. Individuals as well as cultures single out either natural locations or man-made structures for their compelling beauty, imposing ugliness, relative strategic significance, or their promising riches. A space may be endowed with a special function within a cultural system because of its uniqueness. For example, a spot marking the convergence of two or more rivers may constitute an optimum site because of its fertility, for its propitiousness for establishing agricultural settlements. It is not surprising, then, that modern cities have been built on ancient foundations located at key geographical intersections. The richness of the soil, its ability to sustain its inhabitants, makes possible the development and growth of cultures and populations. If some sites are singled out for their obvious economic importance, yet others may be singled out for their strategic, military, or political significance.

The distinction assigned to a place may be transitory, as in the case of Potosí during the seventeenth century, whose importance diminished in direct relation to the exhaustion of its riches. The significance of other locations may endure for centuries, even millennia, primarily because of their crucial locations, as is the case of Gibraltar, a fortress still occupying a highly privileged place in the Western European political imagination. Spaces, then, possess symbolic power and may incite an individual or a nation to an array of emotions and behaviors, which may range from acts of passive contemplation to ones of active exploitation, depending on the function and value assigned to a site. Apart from their political or economic relevance, some sites may also possess profound religious significance for a culture or for members of a certain faith. Perceived as sacred places, these spots are imaginatively endowed with a numinous essence. Lake Titicaca is such a place.

For a historian certain pertinent data may lead to an understanding and assessment of the economic or political significance of a place. The economic importance of a site may be determined by its natural resources (e.g., the petroleum-rich regions of the world), or its political magnitude may be gauged by its status as a seat of government. However, determining how and why a place is considered sacred requires considerably more than access to recoverable data.

Scholars of religious phenomena concur that sacred spaces are set apart from all other places by their direct association with one or more divinities.[1] A locus of supernatural power is a place where believers go and return to commune with the divine. Moreover, the definition of a sacred space depends on the modes of representation that both constitute and are practiced in a culture. This does not preclude a person from having an individual experience of the numinous, that is, from experiencing a personal revelation. However, for that experience to be shared and understood by others, for it to become communal, it must first be conveyed through language. A mountain, for instance, may only be known as a deity if an individual characterizes it as such in some form of language—in written, oral, or other forms of symbolic representation. Although other modes of representation, such as icons and emblems, may transmit the meaning of certain things, language remains their principal means for the intellection of their sense and the ultimate medium for the understanding of all sacred spaces. In the Western iconographic tradition, for example, an image of a woman can represent the mother of god only after the linguistic connection between the iconic signifier and its historically constructed referent is established. Thus, only through language—the indispensable medium of representation—can those who have not personally experienced religious revelation in a sacred place gain access to the sacredness of that place.

Commemorative narratives associated with spaces are among the most common modes of representation in cultures; without them sacred spaces often cease to possess sacredness and, hence, to perform their cultural functions. Regardless of how the sacredness of a space may have originated, a place remains sacred only through commemoration in surviving forms of narrative. These narratives may ultimately have been reduced to a ritual or to an arcane symbol, yet the latter, despite an ostensible isolation, continue to point to a larger plot, story, or design. The fact that narratives with references to Lake Titicaca's hallowedness exist makes it possible to study the sacred dimension of the lake. However, my purpose here is not so much to establish Titicaca's sacredness based on the narratives of the supernatural which envelop it, or to define the perception of the immanently divine essences that motivate the production of those narratives, but rather to examine the constitution of the sacred narratives themselves and the way they represent the lake as a sacred place.

SACRED SPACE AND PROFANE SPACE

[S]*acred* and *profane* are two modes of being in the world, two exis-
tential situations assumed by man in the course of his history. (Eliade
1959, 14)

All definitions and explanations of the sacred must begin with the opposition between the notion of the sacred and that of the profane, two exis-
tential modes that can be understood only in their mutual, yet contradictory, association. There are two parallel and complementary worlds in
the religious thought of traditional societies: the profane world, devoid of
supernatural content, where a person lives without a feeling of depen-
dence on an absolute being; and the sacred world, constituted by a religious experience, a feeling of awe inspired by the presence of supernatural force (Caillois 19–20). Rudolf Otto designates the latter condition
as a sense of something "numinous," a term he coins from the Latin
numen, which represents the Hebrew *qadôsh* and whose meaning is not
totally conveyed by the word *holy* (6). Otto dissociates the numinous
from the moral content usually related to the idea of God as absolute
perfection (6):

[The "Numinous" is] a category of value and of a definite "numinous"
state of mind, which is always found wherever the category is applied. This
state is perfectly *sui generis* and irreducible to any other; and therefore,
like every absolutely primary and elementary datum, while it admits of being discussed, it cannot be strictly defined. (7)

The idea of the numinous, according to Otto, implies nonrational or
suprarational attributes in addition to rational ones. He goes on to say
that, when speaking of God's attributes, we most often stress God's rational qualities because language, a rational system, tends to place emphasis
on them (2). Evidently, that which is ineffable cannot, by definition, be
explained in words. Thus, my concern is not to determine if and how the
numinous has truly manifested itself in certain temples, images, or places
near Lake Titicaca, but rather with the manner in which these temples,
images, heroes, or places are represented in narratives as divinities or as
images with supernatural powers which relate them to the notion of the
numinous.

Eliade (1959, 1963) postulates two modes for perceiving the world,
the sacred and the profane, both of which can be applied to reality.
According to him, any object may be observed from the perspective of

either of the two modes or from both. In his writings on the essence of religious experiences and in his history of religions, Eliade takes as his point of departure the dichotomy between the sacred and the profane. Although he does not dwell on the possible considerations that may underlie or precede this tension, he recognizes in the preface to his book *Patterns in Comparative Religion* that a purely religious phenomenon does not exist: "[B]ecause religion is human it must for that very reason be something social, something linguistic, something economic—you cannot think of man apart from language and society" (xiii). Since my goal is not to investigate the phenomenology of sacred spaces at Titicaca, but rather to analyze the modes used to represent the lake's sacred spaces, it is essential to consider the linguistic aspect of the dichotomy between the sacred and the profane.

Two levels or phases of perception are intimately connected with language. The first phase, which precedes and subtends the profane and sacred modes of conceptualization, is a linguistic universe in which initially things are separated from one another, or from their context, when they are named. Two good examples are the numerous words in Eskimo which refer to snow and the linguistic nondistinction between the colors green and blue in several African languages. The second phase, which arises from specific discursive practices, results in the opposition between the sacred and the profane. Both of these stages are unquestionably culturally determined.

Language does not merely name a given space: it represents the spatial boundaries that a culture considers significant. In other words, to name a space is also to draw cultural boundaries. These boundaries may be naturally defined (a coast marking the separation of the land from the sea) or man-made (the lines separating the directions of travel on a road). Since all space can be segmented into parts that pertain to everyday reality, with each part possessing a different function, Eliade and Van der Leeuw talk about a homogeneous space in the universe of the profane— a space possessing functional or physical distinctions, but lacking qualitative differences. It is thus, in the context of the profane, that Lake Titicaca belongs to the geography of the world.

Lake Titicaca marks the middle point of the Andean mountain range; it is located between the fifteenth and seventeenth parallels of southern latitude and between sixty-eight and seventy degrees of west longitude. At an altitude of 3,835 meters above sea level, Titicaca is the largest lake on the South American continent, measuring 8,288 square kilometers. The Strait of Tiquina divides the lake into two parts, Lago Mayor (the upper lake) or Chucuito, and Lago Menor (the lower lake) or Wiñay-

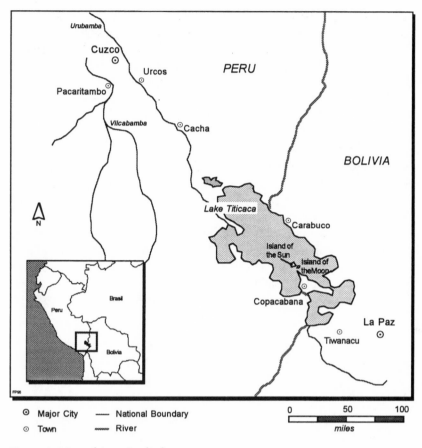

Figure 1. Map of Area Studied

marka (see Figure 1). Numerous fishing and farming villages, primarily of the Aymara culture, surround the lake.[2] Yet, all this superficial data cannot yield insight into the transcendental meaning endowed upon the lake by its inhabitants over time.

THE CONSECRATION OF SPACE: HIEROPHANY

A transcendental experience of space, which neither negates nor alters the physical or functional divisions of the surrounding territory, divides the space into qualitatively different parts, manifesting its heterogeneity (Eliade 1959, 24–25; Van der Leeuw 33). The presence of the numinous, which marks the sanctity of a place, shatters the homogeneity of space to reveal a meaningful central point (Eliade 1959, 36 ff.), separated from the totality, which becomes a locus, or referential "position," that acts as a center to human life and consciousness (Van der Leeuw 393–398).

The numinous may manifest itself through any object (Eliade 1963); that is, any object may become a hierophany. It can manifest itself through a stone (as in the case of the sacred Kaaba of Islam), through a tree (as in Moses' burning bush), through a mountain (as in Sinai), through an image (as in the Christ of Burgos), or through the medium of a person (as in the figure of Jesus Christ). A hierophany may also be a *theophany*, which implies the revelation of a divinity's presence; or it may also take the form of a *kratophany*, which merely reveals the presence of the power of a divinity. In each case, the hierophany transforms the place where it appears, consecrating it, making it numinous and reverential (Eliade 1963, 367).

Lake Titicaca is in this way a paradigmatic sacred place. Nearly all the instances of hierophany which have been identified by historians of religion manifest themselves at some time in or around the lake. In the myths compiled by the seventeenth-century chroniclers, Titicaca is represented over and over again as the scenario of a theophany. Bernabé Cobo confirms the fact:

> Unos . . . dicen que hubo un Hacedor del universo que crió el cielo y la tierra con las diversas naciones de hombres que la habitan; que pasó esto en Tiaguanaco, . . . y los otros en la isla de Titicaca, que está en la gran laguna de Chucuito. (Cobo [1653] 1964, 150)

> [Some . . . say that there was a Maker of the universe that created heaven and earth with all the peoples that inhabit it; they said this happened at Tiaguanaco, . . . and others at the island of Titicaca, which is in the upper lake of Chucuito.] [3]

In this narrative compiled by Cobo, it is the presence of the divinity itself which makes the place sacred, designates it as a fixed point within the territory, and separates it qualitatively from its larger geographical context. This space exists simultaneously within a religious universe and a physical world. Lake Titicaca ceases to be homogeneous within the religious universe because in its new theophanic setting it acquires a transcendental importance. According to Eliade, the homogeneity of space may be understood as an equivalent of primal chaos, where there is no possible differentiation (Eliade 1959, 29). This chaos, which, in my view, is prelinguistic, provides the rationale for establishing a real or imagined central point as an organizing principle, the origin or foundational center of the world—the place where language first appears. The need for an organizing principle, however, is not limited to the religious universe, since it may also be applied to the sphere of the profane; and what Eliade and Van der Leeuw ascribe to the sacred is but one instance which is recognizable through a specific discourse. The manifestation of the sacred sometimes establishes in ontological terms the nature of the world in a religious universe (Eliade 1959, 39). We find one of its discursive representations in the cosmogonic myth compiled by Cobo, in which the "world" finds its origin at Lake Titicaca.

In other examples of sacred places, although the divinity may be absent, its power may nevertheless be manifested, and it is this kratophany which consecrates the place. This type of kratophany appears in some myths concerning Titicaca. A case in point is Inca Garcilaso's account of the absent divinity whose emissaries are the bearers of its power:

> Nuestro Padre el Sol, . . . envió del cielo a la tierra un hijo y una hija de los suyos para que los doctrinase en el conocimiento de Nuestro Padre el Sol, para que lo adorasen y tuviesen por su Dios. . . . Con esta orden y mandato puso Nuestro Padre el Sol estos dos hijos suyos en la laguna Titicaca. . . . (Garcilaso 37–38)

> [Our father the Sun, . . . sent from heaven to earth a son and a daughter of his to indoctrinate them in the knowledge of our father the Sun that they might worship him and adopt him as their god. . . . With this order and mandate our father the Sun set these two children of his in Lake Titicaca. . . .] (Garcilaso 42)

This myth, in marked contrast to the previously cited one, postulates the absence of the divinity at Lake Titicaca and fails to refer to the creation of the world. It does involve, however, an inaugural act—the foundation of a religious belief.

While in the Andean tradition there are many more examples of Titicaca's sacredness, the two just adduced should suffice as indications of the lake's sacredness. Although it may not be immediately evident to occasional visitors who are unfamiliar with these myths, the sacredness of the lake is, nevertheless, an abiding presence to all individuals privy to the lake's numinous quality and its narrative traditions. For some, Titicaca may be no more than a place of impressive beauty by virtue of its deep blue waters that contrast with the arid landscape of the high plateau; for others, it is no more than an imposing view offered by the highest peaks in the Andean cordillera rising from the eastern shore of the lake. Yet for others, especially for those who live there and see it from their cultural perspective, as the Illimani[4] appears to float over the waters of Titicaca as one crosses the Strait of Tiquina, it is easy to understand why the mountain, like others around it, was believed by the ancient inhabitants of the region to be a watchful god. Even today, the Aymara Indians, following long-standing custom, refer to these snowy peaks as *Achachilas* (grandparents), believing they are vigilant deities who protect their homes (Bandelier 8).

SYMBOLS AND STRUCTURES OF SACRED SPACE

Upon coming into contact with the manifestation of the sacred, the religious person consecrates the place symbolically or ritually (Eliade 1959, Chapter 1). The acknowledgment of a divine manifestation may come as a result of an individual religious experience (e.g., God's revelation to Moses on Sinai [Exod. 19:3–7]) or a collective experience (e.g., the manna sent from heaven to the Israelites in the wilderness of sin [Exod. 16:13–16]). The act of divine manifestation itself may prompt in those called upon to experience it an emotional response. But in order to transmit this revelation, it must be represented; this representation, as I have indicated, is a cultural gesture. One can ensure the transmission of such a religious experience either through stories, which eventually become part of a cultural legacy, or through the construction of temples dedicated to the gods, where one can visually portray the idols and images that embody divine power. The Temple of the Sun in Titicaca is a good example of consecration through edification:

> Volviendo a la laguna de Chucuito de que voy tratando, hay muchas islas, es entre todas señalada la de Titicaca de donde la laguna tomó nombre y de quien hay después mucho que decir, pues en ella estuvo aquel famoso adoratorio y Templo del Sol, cuya memoria durará cuanto durare la que estos Naturales tienen de su principio. (Ramos Gavilán 12)

> [Returning to the subject of lake Chucuito which I am dealing with, there are many islands, among them the most remarkable being Titicaca, from which the lake took its name and about which there is much to tell later, since in it was the famous shrine and Temple of the Sun, whose memory will last as long as the Natives remember their origin.]

The sacred space can be conceived as a sort of mental map, which, like its counterpart in the physical world, delineates its constitutive spatial features and demarcates their relative significance. Although sacred in its totality by virtue of the fact that it originated in a divinity, the sacred place possesses a privileged space, normally at its physical center, which is especially imbued with divine power (Van der Leeuw 396–402).

It is clear, then, that narratives about the Maker of the World and the Sun god construe the Island of Titicaca as the scene of a hierophany. A pivotal point in the Andean religious world, the Island of Titicaca, in the words of Ramos Gavilán, is the "más señalada" [most remarkable] among all of the islands in the lake. Its importance, invoked in foundational myths, finds a physical representation in a sumptuous temple that establishes links between material and spiritual culture. One of Ramos Gavilán's most important contributions is his intuition that the sacredness of Titicaca "durará cuanto durare la que estos Naturales tienen de su principio" (12) [will last as long as the Natives remember their origin]; in other words, Titicaca's original religious meaning will survive as long as the myths are kept alive in the culture. Aware that the destruction of the temple or of its idols would fail to eradicate ancient religious beliefs of the Indians, Ramos Gavilán proposes a nonviolent program of evangelization that should be implemented in well-defined stages.[5]

Colonial chroniclers and historians tell us that before the arrival of the Spaniards, the Temple of the Sun on the Island of Titicaca was, for the natives, the most sacred of places, their *sanctum sanctorum*. That it was the "centro del mundo" (Cobo [1653] 1964, 194) is attested to by the name of a place southeast of Titicaca, Taypikala, which in the Aymara language literally means "center of the world" (Imbelloni 48). From this *umbilicus mundi*, as from the center of every sacred spot, power emanates and radiates centrifugally, consecrating all else in creation. In pre-Hispanic times the Indians regarded the Island of Titicaca as the center of creation, where a temple commemorated their supreme divinity; they placed their minor divinities, the guardians responsible for the preservation of creation, along the lake's periphery (see Figure 2).

> Entre los Idolos que se hallaron en este asiento, el principal y más célebre entre los Yunguyos, fue el Idolo Copacabana. . . . Este Idolo Copacabana estaba en el mismo pueblo, como vamos a Tiquina, era de piedra azul vistosa y no tenía mas de la figura de un rostro humano, destroncado de pies y manos, que como a otra figura de Dagon, la verdadera arca . . ., quiso tenerle humillado. Miraba aqueste Idolo hacia el Templo del Sol, como dando a entender que de allí le venía el bien. (Ramos Gavilán 101)

> [Among the idols found in this place, the main and most renowned among the Yunguyos, was the Idol Copacabana. . . . This Idol Copacabana was in the same town, toward Tiquina, it was made out of an attractive blue stone, and it was simply the figure of a human face, without feet or hands, that like another figure of Dagon, the true arch . . ., wanted to humiliate him. This Idol was facing the Temple of the Sun, signifying that from there all its good came.]

Ramos Gavilán makes a connection between the idol of Copacabana, part man and part fish, and Dagon, the Philistine god of agriculture and fertility, which, like a number of deities from universal mythology, symbolizes life-sustaining power because of its association with water. Eliade (1963, 207) writes: "Dragons, snakes, shell-fish, dolphins, fish and so on are the emblems of water; hidden in the depths of the ocean, they are infused with the sacred power of the abyss; lying quietly in lakes or swimming across rivers, they bring rain, moisture, and floods, thus governing the fertility of the world."

Not far from the Copacabana idol was that of Copacati, an image made of "piedra con una figura malísima y todo ensortijado de culebras" [stone with an evil countenance, completely tangled with snakes] (Ramos Gavilán 103), a fertility god worshiped especially during a season of drought. On the western coast of the upper lake, two leagues from the village of Ilavi, there was another idol identified by the same name, "en un cerro el más alto, que ay en toda esta comarca en un repecho que mira hazia donde naze el Sol" [on the highest hill in this district on a slope that faces the sunrise] (Arriaga 87). A god of sustenance, Ilavi was also, then, a life-sustaining deity (Ramos Gavilán 104):

[Era] una estatua de piedra labrada con dos figuras monstruosas, la una de varon, que mirava al nacimiento del Sol, y la otra con otro rostro de muger a las espaldas, que mirava al Poniente con figura de muger en la misma piedra. Las quales figuras tienen unas culebras gruesas, que suben del pie a la cabeça a la mano derecha, y izquierda, y assí mismo tienen otras figuras como de sapos. (Arriaga 88)

[It was a stone statue carved with two monstrous figures, one male, facing the rising of the sun, and the other with a female face at his back, facing the sunset with a figure of a woman carved from the same stone. Both figures have thick snakes, which climb from the foot to the head on both left and right sides, and have also other figures resembling toads.]

Although Ramos Gavilán ascribes a specific function to this idol, its obvious hermaphroditism and the snakes which envelop it mark it as an emblem of fertility. Because of its connection to the cyclical rising and setting of the sun, this deity sacralizes the daily renewal of life. In a religious universe, on a conceptual level, idols such as this signal certain activities in life as sacred events. Moreover, on a physical plane, the material presence of the idols exposes the sacredness of their domain.

Sacred places also possess a cosmogonic value (Eliade 1959, 45; 1963, 375). The notions of sacred and profane separate, in both spatial and temporal terms, the structured and the organized from the formless and the chaotic (Eliade 1959, 29–32). On the one hand, there is an ordered cosmos within the sacred universe, and, on the other, there is chaos and disorder within the profane universe. In his description of the origin of the Temple of the Sun at Titicaca, Bernabé Cobo points to this opposition between order and chaos, which, as in Cobo's own writings, is normally discursively represented through the light/darkness dichotomy:

> El adoratorio del sol que estaba en la isla de Titicaca, era una grande y firme peña, cuya veneración y motivo . . . es que los antiguos afirman que habiendo carecido de *luz celestial* muchos de en esta provincia, y estando los moradores della admirados, *confusos y amedrentados de tan oscuras y largas tinieblas*, los que habitaban la isla sobredicha de Titicaca *vieron salir al sol de aquella peña con extraordinario resplandor*, por lo cual creyeron ser aquel peñasco la casa y morada verdadera del sol . . . y así lo dedicaron y edificaron allí un templo suntuoso para en aquellos tiempos . . . (Cobo [1653] 1964, 190; my emphasis)

> [The shrine of the sun, which was on the Island of Titicaca, was a large solid crag. The reason it was consecrated to the sun and worshiped . . . (is that) the people of ancient times tell of being without *light* from the heavens for many days, and all of the local inhabitants were astonished, *confused, and frightened to have total darkness* for such a long time. Finally, the people of the Island of Titicaca *saw the sun come up one morning out of that crag with extraordinary radiance* . . . thus a magnificent temple, for those times, was constructed there and dedicated to the sun . . .] (Cobo 1990, 91–92; my emphasis)

Not just the sun, but other celestial bodies and phenomena were worshiped as well:

> Así mirando aquestos Indios al Sol, Luna, estrellas, al mar, a la tierra, truenos y relámpagos como a supremos señores los veneraban y adoraban con sacrificios. (Ramos Gavilán 49)

> [In this way these Indians saw the Sun, the Moon, the stars, the sea, earth, thunder and lightning as supreme lords and adored and worshiped them with sacrifices.]

The positioning of the temples corresponds to the position of the stars in the heavens. During the Inca empire, for instance, each deity in the Temple of Titicaca had its own house, the largest being the one occupied by the Sun, which faced toward the sun's position at midday (Ramos Gavilán 48). To the west, opposite the Island of Titicaca, lies the Island of

Coati, where, appropriately, the Temple of the Moon was located. Thus, through these structures, entire territories were consecrated, symbolically constituting a microcosm as they represented the perfect order of the cosmos.

Frequently a threshold both separates and connects sacred and profane spaces. Upon crossing the threshold, which normally occurs subsequent to a ritual of purification (Eliade 1963, 88–189), the believer enters the realm of the divine and experiences god (Eliade 1959, 25). The threshold separating the sacred from the profane may be an object, such as the sculpted portal of a Gothic church, or individuals such as the guardians who usher a pilgrim on his way (Eliade 1959, 25). It is not surprising, therefore, to have an image or the symbols of Saint Peter, the keeper of the keys of heaven, at the entrance of many Catholic churches. Accordingly, in his description of the Temple at Titicaca, Ramos Gavilán highlights its thresholds, liminal spaces, and guardians:

> Antes de llegar a este adoratorio, se había de pasar por tres puertas, que distaban las unas de las otras poco más de veinte pasos; la primera se llamaba Pumapunco, que suena lo mismo que puerta del León porque había allí un León de piedra, que decían guardaba la entrada, y en ésta antes de pasar, se hacía una expiación de pecados, confesándolos al Sacerdote que allí residía.
>
> La segunda puerta tenía por nombre Kentipunco, por estar matizada toda de plumas de tominejos, a quien ellos llaman Kenti, aquí volvían de nuevo a confesarse con otro Sacerdote que guardaba aquella puerta, este aconsejaba a los peregrinos fuesen con devoción si querían ser favorecidos del Sol a quien iban a adorar.
>
> De la tercera puerta era el nombre, Pillcopuncu, que fuera puerta de esperanza, estaba adornada con plumas verdes de un pájaro muy estimado que se trae de los Chunchos, llamado Pillco, que hace muchos visos, en esta puerta que era la última, el Sacerdote que custodiaba ella, persuadía con gran eficacia al peregrino, hiciese muy riguroso examen de conciencia, porque no había de pasar teniéndola agrabada, y sí hacía otra reconciliación con el Sacerdote para esto dedicado. (Ramos Gavilán 48–49)

[Before reaching this temple, one had to go through three gates, separated one from the other by about twenty steps; the first one, called Pumapunco, which means gate of the lion since there was a lion there made out of stone, which they believed guarded the entrance, and at this point before entering, one had to expiate one's sins, confessing them to a priest that resided there.

The second gate, whose name was Kentipunco because it was all adorned with hummingbirds' feathers (Kenti being the word that designates a hummingbird), was where they confessed their sins to another priest that guarded that gate. He advised the pilgrims to be very devout if they were to be favored by the Sun whom they went to worship.

The third gate, the gate of hope, called Pillcopuncu, was adorned with the green feather of a very prized and multicolored bird that comes from the region of the Chunchos, and is known by the name of Pillco. This gate, which was the last one, was guarded by yet another priest who very efficiently persuaded the pilgrims to rigorously examine their conscience, for one could not go through the gate with a guilty conscience; therefore they had yet another confession with the priest assigned there.]

As they approached the *sanctum sanctorum*, the pilgrims performed the rites mentioned by Ramos Gavilán at the end of a series of purifying and expiatory ceremonies. Long before their arrival at the Island of Titicaca, the pilgrims had travelled first through the village of Yunguyo, where, in addition to confessing their sins to a shaman, they fasted in preparation for their entrance into the sanctuary (Ramos Gavilán 12).

From the foregoing discussion, one can readily see how the stories inspired by Lake Titicaca call attention to the sacredness of the lake in general, and to that of the Temple of the Sun in particular, long before the arrival of the Spaniards and the cultural impositions of the Conquest.

THE PERMANENCE OF THE SACRED

Van der Leeuw asserts that "[t]he consciousness of the sacred character of the locality that has once been chosen is . . . always retained" (Van der Leeuw 393). Indeed, experience shows that when a place has been consecrated, either through ritual or by divine revelation, its sacred character generally survives despite drastic changes in the system of beliefs subsequently imposed by spiritual or political upheavals. Conquerors, for instance, have often established their houses of worship in previously sacred places, thus preserving the sacredness of these sites. Examples abound throughout history: pagan temples transformed into basilicas, Hindu temples into mosques, mosques into Christian churches, and churches into mosques.

It is a fact that the inhabitants of the region around Titicaca prior to the Spanish conquest considered the lake a sacred place. It is also known that the early Christian evangelical efforts suppressed the open worship of ancestral gods through their insistence upon the abolition of idolatry, the destruction of temples and idols, the incarceration and banishment of priests, and the prohibition of ancient rituals.[6] Nowadays nothing more than an archeological ruin, the well-known *adoratorio del Sol* has been replaced by the Basilica of Our Lady of Copacabana. Yet both stand as testimony to Titicaca's enduring sacredness.

THE VIRGIN OF COPACABANA: FROM SCULPTURE TO HIEROPHANY

The sanctuary of Our Lady of Copacabana, the patroness of Bolivia, is located in Chucuito, on the peninsula of Copacabana.[7] Every year thousands of pilgrims visit this shrine to the Virgin of Candlemas, especially on February 2, the feast of "Candlemas," and on August 6, Bolivian Independence Day.

The pilgrims, who dance during processions dressed in their traditional costumes, come from the Bolivian-Andean region and from Peru, especially from Arequipa. The Bolivian and the Peruvian *cofradías* (religious brotherhoods) compete for the honor of carrying the Virgin's float during the processions. Representing a wide array of economic and social strata, the pilgrims come from rural as well as from urban areas. Some pilgrimages also take place during November and December, and pilgrims arrive from the provinces of Cochabamba, Oruro, and from the mining towns. At the foot of the image of "Mamita de Copacabana," as the Bolivians affectionately call the Virgin, the pilgrims express their devotion in different ways. Those from the valley of Cochabamba and from the mining towns, for instance, sing Quechua songs during their processions. The rural Indians from the high plateau sing Aymara songs accompanied by panpipes, reed flutes, and drums.[8] Pilgrims from urban centers, many of whom are of European ancestry, express their devotion by singing in Spanish.

Together Copacabana and Lake Titicaca are unquestionably the spiritual and devotional center of this region of the Andes for present-day Catholics, who worship the Virgin of Copacabana as the native inhabitants in pre-Columbian times worshipped Father Sun, the Moon goddess, the Idol of Copacabana, and other divinities.

The Virgin of Copacabana, who has partly replaced the worship of the ancient deities, may be regarded as a new hierophany in the sacred space of the region of Lake Titicaca. However, unlike the ancient Idol of Copacabana, about which not much is known, the Virgin of Copacabana has a long history. In Ramos Gavilán's text, one can trace not only the origin of the sculpture itself, but also the gradual definition of this object as a hierophany and the process of its insertion into the region's culture.

The sculpture venerated in the Sanctuary of Copacabana is an image of the Virgin of Candlemas carved around 1582 by one Francisco Tito Yupanqui, an Indian from the Copacabana region (see Figure 3). This sculpture, which would shortly be acclaimed as the Virgin of Copaca-

Figure 2. A Stele of an Idol Similar to the
Idol of Copacabana

bana, was not immediately recognized as a holy object, and its sculptor
met with many obstacles before it found a place on a church altar. In the
second book of his *Historia del celebre santuario de Nuestra Señora de
Copacabana*, in which he compiles and interprets a series of 132 miracles
attributed to the Virgin of Copacabana, Ramos Gavilán also recounts the
origin of the statue and the circumstances leading to its enthronement in
a church built on a site that had been the very bastion of pre-Hispanic
idolatry, a place he referred to as "un lugar tan abominable por sus maldades y vicios como era Copacabana" [a site as abominable for its evil
and vices as was Copacabana] (Ramos Gavilán 110).

Around 1580, as the area was suffering from a terrible drought, Ramos
Gavilán tells us, the inhabitants of the region "determinaron . . . poner
sus suertes en las manos de Dios, y en la de su madre sus peticiones"

Figure 3. The Virgin of Copacabana with and without Baby Jesus

[decided to put their destiny in the hands of God and made their petitions through His mother] (115). The two rival communities of the Urinsaya and the Anansaya [9] hence decided to choose a patron saint to which a newly-found brotherhood would pray to seek an end to the famine caused by the drought. While the Urinsaya argued for Saint Sebastian, the Anansaya insisted on choosing the Virgin of the Candlemas.[10] It was at this time that Don Alonso Viracocha Inca, then governor of the Anansaya, traveled to Potosí where he met his kinsman Don Francisco Tito Yupanqui, who had already begun to make a sculpture of the Virgin.

Francisco Tito Yupanqui, explains Ramos Gavilán, "pretendía hacer [la imagen], porque de más de la inclinación natural que le llevaba a aquel arte, tenía hecha cierta promesa de dar a su pueblo una Imagen de la Virgen que fuese de su mano; aunque en la demanda gastase, y pade-ciese mucho" [had decided to carve an image because, in addition to his natural inclination to the art of carving, he had made a promise to give his town an image of the Virgin made with his own hands, even if in the process he would spend a lot of money and suffer a lot] (116). Although Ramos Gavilán mentions Tito Yupanqui's desire and determination to make an image of the Virgin with his own hands for his people, he fo-cuses on the pious nature of Tito Yupanqui's project. The Augustinian friar sees Tito Yupanqui's artistic endeavor as an expression of heartfelt devotion, for the sculptor had confessed that, as he labored on the image, he had fasted and constantly prayed to the Virgin. Ramos Gavilán's sym-pathetic attitude toward this expression of Christian piety in an Indian subject contrasts with that of some of his contemporaries. For instance, the Jesuit José de Arriaga, in *La extirpación de la idolatría en el Perú*, published in Lima in 1621—the same year Ramos Gavilán published his *Historia*—cautions the civil and ecclesiastic authorities about any type of manifestation of Christian piety from the Indians. He was convinced that

> . . . a llegado a tanto esta disimulación; o atrevimiento de los Indios, que a acontecido en la fiesta del Corpus, poner una Huaca pequeña en las mis-mas andas al pie de la Custodia del Santísimo Sacramento, muy disimu-ladamente. Y un Cura me dixo que avía hallado las Huacas en el hueco de las Peanas de los Santos del Altar, y otras debaxo del Altar, que las avia puesto el Sacristán, y yó e visto detrás de la misma Iglesia. Como también se averiguó en Huarochirí por el doctor Francisco de Avila, que para ado-rar un Idolo en figura de muger, llamado Chupixamor, y Mamayoc, hazían fiesta a un imágen de nuestra Señora de la Asunción, y para adorar un Idolo varón llamado Huayhuay, hazían fiesta a un Eccehomo. (Arriaga 76)

> [. . . Indian pretense and boldness have come to such extremes that it has happened that in the feast of Corpus Christi, they have furtively put a small idol next to the Host of the Holy Sacrament. And a priest told me that he had found idols in the cavities of the pedestals of the images of the Saints at the altar, and yet others under the Altar, put by the sacristan, and I myself have seen them behind the church. As was found out by Doctor Francisco de Avila, the Indians made a feast to an image of Our Lady of the Assumption in order to worship an Idol shaped as a woman, called Chupixamor, and Mamayoc, and to worship a male idol called Huayhuay, they made a feast in honor of an Eccehomo.]

In Ramos Gavilán's text, however, one does not find even the slightest insinuation of idolatry in Tito Yupanqui's sculpture. On the contrary,

Ramos Gavilán emphasizes the Christian piety motivating Tito Yupanqui's project, a piety which he illustrates with a text said to have been written by Tito Yupanqui himself and given to Ramos Gavilán by the sculptor's kinsmen after his death.[11]

Tito Yupanqui's story tells us that the priests of Copacabana received his first sculptures with neither admiration, enthusiasm, nor alarming suspicion. He recounts the difficulties in creating an image that would be acceptable to the ecclesiastical authorities, which explains why the sculpture that was to be known as the Virgin of Copacabana was not Tito Yupanqui's first work. Before sculpting the famous image that would later be deemed thaumaturgical, Tito Yupanqui already had had one of his sculptures placed on the altar of the church of his village. He writes:

> El primer vez que lo impesabamos, don Felipe de Lion mi hermano con mego, on echora del Vergen di barro, di on vara di grande, in tiempo di on patre quelrrigo, llamado Antonio di Almeda, que mi lo dexo poneldo in altar, in donde lo estava mas que su año con medio, y despues lo vino otro patre llamado bachiller Montoro, que lo vendo esto me hichora que no ista mejor di bueno, que me lo saque mala para voz, y me lo sacaron in el sacristía . . . (Ramos Gavilán 124)

> [The first time that I and my brother, don Felipe de Lion, started to carve an image of the Virgin in clay, of about a yard in length, at the time when a priest by the name of Antonio de Almeda was there, and who told me to put it on the altar, where it was for over a year and a half. Later came another priest named bachiller Montoro who upon seeing my work said it was not as good, that I should take it out, and they took it out to the sacristy . . .]

While one of the clerics, Antonio de Almeda, did not object to placing Tito Yupanqui's sculpture on the altar, the other cleric, Father Montoro, voiced objections, but solely on aesthetic, not doctrinal, grounds. What is also clear in Tito Yupanqui's story, which Ramos Gavilán transcribes "para que se conozca su llaneza, bondad y santa simplicidad" [so that his candor, kindness, and holy simplicity would be known], is his desire to become a sculptor; in Tito Yupanqui's story aesthetic ambitions seem to overshadow piety. Because of Father Montoro's comments about the artistic deficiencies of this early statue, Tito Yupanqui, eager to learn the art of sculpting well, apprenticed himself to one Diego de Ortiz. It was during his apprenticeship that he made the statue that later was to bring him recognition and fame.

Although Ramos Gavilán attributes the making of the statue to Tito Yupanqui alone, the sculptor's story suggests that it was a community enterprise in which all the local inhabitants participated, especially in deciding the Virgin's dimensions, her dress, and the site of her placement:

> todos los Natorales [fueron] a ver los hechoras del Vergen, para sacallo di alli pareciendo buena y lo anduv[ieron] meramdolo los Eclesias ono para ono, y dispues acirta[ron] en la Eclesia dil Santo Domenco, y con hechora dista vergen dil propio sorte dil ropage, e dil neño, e dilo grandura con so candela y di la mesma manera le traemos, dispoes disto nos poncamos a hazer el molde di barro todos tres . . . (Ramos Gavilán 125)

> [all the natives (went) to see the different statues of the Virgin, to copy one that seemed good, and they went from church to church, until they got to Saint Domingo's, where they found an image similar to the one they finally made, with the same dress, with a baby Jesus, and with a candle of the same size, after that all three of them started to make a mold in clay . . .]

It is significant that one man's wish to place an image sculpted with his own hands on the altar be shared by other members of the community, especially since among the three people specifically mentioned by Tito Yupanqui one finds don Alonso Viracocha Inca, governor of the Anansaya. If Ramos Gavilán's transcription is faithful to Tito Yupanqui's supposedly "true" account, it is easy to see in the collective origin of the statue a desire, or perhaps even a need, on the part of the Indians to participate in the newly imposed religion. In other words, the Indians' gesture, in a way, manifested a wish to appropriate the new religion despite its alien dogmas, rituals, and icons. Since Tito Yupanqui's community had already been christianized, the sculpture may be perceived as a tangible display of the Indians' devotion. However, the insistence that they alone make the image, as well as their appropriation of the Virgin, can be understood as an effort to endow it with an autochthonous cultural expression. This was a challenging task, since the Indians needed to conform to European aesthetic standards in order to make their artistic intepretation of the Virgin acceptable to the ecclesiastical authorities.

Not only did Tito Yupanqui and his peers seek to find a model for their statue of the Virgin of Candlemas, but they also sought to understand the frame of aesthetic reference from which the Spaniards had assessed his previous work. Having finished his sculpture, Tito Yupanqui sought Diego de Ortiz's appraisal. Although his teacher complimented him on a job well done, Tito Yupanqui also asked for the opinion of painters who, he tells us, disagreed in their appraisal:

que era mal hecha y otros lo dexeron que era bien hecho, esto [se] lo
dexeron los pentores, e me lo queseron engañar, porque estava el Imagen
acabado, e blanqueado que no lo faltava sino ponerlo con oro . . .
(Ramos Gavilán 125)

[that it was badly made but some others said to him that it was well made.
That is what the painters had said, as they wanted to deceive me, because
the Image was finished, and whitewashed, and the only thing left to do was
to gild it . . .]

What he heard from the critics notwithstanding, Tito Yupanqui considered his sculpture finished and definitely well crafted. There are obvious
discrepancies between his critics, who subscribed to a European mode of
representation, and Tito Yupanqui, an individual who possessed an indigenous artistic vision. Even after having studied and learned the European techniques of representation, Tito Yupanqui produced a sculpture
which, although eventually approved by the Spanish authorities, did not
entirely fit within the Western aesthetic tradition. It was, in fact, a hybrid
piece, the product of an artistic compromise—a sculpture in which native indigenous and European Hispanic elements coalesced in order to
forge a new, intermediary form of representation. I concur with Teresa
Gisbert, a historian of colonial viceregal art, who notes that

Aunque Yupanqui se inspiró en una imagen española, hay que advertir que
existe una gran distancia entre la Virgen de Santo Domingo que le sirvió
de modelo y la de Copacabana. Esta distancia se plasma en el arcaísmo de
la imagen nativa y su calidad de Icono, en ella se advierte que el artista
lejos de expresar el humanismo de su tiempo manifiesta una peculiar manera de arraigo indígena. La Virgen está concebida con esa distancia con
que debieron ver los indígenas las cosas divinas y que proviene de los tiempos anteriores a la conquista. (Gisbert 1980, 100)

[Although Yupanqui's image was of Spanish inspiration, one cannot fail
to notice the immense differences that exist between the Virgin of Santo
Domingo that served him as model and the Virgin of Copacabana. This
distance is evident in the archaic aspect of the native image and its iconic
quality, in it one can see that the artist, far from expressing the humanism
of his time, manifests a particular Indian expression. The Virgin is conceived in a distanced way with which Indians must have viewed divine objects in pre-Conquest times.]

Pertinent to this discussion is Tito Yupanqui's recollection of his visit
to the local bishop to obtain a painting and sculpting license, when he

showed the prelate one of his paintings on wood. Since he sought permission from his Spanish superiors, Tito Yupanqui must have thought that his work abided by the aesthetic canons of European culture. The reaction to his artistic efforts was, however, again not encouraging. Tito Yupanqui explains:

> me lo dexeron que no estaba bien el Imagen, e que lo parece como hombre y lo esta con sus barbas que lo parece barbas, e lo hecharon mocha falta que no es boena, e me lo dexeron que no lo haga no lo haga, e dispoes di quanto lo avia visto el Imagen la Señoria, lo rieron mocho todos e los dimas echando el falta al pentor, e lo meravan quanto lo tenían con sus manos, e me lo tomava cada un Español, e lo reya di merarlo, e lo dexeron que los Natorales no se poeden hazer el Imagenes del Vergen, ne voltos y luego estove medio desmayado, e lo fue espantado amohenado porque lo toxe el Imagen ante el Obespo para que lo riera . . . (Ramos Gavilán 125)

> [they told me that the image was not well made, and that it looked like a man, bearded, or with what looked like a beard, and they found many faults in it. They said it was not good, that I should not make it, and after his lordship saw the image, they laughed a lot, he [the bishop] and all the rest, blaming the painter. Each of the Spaniards took it in his hands, and looked at it, laughing upon seeing it, and they said that the natives cannot make Images of the Virgin, nor sculpt them. I was then dismayed, shocked, and annoyed because I had brought the image to the bishop not for them to laugh at it . . .]

The Spaniards, as this passage shows, objected to the painting on artistic grounds, disregarding all its possible technical merits. Moved not to admiration but to laughter, his critics added insult to injury by suggesting that he paint "monas con so mico" [mother monkeys with their little ones]. In short, the authorities did not consider Tito Yupanqui's art worthy for treating "serious" (i.e., Spanish) subjects. Understandably, Tito Yupanqui was dismayed and annoyed, since this was not the reaction he had expected. For him, his and his people's artistic creations were not "figuras malísimas y monstruosas" [ugly and monstrous figures] (Ramos Gavilán 15), as they were judged by the Europeans and their descendants.

Tito Yupanqui's repeated desire to master and incorporate in his paintings and sculptures European aesthetic principles—which he acknowledges not to understand fully—are of special significance to his story. Even those passages in which Ramos Gavilán alludes to the sculptor's devotion are inextricably tied to Tito Yupanqui's aspirations to produce an art which would find acceptance in Spanish eyes. Ramos Gavilán repeatedly notes how Tito Yupanqui implores divine assistance, either by having a mass said "para que se saliesse bueno esta hechora" [so that this carving will turn out well] (Ramos Gavilán 125) or by frequently going "a la Ecclesia para pedir la meserecordea di nostro Siñior para acertar el pintadura de la Emagen di nostra Señiora y lo dimas, pedendo en me oración licencia para alcanzar este obra, e me lo disse mano para hazer voltos e para ser buen pentor" [to church to ask from God, our Lord's mercy to accept the painting of the image of our Lady and the others, asking in my prayers license to succeed in this work, to give me a good hand, and I made vows so that I would become a good painter] (Ramos Gavilán 125).

On June 4, 1582, having found an acceptable model, Tito Yupanqui began to make his sculpture. While he worked, other members of the community approached him for the related but difficult task of founding a brotherhood to honor the Virgin. It was then, when one of the bishop's servants claimed that "su señor, no daba tales licencias, ni la concedería sino con mucha dificultad y que no llevasen adelante aquel propósito, sino tenían renta para la cofradía" [his Lordship did not give such licenses, nor would he grant it to them so easily and tried to dissuade them from pursuing that venture unless they had the funds to establish the brotherhood] (Ramos Gavilán 116), that Tito Yupanqui tried to obtain the license denied him by the Bishop before starting his apprenticeship in La Paz. Despite this inauspicious beginning, the story as Tito Yupanqui tells it has a happy ending. Three months later, he finished the statue, which received the approval of the Bishop don Alonso Granero, who, in addition to reimbursing the cost of the gold used in the sculpture's gilding, authorized the founding of the brotherhood as well. Although now an official work of art, the statue was not immediately placed on display on an altar.

Since the Anansayas had secured the approval for founding the brotherhood of the Virgin of Candlemas, the Urinsayas had no other choice but to accede to its creation. The rivalry between the two, however, persisted: after the Anansaya's success, the Urinsayas objected to taking Tito Yupanqui's Virgin to Copacabana, and instead insisted on finding a different sculpture in either Spain or in Lima for that purpose. Frustrated with the situation, Don Alonso Viracocha, the governor of the Anansayas, arrived at an entirely unacceptable solution to the conflict: the sale of the sculpture that had exacted so much of Tito Yupanqui's labor and pious effort.

It was at this time that Fr. Francisco Navarrete, under whose care Tito Yupanqui had left his statue of the Virgin, was dazzled by "unos rayos, que salían de la Santa Imagen" [rays coming out of the holy image] (Ramos Gavilán 120). Ramos Gavilán transcribes the friar's words to the sculptor and his friends: "No se hijos qué es esto que veo en vuestra Imagen, que me parece echa rayos de fuego" [I do not know, my children, what it is that I see in your statue, which seems to emanate rays of fire] (Ramos Gavilán 120). This occurrence marks the first step in the statue's transformation from modest native sculpture to hierophany.

To be sure, Francisco Navarrete's words represent through language the sense of the numinous essential to notions of the sacred. The statue's appraisal as a divine sign—that is, as a hierophany—is determined by the ideological and cultural positioning of the interpreting subject. Thus, from his Catholic perspective, Ramos Gavilán interprets Navarrete's experience as a heavenly sign. He sees it as the fulfillment of Saint Cyril's description of the Virgin in his sermon against Nestor:

> Es la Virgen una lámpara que jamás muere, sino que en continuo ser comunica encendidos rayos de luz; es corona de las Vírgenes por quien se alegra el cielo, se gozan los Angeles, los demonios huyen, las gentes y los infieles se reducen a penitencia. Pues los de Copacabana, antes que la Virgen descubriese milagros en su pueblo, se estaban en su Gentilidad, porque como había sido cabeza de Idolatría duraba todavía en ella. Mas a la voz desta Señora, y Santa Imagen: "Ad poenitentiam reducuntur." Es ya su trato dellos el de la penitencia, y dolor de sus culpas, dando del en continuas confesiones. (Ramos Gavilán 120)

> [The Virgin is a lamp that is never extinguished, continuously communicating light rays; it is because of the crown of the Virgins that heaven is gladdened, angels delight, demons flee, people and infidels become penitents. Before the Virgin performed miracles in their town, the people of Copacabana were subsumed in their idolatry, since the place had been capital of the Idolatry, which still persisted there. Yet the voice of this Lady and Holy Image: "Ad poenitentiam reducuntur." It is common to see among them penitence and sorrow for their faults for they go continually to confession.]

One may question the origin of the image of the Virgin of Copacabana, but not the ideology which informs its history. The details in Ramos Gavilán's reconstruction of the origins of the image conform to a Christian worldview. The faith required for salvation in the Christian scheme of things is represented by Tito Yupanqui's profound devotion, which Ramos Gavilán takes pain to demonstrate. The arduous trials an individual must endure for having sinned have their counterparts in the difficulties faced by the sculptor in the course of completing his miraculous image. Even the humiliations that a believer must suffer because of his righteousness and his love of Christ are present in Ramos Gavilán's narrative: in Tito Yupanqui's exposure to the mockery of the Spaniards.

The statue itself conforms, as well, to the traditional iconography of the Virgin in Western Catholicism. Since the early Middle Ages, the Virgin was identified with the woman described in Revelation: "And a great portent appeared in heaven, a woman clothed with the sun, with the moon under her feet, and on her head a crown of twelve stars" (12:1).

Resulting from St. John's apocalyptic vision of the Virgin crowned by stars, Mary came to be iconographically represented with rays of light radiating from her body (Warner 93). The Franciscan's description of the Virgin, as told by Ramos Gavilán, evokes an established iconographical and exegetical Christian tradition which allows one to define the statue as a new Christian hierophany. But there is more. One cannot disregard in this culturally hybrid context a hierophany in the ancient Andean mythology, which Ramos Gavilán describes early on in his *Historia* without detecting its close resemblance to the Christian representation of the Virgin.

Recounting the Inca myth of origins, Ramos Gavilán recalls that a cacique from Cuzco, who in old age had a son who was "rubio y blanco" [blond and white], devised a scheme with a sorcerer to ensure that his child would become a powerful ruler when he came of age. Ramos Gavilán describes the child-turned-ruler in the following passage:

> Llegado el tiempo, congregada la gente . . . y venido el dia al punto que el Sol rayaba el collado y echa la seña apareció sobre todos en pie el dispuesto mozo así vestido y tocado en que el Sol daba de lleno resplandeció de modo que se arrebató los ojos de todos con admiración extraña, y después que los hizo atentos con su vista los admiró más con su habla, porque en voz alta la que bastó para ser oído sin descomponerla les dijo sereno y grave estas palabras: sabed que yo soy el que por vuestro Dios adorais, sin engañaros en esto he querido mostrarme a vosotros bajando del cielo por hallarme obligado de vuestros sacrificios y doliéndome vuestra ignorancia en gobernaros por tantas cabezas, yo soy solo en el Cielo y así quiero que en la tierra haya y no sólo a todos gobierne, siendo respetado como Dios. (Ramos Gavilán 15)

> [When the time came, having the people gathered . . . right at the time when the sun was rising above the mountains, after a sign was made, the young man appeared standing up in front of them. He was dressed from head to toe so that the sun fully shone on him in such a way that startled the eyes of everyone with strange admiration. After he caught their attention with his look he impressed them more with his speech, because in a

loud enough voice to be heard but without breaking it, he said to them these words in a serene and grave manner: You should know that it is I whom you worship as your god. Without wanting to deceive you, I chose to show myself to you coming down from heaven in response to your sacrifices and distressed by your ignorance to govern yourself by so many heads, I am the only one in heaven and so I want that on earth there be just one to govern all of you, and that he be respected like a god.]

It is difficult not to notice the representation of the origin of the Inca dynasty as kratophany and how it resembles the new hierophany embodied in Tito Yupanqui's sculpture of the Virgin of Copacabana. In both instances a transformation of a nonsacred being or object into a sacred being or object occurs: a human being becomes a divine messenger in the Inca myth; and a sculpture becomes a miraculous mediator in the story of the Virgin of Copacabana. The astonishment that both produced was comparable, as were their objectives: to reveal a new form of life. That both are considered revelations is also evidently clear. In order to establish the difference between the two, Ramos Gavilán, acting as the advocate of Christian orthodoxy, attributes the Inca hierophany to the Devil and the image of the Virgin of Copacabana to God. Within Ramos Gavilán's ideological construct, the Inca hierophany cannot be but false, and it is replaced and corrected by the Christian, and hence "true," hierophany of the Virgin.

Official policy, as part of a program to supplant the Indians' idolatrous beliefs with the Christian faith, dictated the establishment of Catholic churches in places that had formerly been considered sacred by the Incas. A decree of the First Council of Lima from 1552 states:

Constitución 3a—Que las guacas sean derribadas, y en el mismo lugar, si fuere decente, se hagan iglesias.

Item porque no solamente se á de procurar hacer casas e iglesias donde nuestro Señor sea honrado, pero deshacer las que están hechas en honra y culto del demonio, pues allende de ser contra ley natural, es gran perjuicio e incentivo para volverse los ya cristianos a los ritos antiguos, por estar juntos los cristianos con padres y hermanos infieles, y a los mismos infieles es grande estorbo para tornarse cristianos: (f 27) Por tanto, S.S. ap. mandamos que todos los ídolos y adoratorios que hobiere en pueblos donde hay indios cristianos sean quemados y derrocados; y si fuere lugar decente para ello se edifique allí iglesia . . . (Concilios Limenses 8)

[Constitution 3a—(It is ordered) that the *guacas* be demolished, and in the same place, if it were decent, churches be built.

Item: Because not only should one erect houses and churches where our

Lord is worshiped, but one should demolish the ones built in honor of and worship of the devil, since besides being against natural law, it is a grave danger and incentive for those already christianized to return to their ancient rites, to be near infidel parents and siblings; and for those infidels it is a major obstacle in the path to become christians: (f27) Thus, we order that all idols and temples that might be in towns where Christian Indians live be burned and demolished; and if it were a decent and suitable place erect a church there . . .]

The missionaries' objective was not only to appropriate the Indians' sacred places but also to impose upon the infidels a Christian God and a complete celestial hierarchy in which the figure of the Virgin played a prominent role. It was the missionaries' belief that a "physical" change, embodied by the placement of their Christian deities at sites formerly occupied by Indian deities, would help realize a "spiritual" conversion. If conversions did take place, and in large numbers, the coincidence of motifs in both iconographic traditions such as the beams of light and luminescence, which in both cultures were considered signs of supernatural power, paved the way to syncretism. Indeed, in several iconographic representations of the Virgin, especially from the seventeenth century, the Pachamama—the Andean goddess of the earth—and the Virgin share the same artistic space in a syncretistic manner (see Figure 4). Gisbert notes that

Varios estudios antropológicos hacen hincapié en esta identificación, escasa en representaciones plásticas que la materialicen; sólo en tiempos virreinales fue representada la Virgen María como Madre Tierra en forma explícita. El ejemplo más importante es el cuadro existente en el Museo de la Moneda (Potosí) donde María y el Cerro de Potosí son un todo. En el lienzo se muestra la montaña con rostro femenino y un par de manos con las palmas abiertas. Es la imagen de María inserta en el Cerro y coronada por la Trinidad. (Gisbert 1980, 17)

[Several anthropological studies underscore this identification, which is seldom materialized in plastic representations; it was only in colonial times that the Virgin Mary was represented explicitly as Mother Earth. The most important example is the painting found in the Museum of the Moneda (Potosí), where Mary and the Mountain of Potosí are one and the same. In the canvas the mountain is shown with a feminine face and with open hands. It is the image of Mary inserted in the mountain and crowned by the Trinity.]

Gisbert argues that, since the Virgin replaced the protective gods embodied in the mountains and because these were made of soil, it was logi-

Figure 4. The Syncretic Representation of the Virgin

cal to identify the Virgin with *tierra* (earth, soil). She argues further that the worship of the Pachamama in Copacabana had by then been well established and thus facilitated the identification (Gisbert 1980, 21). Although it may be possible that a syncretism of this sort may have taken place, what happened in Copacabana was, as we shall see, much more complex.

If by syncretism one means the reconciliation or union of different doctrines, I do not believe that this was the case with Copacabana, nor was it Ramos Gavilán's intention to suggest such an occurrence. Gisbert observes that the Augustinians, "para desterrar el culto gentílico que allí se practicaba" [in order to eradicate the gentile cult that was practiced there], enthroned the Virgin of Copacabana and the Virgin of Pucarani. She goes on to say:

> Si en un principio María es síntesis que engloba el culto de muchos sitios y dioses prehispanos, una vez entronizada recomienza el proceso de diso-ciación, pues es ya Copacabana, Pucarani, Reina, Purificada, Candelaria y Virgen de la Gracia. (Gisbert 1980, 22)

> [If at the beginning Mary is a synthesis that encompassed the cult of many pre-Hispanic sites and deities, once enthroned the process of dissociation begins, and she becomes (Virgin of) Copacabana, (Virgin of) Pucarani, Queen, Purified, Candlemas and Virgin full of Grace.]

While one may affirm that the Augustinians sought to suppress the idolatrous cults by replacing the ancient gods with Christian divinities, it is highly problematic to talk about a process of dissociation, or of a for-mer association, without considering whether, from the perspective of both indigenous and Christian religions, a complete separation was, or was not, possible. A substitution entails the replacement of one thing by another, resulting in the absence of that which was replaced. The cult of the Virgin of Copacabana, or any of other representations of the virgin or saints enthroned in the region, did not put an end to the cult of the Pachamama: to this day the rites to the Pachamama persist alongside Christian rites in the Bolivian high plateau. The *challa*, a ritual of the Pachamama, is performed periodically to express gratitude for, or to so-licit, the Pachamama's benevolence (Paredes 127). In Peru, José María Arguedas writes that

> En el departamento de Cuzco, como en casi todos los de la sierra del Perú, los indios todavía siembran y cosechan entre fiestas y ceremonias. Los ritos antiguos principales no han desaparecido, ni aun en regiones donde el ferrocarril ha transformado los pueblos y ha multiplicado el comercio. (Arguedas 85)

> [In the department of Cuzco, as in almost all the ones of the Peruvian hills, Indians still seed and harvest with feasts and ceremonies. The main ancient rituals have not disappeared, not even in regions where the railroad has transformed towns and increased commerce.]

The persistence of ancient forms of worship, with their distinctive indige-nous rituals, attests to the nonexistence of the complete syncretism of Pachamama and the Virgin.

I propose, then, that the study of these divinities be approached from a wider perspective and a broader system of beliefs that allow one to consider whether such a synthesis might even have been theoretically possible. An essential difference between the Andean religions and Christianity is that the latter has no place for any other deity. Acosta points out:

> [El] oficio del predicador cristiano es enseñar la fe e instruir en las costumbres. Es necesario comenzar por la fe sin la cual es imposible agradar a Dios, de la cual es autor y consumador Jesucristo. El primer y principal cuidado del ministro evangélico ha de ser, pues, anunciar a Cristo a las gentes, *no habiendo otro nombre que haya sido dado a los hombres para conseguir la salvación.* Y nadie puede poner otro fundamento, ni hay otra puerta y otro camino para la vida eterna . . . (Acosta [1590] 1952, 422)

> [The task of the Christian preacher is to teach the Faith and instruct in its customs. It is necessary to begin with the faith without which it is impossible to please God, a faith whose author and perfecter is Jesus Christ. The first and main goal of the evangelic minister has to be announcing Christ to the peoples, *there is no other name that has been given to man for attaining his salvation.* And nobody can present another foundation, nor is there another door nor another way to eternal life . . .]

Acosta, as well as other theologians of the sixteenth century, had many arguments against idolatry, one of which is the following:

> [L]os ídolos de los gentiles son de madera, piedra o metal, a los que dió forma el arte por industria de hombres y favorecida por la codicia de los sacerdotes o el imperio de los reyes. Y los hombres no pueden hacer a los dioses, siendo ellos de mejor especie que las cosas que fabrican. Si la idolatría es sobre cosas celestes o cuerpos de la naturaleza, se puede fácilmente demostrar por la sustancia de que constan y los movimientos a que están sujetos que son muy ajenos a la naturaleza de Dios. (Acosta [1590] 1952, 466)

> [(T)he idols of the gentiles are made out of wood, stone, or metal, to which art gave shape because of human industry and which were favored by the avarice of the priests or the empire of the kings. And men cannot make gods, being themselves of a better kind than the objects they make. If idolatry is based on celestial bodies or nature, based on the substance of which they are made and the movements to which they are subject, it is easy to demonstrate that they are not part of God's essence.]

Non-Christian deities, considered demonic, were excluded from the Christian pantheon. Thus, elimination rather than assimilation of the Pachamama (or of any other indigenous religious representation) conforms better with the tenets of Christianity. The Andean creed, however, unlike Christian dogma, did allow for the adoption of new deities:

> Sabemos que los Inkas iban encontrando nuevos y numerosos dioses en cada pueblo recién ocupado. Pero empleaban con ellos un comportamiento peculiar, en nada parecido al que se observa en la historia del Viejo Mundo. No arrasaban los adoratorios, ni destruían las efigies de las deidades lugareñas, ni prohibían los ritos ni imponían a la fuerza las creencias del Cuzco. No echaban mano de la hoguera ni de ningún género de tormento para que se obligase a la gente a creer en el Sol o en Tijsi Wiraqocha. Al contrario, con la sola condición, de reconocimiento a la divinidad del Sol, otorgaban una entera libertad de cultos. . . . Aún mas. El dios principal era llevado al Cuzco, donde, en unión de otros iguales, era colocado y honrado en un templo construido con ese objeto. (Lara 46–47)

> [We know that the Incas found new and numerous gods in each of the towns they occupied. But they behaved toward them in a peculiar way, quite dissimilar from what we observe in the history of the Old World. They did not demolish the temples, nor destroy the effigies of the local deities, nor prohibit the rites or impose by force the beliefs from Cuzco. They did not use the stake or any other sort of torment to force the people to believe in the Sun or in Tijsi Wiraqocha. On the contrary, with the sole condition that they recognize the Sun's divinity, they gave complete freedom of worship. . . . Still more: The main god was taken to Cuzco, where, together with others, it was placed and honored in a temple built for this purpose.]

In the Andean religious universe, with its natural tendency to adopt new deities, substitution or syncretism would be unnecessary; the adoption of Christian deities on the part of the Indians would have been an unimpeded, culturally innate impulse. The program of Christianization to which the Indians were subjugated proscribed, but did not eradicate, this religious practice. The flexibility of Andean religious beliefs allowed the two creeds to coexist in the religious practices of the Indians because, as Pedro Borges, in his *Métodos misionales de la cristianización de América, Siglo XVI* (1960), observes,

> [Había] una coexistencia de dos religiones yuxtapuestas, por medio de las cuales los indios intentaban compaginar el cristianismo con el paganismo, practicando en ocasiones el uno sin dificultad para practicar en otras ocasiones el otro. Los indios quisieron cumplir al mismo tiempo con dos religiones opuestas: ser cristianos pero sin dejar por ello de ser paganos.[12] (Borges 521–522)

[There was a coexistence of two juxtaposed religions, through which the Indians tried to conform paganism to Christianity, practicing one or the other without any difficulty. The Indians wanted to follow at the same time the two opposite religions: being Christians without necessarily ceasing to be pagans.]

Christianity's basic premises disallowed the possibility of the practice of religious syncretism. But because of Spanish repression, the Indians may have found in a sort of syncretism the only way to preserve certain aspects of their ancient beliefs and divinities. This may explain the existence of some iconographic representations that may perhaps be considered syncretic. However, the unsustainability of the internal contradictions resulting from the union of incompatible attributes of the autochthonous and Christian divinities may have led eventually to what Gisbert defines as a dissociation. I contend that these two practices— syncretism and dissociation—do not accurately describe the process of *mestizaje*, or hybridization, either in the realm of religion in particular or in that of culture in general.

In their accounts of the Pachamama, some missionaries, among them Ramos Gavilán and Arriaga, not only associated her, as the Indians did, with agriculture, fertility, and the Andean woman but also regarded her, following the Christian tradition, as an Eve-like figure who embodies lasciviousness. In what follows, I will examine some representations of the Pachamama, Andean women, and the rites of fertility in key colonial texts.

In the second chapter of José de Arriaga's *Extirpación de idolatrías del Perú* (1621), titled "Que cosas adoran oy en dia los Indios, y en que consiste su idolatría" [On the Worship and Idolatries of Indians Today], the Jesuit observes that:

A Mamapacha, que es la tierra también reverencian especialmente las mugeres, al tiempo que an de sembrar, y hablan con ella diziendo que les dé buena cosecha, y derraman para esto chicha, y mayz molido, o por su mano, o por medio de los hechiceros. (Arriaga 1621, 20)[13]

[Pachamama, who is Earth, is revered especially by women at the time of seeding; they speak to her asking for a good harvest, they spill *chicha*, and ground corn; sometimes this is done by the women themselves, and other times the sorcerers do it for them.]

Another rite, mentioned by Ramos Gavilán, was the game of *Panuco*, which took place in Cuzco and in Copacabana during February. In this game, the Indians made very large balls of esparto grass that they rolled away from the village in order to roll up and cast out all sickness from the community. It was, says the Augustinian friar, a festival of great rejoicing which involved a ritual bath, since "aquellas aguas dejaban salvo-conducto, contra todas las enfermedades, quedando libres y limpios de ellas" [those waters gave them security, against all diseases, finding themselves free and clean of them] (Ramos Gavilán 71). During this festival, which continued through the night, there were "grandes las ofensas que contra Dios se cometían, porque la misma noche, les daba licencia para las maldades que en juegos nocturnos suelen suceder" [great offenses that they committed against God, because night itself gave them license for the wickedness that frequently occurs in nocturnal games] (Ramos Gavilán 71).

For Ramos Gavilán, lust was the worst possible Indian trait. The Devil, in complicity with women since the Fall, led the latter to a sinful life. Ramos Gavilán's circular reasoning and network of associations have biblical resonances and may be summarized as follows: idolatry was the work of the Devil; women, because of their intrinsic lasciviousness were the Devil's accomplices, and hence a conduit of idolatry. With his type of reasoning, Ramos Gavilán, and others like him, cannot but consider lustful all rituals involving women. Bernabé Cobo, in his *Historia del Nuevo Mundo* (1653), discusses women's perceived role in the propagation of wantonness:

> Nunca conocieron el resplandor y hermosura de la castidad, para hacer estima della; antes les era muy ofensiva la virginidad en sus mujeres, porque decían que las que estaban doncellas no habían sido de nadie queridas; si bien pienso eran raras las que conservaban su integridad hasta tomar estado, lo uno por criarse desde niñas con toda libertad, sin que los padres cuidasen de su recogimiento, recato y honestidad, ni les prohibiesen el salir de casa cada y cuando querían e irse solas adonde se les antojaba, . . . y lo otro porque por librarse de la infamia en que las castas solían incurrir sólo porque lo eran, ellas mismas fácilmente se dejaban desflorar. Tan lejos estaba de tenerse por delito ni aun para reprehenderse ningún exceso que en esto hubiese. (Cobo [1653] 1965, 22)

> [Because they never knew the splendor and beauty of chastity, they never appreciated it; indeed, the virginity of their women was very offensive to them. They said that those who were virgins had never been loved by anyone. As a matter of fact, very few remained virgins until the day of their marriage. This was so, first of all because since childhood they were brought up with complete freedom. Their parents did not shelter them or

look after their modesty and chastity. Nor did they prohibit them from going out by themselves whenever and wherever they wanted. . . . Second, they consented to being deflowered because they wanted to be free of the shame which the chaste had to endure simply for being virgins. Hence, no excess in this respect was considered a crime or, for that matter, considered reprehensible.] (Cobo 1979, 29–30)

Ramos Gavilán's view on Indian women resembles Cobo's. In the former's case, however, it also seems to be shaped by a general misogyny, as evident in a comment in a passage about the indiscretion of one of Topa Inca's concubines who failed to keep a secret the Inca had confided in her:

No puedo aunque sea de paso, y a costa de alguna digresión, dejar de decir, como muchas y aún las más veces son las mujeres la causa de las mayores ruinas, porque no solo pretendo mover los corazones de los que este libro leyeren, a la devoción de Copacabana, sino también advertirles de lo que convenga a la honra de Dios y provecho del alma. (Ramos Gavilán 20)

[I cannot fail to mention, in spite of it being somewhat a digression, that many and even the majority of times women are the cause of the biggest ruins, for I not only intend to move the hearts of those who read this book to the devotion to Copacabana, but also advise them about what is appropriate for the honoring of God and the benefit of their souls.]

While the Indians denigrated virginity, Christians exalted abstinence and the state of sexual purity, revering virginity in the figure of Mary. Ramos Gavilán, like other missionaries, expressed admiration and respect for all women, including Indians, who were virtuous, pure, chaste, and modest, virtues embodied in the Mother of Christ, who was the ideal model of female perfection. A case in point is found in the chapter on Virgins of the Sun. He tells the story of a 120-year-old woman who lived around 1611 in the village of Viacha, and whom no man had dared to approach in deference to her having once been a Virgin of the Sun. The priest who heard her final confession, upon learning that she was a virgin, promptly baptized her. Ramos Gavilán comments:

[Dios] quiso honrar a esta pobre India, por la limpieza que conservó en vida, guardando perpetua virginidad, que hasta en los gentiles la respeta Dios, que mandó a Josué pasase a cuchillo todos los culpados y a vueltas todo el pueblo, solamente le exceptuó las vírgenes. (Ramos Gavilán 65)

[(God) wanted to honor this poor Indian, for the cleanliness she kept during her life, and for always keeping her virginity, which God respects even in the gentiles, as he ordered Joshua to pass beneath the knife all the guilty ones and all the people, except the virgins.]

It was Ramos Gavilán's contention, moreover, that the Virgin of Copacabana not only replaced the ancient gods, but that she also changed, through the emulation of her virtuous example, the behavior of the Indians:

> Ya gracias sean dadas al omnipotente Dios, y a la esclarecida reina de los Angeles, la Virgen de Copacabana, que en este asiento de donde ella es Patrona, no hay rastro de Idolos ni de apachetas, ni de cosa que huela a idolatría, porque como los Naturales de aqueste lugar y de casi toda su comarca han visto tantas maravillas y milagros que la Virgen ha obrado en favor suyo, olvidados de sus locas ceremonias y ritos supersticiosos acuden a ella, que como verdadera Madre y Señora jamás se cansa de favorecerlos, con larga mano. (Ramos Gavilán 70)

> [Thanks be to the omnipotent God, and to the Queen of angels, the Virgin of Copacabana, that in this place where she is patroness, there is no trace of idols and *apachetas*, nor anything that might smell of idolatry, because since the natives of this place and surrounding places have seen the many wonders and miracles that the Virgin has performed for them, having forgotten their crazy ceremonies and superstitious rituals they come to her, who as the true mother that she is, never tires of favoring them with an open hand.]

Women's supervision of the agricultural rites dedicated to the Pachamama would doubtless have suggested to missionaries like Ramos Gavilán that the worship of the Pachamama would indeed arouse lasciviousness. It is this association with lust which renders impossible the Pachamama's syncretization with the Virgin Mary; unlike the Mother of Christ, the Indian deity is not virginal, chaste, or pure. The union of these two feminine deities results in a set of internal contradictions that are impossible to reconcile. Although a long tradition of Christian hermeneutics has permitted the invocation of a type through the presence of an antitype, the opposition between Virgin Mary and Pachamama cannot be reduced to these terms. For Christians, the cult of Pachamama must, because of its demonic nature, be denied and eliminated. To the Andean Indians, Pachamama remains a pivotal figure that links the natives not only to their immediate experience but also to their ancestral and mythical past.

However, Christian assimilation of other indigenous divinities was possible. For instance, the belief in a god, like Tijsi Viracocha, who created the entire universe, was easily incorporated into the idea of God the Father in Christian doctrine. Since it was believed that only the name, not the concept, was wrong, the insertion of the Indian deity into a Christian framework did not pose a problem. However, unlike Viracocha, the lascivious Pachamama was not assimilable. The fact that both Pachamama and the Virgin were feminine sacred figures and that both stood for motherhood and sustenance was simply not enough to collapse one into the other. The lasciviousness that Pachamama evoked made it necessary for the missionaries to mount an effort to eliminate her cult, rendering impossible an assimilation that would doubtless have led to heresy.

What may sometimes appear to be syncretism can in fact be attributed to the presence of certain modes of representation universal to all religions. Formal and symbolic elements common to all religious phenomena, such as sacred time, sacred space, and sacred water, may, however, have a different cultural or ideological significance, or both, depending on the system of belief in which they manifest themselves. The program of evangelization of the Indians in general, and Ramos Gavilán's vision in particular, involves emptying forms and symbols of their pre-Christian religious contents and then filling them with strictly Christian meaning. Not surprisingly, then, Ramos Gavilán expresses admiration for the pious and respectful conduct of the Indians in their temples, which he singles out as something to be emulated by less devout Catholics, because this is a trait both religions esteem very highly:

> Después de haber puesto los Idolos en sus lugares iban descalzos y sin mantas, y postrábanse ante ellos, adorándolos. Daba principio a esta adoración el más principal que se hallaba en la fiesta. Instrucción harto necesaria para que el cristianismo reconozca la humildad con que debe celebrar el sacrosanto misterio del altar, y que el más autorizado piense que postrarse ante el Santísimo Sacramento es lo que le autoriza más. (Ramos Gavilán 93)

> [After putting their idols in their proper place, they went without shoes and without shawls, and prostrated themselves before them to worship. This ceremony was led by the most important person that was present at the feast. This is a necessary example in which Christians should recognize the humbleness with which one must celebrate the sacred mystery of the altar, and the most powerful person should realize that to prostrate himself before the Holy Sacrament is what gives him his power.]

The Indians' piety, worthy of emulation even by Christians, would in turn facilitate the natives' conversion to Christianity, as would the recontextualization of some of their religious symbols. The rays of light to represent divinity, for instance, which in the pre-Christian Andean system were identified with Father Sun, begin to be associated with the Christian God.

Many of the religious practices of the Indians, such as fasting and confession, are also given a new significance in the context of the evangelization. Their pilgrimages, for instance, underwent a transformation. In times of difficulty, such as droughts, the ancient inhabitants of the Titicaca region would set forth on pilgrimages to the temples of their deities, like Copacabana or Copacati, the gods of fertility, to seek divine intercession. To this essentially agricultural ritual, Christian doctrine added the concept of an afterlife in which one would either achieve eternal bliss or everlasting damnation. According to Catholic doctrine, although humanity must expiate its sins, the rigors of atonement may be reduced, or completely forgiven, by means of indulgences, which the Pope, as the Vicar of Christ, has the power to grant.

A system of indulgences had existed in Christendom since the High Middle Ages. It was Pope Urban II who, in 1095, proposed plenary indulgences for those who participated in the First Crusade. Some thirty years before, around 1063, Pope Alexander II had granted similar dispensations to Spaniards and other Christians who fought against the Moors in Spain. Since the eleventh century, then, a system of indulgences had developed and flourished in the Christian West. Indulgences were routinely granted to pilgrims who visited sacred places, to believers who collaborated in the building of churches, or to those who were willing to pay for them in the form of charitable donations (Walker 347). Pope Clement VII granted plenary indulgence to the brotherhood of the Virgin of Copacabana in a bull dated 14 August 1604 (Calancha). By granting this privilege to the members of the brotherhood, the Church recognized the hierophanic quality of the image of the Virgin, and, therefore, the sacredness of the place where it was to be found. At the same time, this legitimizing gesture guaranteed the power of the Virgin of Copacabana for those who would invoke her assistance. The new Christian belief in the need to purify the soul prior to its entrance into Paradise left the natives little choice but to invoke the intercession of the Virgin, since the ancient gods possessed no jurisdiction over an afterlife. Had the Virgin's attributes been the same as those of the ancestral indigenous gods, the new hierophany would have been rendered superfluous. Yet, despite their differences, both divinities managed to share some attributes. In several narratives recording the miracles of the Virgin of Copacabana compiled by Ramos Gavilán, for instance, the Virgin, like the ancient gods of fertility, provided rain in times of drought (Ramos Gavilán 129–131).

When the Augustinian Ramos Gavilán arrived in Copacabana in 1617, the image of the Virgin had been enthroned on the altar as a sacred object for some time. The miracles attributed to the image had made possible its transformation from a religious objet d'art into a hierophany; in the eyes of believers, the miracles were a manifestation and confirmation of supernatural power.

As compiled by Ramos Gavilán, the long series of narratives about the miracles of the Virgin of Copacabana begins with an incident interpreted as a divine sign to build the Virgin's shrine in Copacabana. According to the story, once the conflict between the Urinsayas and the Anansayas had been resolved through the mediation of Don Gerónimo Marañón, the Corregidor of Omasuyos and the village of Copacabana, it was decided to move the statue of the Virgin from La Paz to Copacabana. On the day the image was carried on a litter to its new site, a heavy cross fell on the head of the Corregidor, who led the procession as the faithful entered the village. Ramos Gavilán describes the incident with the following words: "y con ser pesada la cruz no le hizo daño alguno, cosa que admiró a todos y se tuvo por milagro, y fue razón que la Virgen lo hiciese, con quien libró de olvido su retrato" [despite its weight, the cross did not hurt him, a fact that astonished everyone and was taken for a miracle, and the Virgin had reason for doing it, for it was he who had saved her portrait from oblivion] (Ramos Gavilán 124). Because of this miraculous event, the Augustinian tells us, "empezaron los fieles a venerar la Santa Imagen" [the faithful began to worship the Holy Image] (Ramos Gavilán 124).

The representation of this incident as a thaumaturgical event, along with subsequent narratives of other miracles, created an outpouring of devotion for the Virgin of Copacabana which gradually began to form part of local culture.[14]

In light of the foregoing discussion, one can say that the portrayal of an object as a hierophany depends on both the way in which it is represented and the meaning attached to this representation by a culture or an ideology. Both verbal representation and its interpretation are engaged here in a dialectical relationship: in the absence of mediation by each of these, the object (be it the Inca Manco Capac or the statue of the Virgin of Copacabana) would exist only in what Mircea Eliade calls the profane world.

COPACABANA AND THE AUGUSTINIANS

Just as the temples of native divinities had their priests, Copacabana too had its own sacerdotal group, who in addition to being in charge of the cult of the Virgin, took charge of the conversion of the region's inhabitants to Christianity. Although this had been customary in the Spanish

Crown's evangelical mission since the beginning of the Conquest of America, the circumstances at Copacabana are significant because the Augustinians were the ones who began to supervise the shrine almost immediately after the image arrived there. As we will see, Augustinian ideology provided people like Ramos Gavilán and Antonio de la Calancha a context from which to interpret the religious and political reality of the Andean region, and this, in turn, led to an evangelizing mission which was unusual and quite different from those initiated by other orders like the Dominicans and the Jesuits.

Ramos Gavilán tells us that large numbers of devotees came to what was then no more than a small church with a solitary secular priest, Father Montoro. Because of the ever-increasing renown of the Virgin, the ecclesiastical authorities saw fit to remove Montoro from his post and have a religious order take charge of the parish. Although not the first to be asked, the Augustinians gladly accepted the invitation. Ramos Gavilán states:

> Agradecida la Emperatriz del cielo de la humildad con que los Religiosos Agustinos reciben estos continuos favores, se sirvió de que en este nuevo mundo no perdiesen el oficio, para que ella tan de atrás los había escogido, y así viendo que este Copacabana, no subía tan aprisa como era justo el culto que se le debía, y que su amor podía ser se resfriase, por esto habiéndose esta Santa Imagen servido primero de las vistosas flores de Clérigo, quiso que no se quedase sola en flor su devoción, y así por orden que ya el cielo tenía dado, trajo a su casa las Africanas manzanas, digo los frayles Agustinos, con cuyo buen olor, ejemplo y continua doctrina, creciese aquella tierna devoción, que todavía había menester arrimos para no desmayar. (Ramos Gavilán 143)

> [The Empress of Heaven, recognizing the humility with which the Augustinian friars receive these continuous favors, was glad to see that in this New World they would not lose this mission, for which she had chosen them so long ago. Seeing that in Copacabana, the devotion to her did not grow so rapidly—as she deserves—and so that this love would not diminish, the image served herself first the attractive flowers of a clergy, but she did not want to keep only flowers of devotions, but brought fruits; that is why she brought to her house the African apples, meaning the Augustinian friars, who with their good smell, example, and continuous doctrine, would nurture there a tender devotion, which needed to be sustained and not to wilt.]

It is quite clear that the late medieval debate between Augustinians, Dominicans, and Franciscans concerning the Immaculate Conception resonates in this passage. Understandably, given their interest in the Virgin, the Augustinians would not miss the opportunity to play a key role in the evolving new cult to the mother of Christ.

The Augustinians, Ramos Gavilán reminds us, were also the ones who had long ago been chosen to disseminate and nourish the newly emerging cult of Christianity. For this reason they are not "flowers," like Father Montoro, but "fruits" of the Church, which provide both seed and nourishment for the faithful. Moreover, the metaphor of "African apples" suggests as well the providentialist vision of having been chosen to christianize the Indians. The adjective "African" obviously refers to Saint Augustine's birthplace; and the fact that they are "apples" remands us to the Tree of Knowledge in the Garden of Eden, which bore the forbidden fruit tasted by Adam and Eve. According to the fathers of the Church, Eve, in complicity with the Devil, was responsible for humanity's Fall by offering the apple to Adam. The Virgin Mary, as the second Eve, crushes the serpent's head as she undoes the curse of Genesis and foreshadows the birth of the Redeemer.[15] Saint Justine writes:

> [Christ was born of the Virgin] in order that by the same way in which the disobedience caused by the serpent took its beginning; by this way should it also take its destruction. For Eve, being a virgin and uncorrupt, conceived the word spoken of the serpent, and brought forth disobedience and death. But Mary the Virgin, receiving faith and grace . . . [gave birth to him] . . . by whom God destroys both the serpent and those angels and men that became like it . . . (as cited by Warner 100)

Ramos Gavilán sees the Augustinians as these new fruits of redemption, as the "apples" of salvation of the Second Eve as she is portrayed in the Virgin of Copacabana, who has come to offer the Indians succor and rescue them from the demon, idolatry. He thus proffers a providentialist explanation of the Augustinian presence in Copacabana.

What Ramos Gavilán considered to be part of a providential scheme was actually authorized by a royal decree on 7 January 1588. On that date Philip II "mandaba dar y que se diese la doctrina, y beneficio de Copacabana a la Orden de San Agustín, y que se le entregase la Santa Imagen, con todo lo perteneciente a ella, conforme al Patronazgo Real" [mandated that the church of Copacabana, with all its benefactions, be given to the Order of Saint Augustine, and that the Holy Image be entrusted to them with everything that belonged to it, in accordance with the Royal Patronage] (Ramos Gavilán 144). Ramos Gavilán's providential interpretation apparently failed to convince the Viceroy, the Conde del Villar, whom he quotes as saying "que se le hacía agravio al Padre Antonio de Montoro quitarle aquella doctrina, e Imagen, que tanto trabajo le había costado" [that it was unfair to take away from Fr. Antonio Montoro the church and the Image for which he had worked so hard] (Ramos Gavilán 144). The tension that existed between the viceregal authorities, most of whom were Spanish, and the Augustinians, most of whom were creoles, may explain the motivation behind the Viceroy's statement.[16]

The Augustinians took charge of the evangelizing mission in Copacabana on 16 January 1589 (Calancha 283) and remained there until 16 May 1826, when the civil authorities of the recently liberated Alto Perú (now Bolivia) removed them from the parish where on 6 April 1614 they had enthroned the image that Tito Yupanqui had sculpted for the church's high altar (Villarejo 353).

In 1631 the Augustinians began the construction of a basilica on the site, at the most imposing spot in the village of Copacabana. Its central nave and the high altar's *retablo*, fashioned by Don Carlos Acostopa Inca, were finished twenty years later. The basilica of Our Lady of Copacabana has eclipsed the Temple of the Sun in Titicaca, but the latter's sacredness has endured despite the ideological changes which have occurred through the centuries.

The cult of divinities of the various cultures that have inhabited Titicaca attest to the sacredness of the region. Each of these cultures has possessed specific modes for the representation of its beliefs (idols, images, rites, buildings, and narratives), and each in this way represents an avatar of the sacred, ranging from Viracocha to the Virgin of Copacabana. At different times the manifestations of the sacred were assimilated by newly arrived cultures that came to the area; at other times, they were simply supplanted. In the following chapter I will examine how the sacredness of the lake was represented in different narrative cycles belonging to disparate cultures.

2

The Kolla Narrative Cycle

TOWARD A SACRED HISTORY OF LAKE TITICACA

The peoples who have inhabited the region of Lake Titicaca have represented the sacredness of this place by resorting to various modes of representation: idols, temples, rites, and myths, among them. Numerous documents from the sixteenth and seventeenth centuries also include stories about Lake Titicaca which attest to its continuing religious significance for the different cultures that have flourished upon its shores.

These stories mark the permanence of Lake Titicaca's sacred nature. They constitute an attempt to represent a place in the continuous cosmic order for the region despite the discontinuities caused by periodic invasions perpetrated by other cultures. Three narrative cycles mark the lake's sacredness and correspond broadly to three clearly recognizable periods in the history of the region: the period preceding the Inca conquest, the Inca period, and the Christian period, which resulted from the Spanish conquest of Peru in 1532.

A close examination of these stories reveals the intertwining of new plots with tales belonging to previous narrative cycles. In its appropriation and recontextualization of elements from the old stories into its own narratives, the politically empowered group of a given moment guarantees continuity with the culture it seeks to dominate.

In the Lake Titicaca region, each culture, according to its perception of the sacred, has staked out and practiced its own ritual behavior. As a discrete cultural act, a culture's sacredness can then be studied in the stories on the subject written either by individual authors or gathered collectively in the oral tradition.[17] Since past oral traditions have come down to us only in the writings of colonial authors, however, the collected stories have passed through the ideological and cultural filters of their compilers. As a result, what we have are "contaminated" versions that do not faithfully represent early Andean thinking. Henrique Urbano's comments about the Andean myths of origins apply to the sacred narratives of Lake Titicaca:

> Todos o casi todos han sido recogidos en base a preocupaciones políticas y religiosas muy distintas de las nuestras. Esas preocupaciones formaban parte del arsenal político y religioso de la península ibérica, y habían sido aplicadas anteriormente en otros territorios conquistados. Quizás por eso, fue con algún escepticismo que los primeros recopiladores escucharon las explicaciones de los informantes y guiaron sus dilatadas encuestas. De igual manera, borraron de su escritos muchos materiales que hoy día nos privan de conocimientos indispensables para una visión cabal del problema mítico andino. (Urbano 1981, xvi)

> [All or almost all have been compiled because of political and religious preoccupations which were quite different from ours. These preoccupations formed part of the political and religious arsenal of the Iberian peninsula, and had been applied to other formerly conquered territories. Perhaps for that reason, the first compilers listened with a certain skepticism to the long explanations of their informants and directed their surveys with the same feeling. In the same way, they erased from their writings materials that today prevent us from achieving a basic knowledge in order to have an appropriate view of the Andean mythical problem.]

Mindful that the only textual sources available to us are collections of indigenous stories which have been contaminated by European elements, I can only offer speculative readings and conclusions. Nevertheless, the exercise is a fruitful one.

In the stories which have come down to us, one can see that the recognition of a hierophany on the part of the members of a given culture involves establishing a relationship between a natural and a divine order, as in the case of observing the cosmos and attributing its creation to one or several Gods.[18] Individuals or groups may, likewise, link the social order with the divine order, and not necessarily for religious reasons. They may do this to ensure their own survival or the domination of peoples inside or outside their culture. Such is the case in the history of the Andes: the Incas, who were a privileged caste, used religion and religious narratives to impose their supremacy on other Andean ethnic groups, just as the Spaniards would do in the same area years later. The establishment of a link to a divine order allows the politically empowered entity, be it an individual or a group, to impose its sociopolitical order on others and thus to secure its hegemony.

Elements comprising the divine, natural, and social orders are always culturally specific; what in one culture may be an integral part of the natural order may belong to the realm of the divine in another. The ways in which these orders relate to one another are also cultural constructions determined by specific perceptions and needs. Theistic cultures, for instance, establish an intimate relationship between the divine and the social orders. Social and political changes may result from the redefinition of these relationships.

In stories examined here, all of which establish and represent the relationship between the natural, divine, and social orders, the conquering cultures inscribe themselves into a divine order, which justifies an alteration of the existing power relations and the imposition of a new social order. In these stories, Lake Titicaca—a sacred space—is the pivotal point around which the narratives revolve.

The three cycles of sacred stories associated with Lake Titicaca have in common explicit or implicit references to some kind of initial chaos which a divine intervention attempts to organize. In the first narrative cycle, as a result of Tici Viracocha's intercession, natural and human order replaces the initial chaos of the cosmos. The darkness surrounding the earth yields to the sun, moon, and stars. Man, now settled in a definite place, begins to wear clothing and embraces a religion. After the establishment of this natural order, political chaos appears on the scene in the second narrative cycle. Following a divine mandate, Manco Capac arrives and imposes a civil order symbolized in the utensils, arms, seeds, and clothing of Inti's messengers. If for the natives the Andean world has achieved at this juncture political and social stability, for the Christians, whose views appear in the third cycle, that universe is fraught with moral chaos: the intervention of the devil, they claim, has led to a corruption of customs, which the Apostle Saint Thomas, messenger of Christ, unsuccessfully seeks to correct. Moral order can only be achieved with the successful completion of a Christian evangelical mission. With the miracles of the Virgin of Copacabana, the final avatar of all sacredness at Titicaca, the moral order of the third cycle falls into place.

The "meaning" attached to the stories from each cycle changes depending upon who the interpreter is and what the circumstances are. The stories from the first cycle, which invoke a pre-Inca Golden Age, during the Inca hegemony generate on the part of the Kollas a discourse of longing and resistance. The same narratives of the first cycle, interpreted by the Incas as a reflection of a period of chaos, evoke, as they later did for the Christians in the case of the Incas, a discourse of domination. Likewise, the stories of the second cycle, during the Spanish conquest, generate on the part of the Incas a discourse of longing and resistance. Not surprisingly, then, the stories from both "native" cycles engender on the part of the Spaniards—who saw only political and moral chaos in the New World before their arrival— a discourse of domination. The Christian narratives, furthermore, trace a teleology that, with the promise of eternal salvation, produces a discourse of hope.

The chronicler Ramos Gavilán was one of many Augustinians who recognized the importance of establishing a continuity between the Christian present and the Andean past in order to achieve the goals of the evangelical mission in the New World. His *Historia* encompasses a cultural project that opposes the official policy on the extirpation of idolatries which was in effect in the Andes during the last decades of the sixteenth century and in the beginning of the seventeenth.

Although I situate each narrative cycle examined within a specific historical time period at Lake Titicaca, the hierophantic history I propose does not hinge on chronology. Hierophantic periods, as I see them, are discrete historical moments in which discourses of domination and subjection intertwine. Each new conquest produces not only a political rupture but social and religious ones as well. These ruptures, however, tend to be minimized through the recontextualization of "old" stories. The new stories constitute an effort on the part of the dominating culture to establish a continuity of a teleological nature with the cultural past.

NARRATIVE CYCLES AND HISTORICAL PERIODS

It is possible to identify at least three cycles of sacred narratives in the Titicaca region, and each of them fluctuates between myth and history. The first is the Kolla cycle, which includes stories from the Kollasuyo before the Inca expansion into the region. The second is the Inca cycle, which includes stories that link the Incas to Lake Titicaca; and the third is constituted by the Christian cycle, which includes stories with a Christian content.

Although each cycle corresponds to a specific moment in history, their chronology may often be blurred. The temporal limits of the cycles may expand, resulting in an overlap of their chronology; or two chronologically distant cycles may merge, resulting in a narrative unit despite the temporal gap that separates them.

In my history of the sacred at Lake Titicaca I include in the Kolla cycle the creation myths in which Viracocha is a protagonist, and in which there is no mention of the Incas. Although some may argue, following Henrique Urbano, that these myths may be considered contemporary to those of the Incas, I argue that, because the Inca presence at Titicaca came later, the myths about Viracocha preceded those of the Incas.[19]

THE KOLLAS

The name of each of the four parts of the Inca empire—the Tahuan-tinsuyu—corresponded to the most important cultural group that lived in each of the four regions comprising the empire. Kollasuyo, the south-ern quarter of the empire, in which Lake Titicaca is located, derived its name from the ancient Kolla ethnic polity that encompassed the territory northeast of Titicaca, whose capital was Hatuncolla.[20]

Although not all the natives who lived in the surrounding areas of the lake, and who mainly spoke the Aymara language, belonged to this eth-nic group, the term Kolla has been customarily applied to all of those who inhabited the Kollasuyo. For example, the Lupacas, the Omasuyos, and the Pacajes fall within the broad category of "Kollas." I use the term Kolla, then, in this broad sense to refer to all groups, including the great pre-Inca ethnic polity of the same name.[21]

The first pre-Inca period may be subdivided into chronological mo-ments if we consider the different ethnic cultures that lived in the Titicaca area throughout history. Bouysse Cassagne, using geological and archeo-logical evidence, constructs a chronology of Lake Titicaca that indicates the climate, the levels of the lake, and the cultures that lived in the region. Table 1 is an abridged version of one of her tables.

The geographical location of the lake constitutes one of the reasons for its cultural importance:

Situado sobre el eje mediano del altiplano, el lago constituye, con Tiawa-nacu, un lugar de mediación (*taypi* en aymara) entre las dos orillas: al este entre el lago y la Cordillera Real cercana, el Umasuyu; al oeste, solidaria y a la vez contradictoria, la orilla opuesta del Urcosuyo. En tiempo despe-jado, desde la isla del Sol (Titicaca) y de la Luna (Coati), es el arco nevado de la Cordillera Real el que parece constituir la frontera entre el lago y el cielo de tan cerca que parecen. Hacia el sud, la península de Copacabana se aproxima a la de Huata, estando ésta separada por el estrecho de Tiquina. La masa de las aguas está, de este modo, dividida en dos por ese brazo de tierra: al norte, el lago de Chucuito o lago de Pukina (según la antigua terminología); y al sud, el lago de Wiñaymarca (el país de la Eternidad en Puquina y Aymara); de suerte que el estrecho de Tiquina es esa puerta estrecha que comunica entre sí a dos universos acuáticos, e indi-vidualiza dos cuencas. Es el paso obligado porque es el más estrecho de una orilla a la otra. Para la gente del Urcosuyo, el control del estrecho, vale decir de la península de Copacabana y de las islas de la península de Huata, marcan el acceso a las tierras templadas de los valles y a las

Chronology	Climate and Changing Levels of the Lake	Cultures	Languages
10000 BC to 2500 BC	Changes from flood stage to completely dry	Viscachani, Laguna Hedionda, Laguna Colorada	Uru, Choquela
2500 BC to 250 BC	Greater humidity, the lake begins to rise	North: Pucara (ca. 1100–100) South: Chiripa (ca. 500–100)	Pukina (?)
250 BC to 1000 AD	Last phase of rising lake levels	Tiawanacu	Pukina
1100 AD to 1200 AD		Chullpas	Diffusion of Aymara
1200 AD to 1400 AD		Aymaras, Lupacas, and Collas	Aymara, Pukina and Uru
1400 AD to 1500 AD	The cycle of the rising of the waters comes to an end	Inca occupation	Highlands: Aymara Valleys: Quechua (*mitimaes*)
1528 to present	Slight lowering of the lake's levels	Arrival of the Spaniards	Highlands: Aymara/ Spanish. Valleys: Quechua/Spanish

Table 1. A Chronology of the Cultures in the Lake Titicaca Region

planicies amazónicas; y para los de la orilla del Omasuyo, el dominio de las riquezas de las costas del Pacífico. . . . para los habitantes de Tiwanacu, al sud, el estrecho significa también el paso hacia la gran cuenca lacustre y a las tierras más al norte. . . . pero por las mismas razones, los habitantes de las orillas septentrionales tenían interés en controlar la península. (Bouysse Cassagne 1988, 31)

[Situated on the median axis of the high plateau, the lake, together with Tiwanacu, constitutes a place of mediation (*taypi* in Aymara) between the two shores: to the East, between the lake and the nearby Cordillera Real, the Umasuyo; to the West, solidary and at the same time contradictory, the opposite shore of Urcosuyo. On a clear day, from the Island of the Sun (Titicaca) and the Island of the Moon (Coati), the snow peaks of the

Cordillera Real seem to be the frontier between the lake and the sky, they appear to be so near. Toward the south, the Copacabana peninsula is close to the Huata peninsula, both separated by the strait of Tiquina. The water mass is therefore divided in two by this piece of land: to the north, the lake of the Chucuito or Pukina Lake (according to ancient terminology); and to the south, the lake of Wiñaymarka ("the land of Eternity" in Puquina and Aymara); the Tiquina strait is that narrow gate that communicates between two aquatic universes and individualizes two basins. It is the necessary passage from one shore to the other because it is the narrowest. For the people of Urcosuyo, the control of the straits, that is of the Copacabana peninsula and the islands of the Huata peninsula, signify the access to the temperate lands of the valleys and the Amazonian lowlands; and for the people of the Omasuyo shore, the dominion of the riches of the Pacific coast. . . . for the inhabitants of Tiwanacu, in the south, the strait means the access to the large river basin and to the northern lands. . . . for the same reasons, the inhabitants of the southern shores were keen on controlling the peninsula.]

The location of the lake and its importance in the daily lives of the natives, in terms of agriculture, fishing, and politics, made it an exceptional place, which was coveted by those who wished to exercise control of the region. Hence, "quien controle ese centro neurálgico, controlará potencialmente, a la vez, las riquezas y los dioses, y juntará las dos mitades antagónicas del Universo (derecha/izquierda, alto/bajo, hombre/mujer)" [whoever controlled this vital center would potentially control both wealth and the gods at the same time. This would unite the two opposing halves of the universe—right/left, high/low, man/woman] (Bouysse Cassagne 1988, 32).

As I noted in Chapter 1, scholars of religious phenomenology describe a sacred space as a place that mediates between the divine and the human; the notion of Aymaran *taypi* assigned to Lake Titicaca is a cultural representation of this phenomenon. All the different cultures from the region left evidence that the site had a religious significance. For example,

hacia el año 1000–1200 d.d.c. aparecieron unas construcciones funerarias, generalmente en formas de iglú, las *chullpas*, que se superpusieron a los templos y a los lugares de culto. Este notable cambio estilístico al final del Tiwanacu expansivo, interpretado como el reflejo de un cambio en las prácticas religiosas, como consecuencia de diferencias étnicas, nos incita hoy a considerar, que el estudio de los fenómenos religiosos debe estar ligado a las diversas olas de ocupación del altiplano. (Bouysse Cassagne 1988, 44–45)

[toward the year A.D. 1000–1200 funerary constructions appeared in the form of igloos, the *chullpas*, that were superimposed on the temples and places of worship. This noticeable stylistic change at the end of the Tiwanaku expansive, interpreted as a change in the religious practices due to ethnic differences, invites us today to consider that the study of the religious phenomena must be linked to the diverse waves of occupations in the plateau.]

Archeological findings indicate that the Titicaca region had a religious significance for all its inhabitants, beginning with the Pucara, who were followed, successively, by the Chiripas, Tiahuanacus, Chullpas, Collas, Aymara, and Lupacas.[22] Different languages correspond to the different time periods. Pukina, the language spoken in the beginning (and still in use as late as the colonial period), was followed by the Aymara language with the arrival of the Lupacas, who came from the Coquimbo region of Chile and were attracted by the fame of the Island of Titicaca, where the solar cult seems to have had already a long history (Bouysse Cassagne 1988; Hyslop 1976; Gisbert, Arze, and Cajías 1987). Each culture left a wake of myths and legends. Each marked this place with its idols and religious buildings in such a manner that one can read, as if in an eternal book, both the supreme importance of religion in the area and the successive periods of its sacred history. Bouysse Cassagne believes that proof of its religious significance lies in the

> obsesión, tan particular al hombre de esta región, de privilegiar ciertos lugares, de sacralizarlos de modo que la escritura del mito reenvía muy directamente . . . a la arquitectura de una cierta geografía religiosa donde cada una de las sucesivas invasiones tuvieron que inscribirse. Los mitos tratan de dos lugares esencialmente: Tiwanacu y una isla del lago Titicaca. . . . Y es allí donde los primeros ocupantes del lago . . . los Aymaras y después los Incas, inscribieron como en un palimpsesto una parte importante de su historia. (1988, 27).

> [obsession, so particular to the man of this region, to privilege certain places, to sacralize them in such a way that the myth redirects very directly . . . to the architecture of a certain religious geography where each one of the successive invasions had to inscribe itself. The myths deal especially with two places in particular: Tiwanacu and an island on Lake Titicaca. . . . And it is there where the first inhabitants of the lake . . . (then) the Aymaras and later the Incas, wrote like on a palimpsest an important part of their history.]

One could perhaps attribute certain elements of the myths of origin, which have come down to us in sixteenth- and seventeenth-century texts, to one or another indigenous culture. Bouysse Cassagne, for instance, correlates the "flood" mentioned in the myths with the rising of the lake's surface during the Pucara period. Geological studies and archeological findings confirm the occurrence of such an event during that period, which was immortalized in myths and legends (Bouysse Cassagne 1988, 43). Using this type of approach, one could establish a chronology of the different elements that shape the myth. And if one were to discover that analogous events occurred in subsequent periods (i.e., Inca and Christian), then it would be possible to trace in the indigenous myths a pattern of superimpositions, appropriations, and recontextualizations of elements from one culture to another—the result being an atemporal cultural resonance among the myths that suggests a certain continuity in them across time. Although with the aid of archeological and historical data it is possible to establish the existence of successive ethnic occupations in the Titicaca region during the pre-Inca period, I will nevertheless group this time period into one narrative cycle.

For the reconstruction of this narrative cycle, I have considered sixteen different versions of the origin myth compiled between 1550 and 1653.[23] All these stories mention Lake Titicaca as the primeval place, the beginning of all things. A structural analysis of these narratives permits the construction of a master narrative, which in turn allows a distillation of extraneous elements introduced in the myths by, in all likelihood, their interpreters, who, consciously or unconsciously, inscribed their ideologies or self-interests in their transcriptions. At the same time, this master narrative facilitates the study of the differences among the various versions of the stories.

MASTER NARRATIVE: VIRACOCHA AND THE CREATION

Viracocha appeared in the region surrounding Lake Titicaca. Darkness reigned as neither the sun nor moon had yet been created. He passed through Tiwanacu, where he created giants and mankind, along with animals and all things. Viracocha prescribed certain rules of conduct which his creatures were to observe. Because of humankind's disobedience, Viracocha sent a flood that destroyed everything, save for some privileged individuals who managed to escape punishment. When the flood receded, Viracocha traveled to Titicaca and created the sun, moon, and stars. He formed the different lineages of humankind with the clay of Tiawanaco and gave each group its clothing, language, songs, agricultural systems, and religion. Viracocha sent some of the individuals he had just created to the tops of the mountains, others to the rivers and springs, and still others into caves. This is how the different lineages originated. After he finished his creative labors and populated the earth,

Viracocha set off on a journey throughout the different regions of the Andes. He went from one region to the next revealing himself as their creator, though not all recognized him. In Cacha the people attempted to kill him, and Viracocha punished them with a rain of fire that he then extinguished with his staff, answering the pleas of the penitent offenders. When his mission on earth was finished, Viracocha disappeared into the sea.

Viracocha Appeared in the Regions Surrounding Lake Titicaca

Although all of the chroniclers mention a creator, the name "Viracocha" appears in only thirteen of the sixteen versions. In several narratives it appears simply as Viracocha (Sarmiento de Gamboa [II], Gutiérres de Santa Clara, Cobo [III], Calancha, Acosta);[24] in others, it appears together with four other appellations: Con Ticsi (Las Casas, Betanzos, Cieza de León, Molina), Pachayachachic (Sarmiento de Gamboa [I], Molina, Acosta [II]), and materializing as Tonapa and Taracapa Viracochanpachayachican or Pacchan and Bicchhaycamayoc Cunacuycamayoc (Santacruz Pachacuti Yamqui).

Henrique Urbano includes the different semantic contents that chroniclers and grammarians of the colonial period attributed to the word *Viracocha*. Table 2 presents a synopsis of several different meanings given to the word by various chroniclers and grammarians of the time.

Domingo de Santo Tomás and Holguín were not alone in their translation of *Viracocha* as "Christian," nor were they alone in relating it to the Spaniards. Other authors also mention that the Indians called the Spanish Viracochas.[25] There are several different reasons the Indians called the Spanish Viracocha, but they are not immediately relevant to the discussion here.[26] All other meanings connote an extraordinary being, which the chroniclers transcribed or represented using the words *god*, *maker of the world*, or *creator*.

Urbano notes that the stories compiled by the chroniclers were imbued with their political and religious preoccupations, among them "la búsqueda afanosa de una creencia en un dios 'único y creador' que de alguna manera mostrara los rasgos del Dios de la tradición judeocristiana" [the painstaking search for a belief in one omnipotent god that would somehow exhibit the characteristics of the God in the Judeo-Christian tradition] (Urbano 1981, xvi). This is why, Urbano goes on to explain (xxv), the commentaries of the chroniclers about Viracocha tend to subsume the god into just one individual whose primary purpose is to be the "criador y hacedor de todas las cosas" [creator and maker of all things].

Bertonio attributes *Viracocha* to the Incas, which would make it a Quechua word. In his *Vocabulario de la Lengua Aymara*, the term ap-

Source	Meaning
Bartolomé de Las Casas (1550)	Condici Viracocha, que en la lengua del Cuzco suena "Hacedor del Mundo" [Condici Viracocha, which in Cuzcan language means "Creator of the world"]
Domingo de Santo Tomás (1560)	Cristiano [Christian]
Holguín, D.G.	epicteto del sol honroso nombre del Dios que adoravan los indios y de ay yguallandolos con su Dios llamauan a los españoles Viracocha. [epithet referring to the sun, name of the god worshiped by the Indians and from that meaning, equating Spaniards with their God, they called them Viracocha.]
Sarmiento de Gamboa (1572)	Viracocha Pachayacachi, que quiere decir Criador de todas las cosas [Viracocha Pachayacachi, which means Creator of all things]
Cristóbal de Molina, "El Cusqueño" (1575)	Tecsi Viracocha, que quiere decir Incomprensible Dios [Tecsi Viracocha, which means Unintelligible God]
Acosta (1590)	un supremo señor y hacedor de todo, al cual los del Perú llamaban Viracocha [a supreme lord and maker of everything, whom the people of Peru called Viracocha]
Bertonio (1612)	significa sabio segun los ingas, o fue nombre proprio de uno de aquellos antiguos muy savio [it means wise according to the Incas, or it was a proper name of a very wise ancestor]
Cobo (1653)	daban a la primera causa títulos y nombres de gran excelencia: los más honrosos y usados eran dos: Viracocha el uno, y el otro Pachayachachic [they assigned to the First Cause titles and names of great excellence: the most honorable and used were two: one was Viracocha, and the other Pachayachachic.]

Table 2. Viracocha: Its Various Meanings in the Sixteenth and Seventeenth Centuries

pears only in the first section—Castilian/Aymara—where it is translated as "español." But in defining the word *dios*, Bertonio provides ten different expressions, each one with a different meaning: eternal God, God without beginning and end, all-powerful God, God of the universe, God obeyed by all, God who gives life to all mankind, God creator of all things, God of infinite glory, God of infinite majesty, God the impartial judge, God of infinite mercy. Clearly, Bertonio tries to find words and phrases that could represent the idea of a Christian god in the Aymara language. But, in addition to these expressions, Bertonio (1612) registers another entry for the word *Dios*:

> Dios fue tenido destos indios uno a quien llamauan Tunuupa, de quien cuentan infinitas cosas. Dellas muy indignas no solo de Dios, sino de qualquiera hombre de razon, otras que tiran a los misterios de nuestra santa fe. Mucho haria al caso declarar a los indios los enbustes de Tunuupa para que todo lo que del cuentan se vea claramente ser fabula y se desengañen. En otras tierras o prouincias del Peru le llamaban Ecaco . . . (Bertonio 192)

> [These Indians had as God someone called Tunuupa, about whom they tell endless things. Some of them very offensive not only to God, but to any man of reason, some others relate to the mysteries of our holy faith. It would be very worthwhile to disclose to the Indians the lies of Tunuupa so that everything that they say about him be shown to be fables and the Indians realized the truth. In some other lands or provinces of Peru they called him Ecaco . . .]

According to Bertonio, the Kollas identified their God as Tunupa. The myth of Tunupa, which I will discuss in the chapter on the Christian narratives, is similar to that of Viracocha. Ramos Gavilán and Antonio de la Calancha recontextualize the Tunupa myth within the Christian tradition and represent this hero as one of Jesus Christ's apostles.

In all sixteen versions that I have considered, Santacruz Pachacuti Yamqui's is the only one to invoke the name of Tunupa. He mentions it along with other appellations: "le llamaban Tonapa o Tarapaca, Viracochapachayachicachan o Pacchan y Bicchaycamayoc Cunacuycamayoc" [they called him Tonapa o Tarapaca, Viracochapachayachicachan o Pacchan and Bicchaycomayoc Cunacuycamayoc]. Santacruz Pachacuti provides these as alternative names for the same hero. It is thus not unreasonable to hypothesize that Tunupa was the name of the hero in the Kolla myth.

In Santacruz Pachacuti's tale, Tunupa also appeared in the Titicaca region—in the Kollao. Ramos Gavilán records a similar story, though it is clearly recontexualized within Christianity. He tells us that the inhabitants of the Peruvian highlands had the time-honored tradition that an extraordinary personage called Tarapaca (one of Christ's disciples, according to Ramos Gavilán) had visited the Titicaca area. He also affirms that the appearance of the Incas came relatively late (Topa Inca was the first to visit the lake). Therefore, the presence of the hero Tunupa or Tarapaca predates the Inca expansion, and his identification with one of Christ's disciples dates the event at the beginning of the Christian Era.

Gisbert notes the following regarding Tunupa's cultural identity:

> Tunupa es un dios aimara, celeste y purificador, relacionado con el fuego y con el rayo. Con posterioridad la imagen de Viracocha, Dios creador, se le superpone heredando todas sus cualidades positivas, y dejando para Illapa los poderes negativos como agente destructor y activo que domina el fuego del cielo. (Gisbert 1980, 35)

> [Tunupa is an Aymara god, heavenly and purifying, related with fire and lightning. Later the image of Viracocha, God creator, was superimposed on him, keeping all the positive qualities, and leaving the negative powers to Illapa, as a destroyer and active agent who rules celestial fire.]

According to Gisbert and Ponce Sanjinés, Viracocha replaced Tunupa, which suggests that, at one point in time, Tunupa and Viracocha must have been two separate gods. Gisbert assigns positive qualities to Viracocha—the ones associated with creation—and to Illapa the negative ones. We will soon see that the separation of qualities into positive and negative cannot be sustained when we consider the different versions of the myth that have been preserved. Furthermore, a Manichean separation between a creator and a destroyer seems to be a Western imposition on the Andean view of the cosmos, where a fundamental equilibrium exists between positive and negative forces. Opposites do not necessarily exclude one another but are instead complementary (Van den Berg and Schiffers 301). Illapa was associated with rain and thus with fertility and life and at the same time with death; the mummified bodies were called *yllapas*, according to Albornoz.[27] Nor do I believe that one can maintain that a complete replacement occurred, since contemporary versions of the myth (Santacruz Pachacuti and Ramos Gavilán) compiled in the Kollao region refer to this god as Tunupa. It seems more likely that the existence of both names reflects a linguistic difference in the naming of a pan-Andean divinity which, like the Hindu god Brahma, has the attributes of creator and destroyer simultaneously.[28]

If for the Aymaras Tunupa was the name of one of their gods, as Bertonio claims, and if the "story," as Ramos Gavilán's Aymara informants related it to him, was in essence the same as that of Viracocha's, it is possible to argue that this is one of the Kolla myths of origin. Since *Viracocha* is a Quechua word, perhaps it replaced the name of a previous god or the stories that have come down to us are an amalgamation of similar myths that evolved after the Incas had conquered the region. Even if this were not true, however, the myth clearly refers back to a primeval time when all things originated. The fact that this initial moment is associated with Lake Titicaca is of paramount importance.

Urbano makes a distinction among four "Viracochas": Pachayachachi o Yachachi,[29] Imaymana,[30] Tocapo,[31] and Taguapaca or Taguapica,[32] each performing different functions. By comparing the different versions, Urbano also shows that these Viracochas appear in a hierarchal relationship, headed by Viracocha Pachayachachi, the principal figure, with the others as his children or as his assistants or servants. In addition to these, other names were associated with Viracocha: Tecsi, Ticci, Tici, Contici, Tonapa or Tunupa.

The functions of the principal figures, according to Urbano, were the following:

> *Pachayachachi o Tecsi Viracocha* representa la sabiduría o la capacidad de ordenamiento del mundo y de las cosas, de las cuales participan también los dos hijos héroes, Imaymana y Tocapo. (Urbano 1981, xxxii)

> [*Pachayachachi or Tecsi Viracocha* represent wisdom or the capacity to order the world and things, a capacity which his hero children, Imaymana and Tocapo, share.]

> Las funciones de *Imaymana* son significativas: poderes mágico-curativos y, quizá agrícolas. Imaymana es aquél "en cuyo poder y mano están todas las cosas." (Urbano 1981, xxxii)

> [The functions of *Imaymana* are significant: magical-curative powers, and perhaps agricultural. Imaymana is the one "in whose power and hands is everything."]

> [*Tocapo*]: Las funciones del tercer héroe . . . tienen algo que ver con la producción de tejidos finos, empleados sobretodo en las prácticas rituales, ya sea por los oficiantes encargados de ejecutar los ritos, ya sea en las ofrendas entregadas a las diferentes wakas. (Urbano 1981, xxxiii)

> [[*Tocapo*]: The functions of the third hero . . . have something to do with the production of fine textiles, employed above all in ritual practices, by the officiating priest in charge of the rituals, or given by them as offerings to different deities.]

Besides assigning a specific function to each hero, Urbano's structural model traces for each of them a specific route through the Andes whose starting point is Lake Titicaca or Tiwanaku.

We still must clarify Tunupa's role in this paradigm, keeping in mind that, according to Bertonio, he is a Kolla deity or hero. Urbano explains that

> el personaje Tunupa recorre un espacio en el que a veces se confunde con Taguapaca y a veces con Pachayachachi, hecho éste que sugiere que, en realidad se trata del mismo héroe con funciones semejantes a las dos caras del Viracocha principal y de Taguapaca. (Urbano 1981, xxxii)

> [the character Tunupa traverses a space in which sometimes he is confused with Taguapaca and sometimes with Pachayachachi, which suggests that it really is the same hero with functions similar to the two different faces of the main Viracocha and of Taguapaca.]

Cieza de León (1553) states that the Kollao people called Ticciviracocha by the name Tuapaca. Ramos Gavilán (1621) says that Tunupa was also called Taapac, "son of the creator." Since he depicts him within a Christian context, as we will see presently, he assigns to Tunupa positive characteristics, making him a saint. However, the same character, with the names of Taguapica o Taguapaca, is transformed in the versions by Las Casas (1550) and Sarmiento de Gamboa (1572) into a god with a negative characteristic, namely, disobedience. Urbano explains the contradiction:

> No hay, por cierto, ninguna razón filológica para decir que Taguapaca y Tunupa o Tonapa son dos nombres de un mismo héroe. Pero algunos relatos y textos antiguos sugieren que se trata de un solo personaje, pese al hecho de que en algunos de ellos recibe tratamiento contradictorio: rebelde y castigado por su desobediencia, y bondadoso, muerto por la maldad de las gentes a quienes predicaba. Es esta doble tradición o lectura recogida por los cronistas que Bertonio ejemplifica cuando define lo que era "dios" para los indios. (Urbano 1981, xxix)

> [Certainly there is no philological reason to say that Taguapaca and Tunupa or Tonapa are two names of the same hero. But some narratives and old texts suggest that we are dealing with a single character, in spite of the fact that in some of them he receives a contradictory treatment. In some he is rebellious and punished for his disobedience, and in others he is kind, and is killed by the malevolence of the people to whom he was preaching. It is this double tradition or reading rendered by the chroniclers that Bertonio exemplifies when he defines what "god" was for the Indians.]

Here, Urbano refers to Bertonio's definition for *dios* in the Aymara language of the Kollao. This differentiation seems unimportant to Urbano, since he uses Bertonio's definition under the assumption that it applies to all Indian traditions without regard for their different ethnicity. However, with reference to Tunupa, this distinction is crucial because it justifies a separation between pre-Inca and Inca myths and supports the recognition of three different narrative cycles.

The double reading alluded to by Urbano originates in the dissonance among the versions, which, according to him, is exemplified in the part of Bertonio's definition of God that was "offensive not only to Him," "but to any man of reason." The "offensive" things to which Bertonio refers are two female marine creatures, Quesintu and Umantuu, with whom Tunupa had sinned, an episode which is completely transformed in Ramos Gavilán's christianized version. These aquatic female beings become "una señora muy hermosa, que puesta sobre la balsa, libró al santo y le acompañó navegando con él" [a beautiful woman who, from a boat, saved the saint and sailed away with him] (40). This transformation has a double function in Ramos Gavilán's story: first, it eliminates all the negative or sinful connotations in order to represent Tunupa as a Christian apostle; and second, it foreshadows the Virgin of Copacabana, who is to reign in the region in the future.

Classical mythology, European folklore, and medieval bestiaries had represented a being half woman, half fish, the siren, as a figure that symbolizes the beauty and temptation that would lead man to destruction (Cirlot 1982, 415). Following this iconographic tradition, it would not be unusual, then, for Bertonio or other chroniclers to demonize Tunupa or Taguapaca, attributing to them sinful or negative characteristics when dealing with episodes involving Quesintu and Umantuu.

However, when viewed from an indigenous frame of reference, the episode represents something else. Quesintu and Umantuu, which are Aymara names for two types of fish common to Lake Titicaca, constituted an essential part of the diet of those who lived on the shores of the lake. The link between the origin of these fish and one of their gods must be seen as the sacralization of quotidian needs, a phenomenon similar to the transformation of unusual agricultural products into sacred objects. Arriaga notes:

> Las Conopas, q' en el Cuzco, y por allá arriva llaman Chancas; son propiamente sus dioses Lares y Penates . . . estas son de diversas materias y figuras, aunque de notable, o en la color, o en la figura. . . . Ay también Conopas más particulares, unas para el maiz, que llaman Zarapconopa. . . .
>
> Zaramamas, son de tres maneras, y son las que se quentan entre las cosas halladas en los pueblos. La primera es una como muñeca hecha de

cañas de maiz. . . . Otras son de piedra labradas como choclos, o mazorcas de maiz. . . . Otras son algunas cañas fértiles de maiz, que con la fertilidad de la tierra dieron muchas maçorcas, y grandes, o quando salen dos maçorcas juntas, y estas son las principales, Zaramamas, y assí las reverencian como a madres del maiz. . . . A este tercer género no le dan la adoración, que a Huaca, ni Conopa, sino que le tienen supersticiosamente como una cosa sagrada. (Arriaga 26–29)

[The Conopas, which in Cuzco and in the mountains are called Chancas, are household deities and Penates. . . . They are made of different materials and in different shapes, yet remarkable in color or in shape. . . . There are also some particular Conopas, some for corn called Zarap-conopa. . . .

Zaramamas are of three kinds and are among the things found in towns. The first is like a doll made out of corn canes. . . . Others are made out of carved stones shaped as ears of corn. . . . Others are fertile corn canes, which with the fertility of the land gave many and large ears of corn, or when two ears come together, and these ones are the most important Zaramamas, for they are revered as mothers of corn. . . . This third kind is not worshipped as a huaca, nor Conopa, but it is superstitiously held as a sacred object.]

These *zaramamas*, like the story of Quesintu and Umantuu, embody a mode of representation of the sacred: the transformation of common elements of Andean culture into something holy. Thus, the interpretation of the story of Quesintu and Umantuu as an instance of immorality arises from the imposition of a foreign perspective. Andeans would not have interpreted the incident as immoral because their views on sexuality differ greatly from Catholic views.[33]

In Chapter 1 I discussed Ramos Gavilán's attitude toward sexual behavior and how he associates it with humanity's fall and sin. This attitude, shared by other chroniclers, explains the purging of episodes they deemed immoral in their attempt to Christianize the myths and find among the Andean gods a "dios único y creador" [a single creator god] or one of Christ's apostles. However, if we interpret Quesintu and Umantuu's episode as a representation of sustenance from the waters for mankind, and if we recall that Viracocha is depicted as having emerged from the lake (Acosta 63), as well as that his name means "espuma del mar" [sea foam] (Gutiérres de Santa Clara; Calancha 209), we can then see that the myths and the aquatic symbolism associated with Lake Titicaca respond to a mind-set that is common to all religions:

Principle of what is formless and potential, basis of every cosmic manifestation, container of all seeds, water symbolizes the primal substance from
which all forms come and to which they will return either by their own re-
gression or in a cataclysm. It existed at the beginning and returns at the
end of every cosmic or historic cycle; it will always exist, though never
alone, for water is always germinative, containing the potentiality of all
forms in their unbroken unity. In cosmogony, in myth, ritual and iconography, water fills the same function in whatever type of cultural pattern we
find it; it precedes all forms and upholds all creation. (Eliade 1963, 188)

All renditions of the cosmogonic myth that I have considered indicate
that Lake Titicaca is a primeval place. The variants coincide in their pre-
sentation of an extraordinary being who appears at the lake and performs an organizing or creative function and who also becomes multiple
beings with similar but limited functions. This extraordinary being, who
was called Viracocha in the Quechua language, seems to have been
Tunupa, the god of the Aymara Indians who lived in the region hundreds
of years before the arrival of the Incas.

The Reign of Darkness

Five accounts of the myth (Betanzos, Cieza de León, Sarmiento de Gamboa, Acosta [II], and Cobo [III]) speak explicitly of darkness, since neither the sun nor the stars had yet been created. The representation of a
time dominated by the absence of light provokes a chain of associations
connected with the idea of darkness.

The most basic Spanish dictionary includes among its synonyms for
oscuro the following words: *abstracto, caliginoso, confuso, enrevesado,
fulginoso, inconexo, inextricable, misterioso, vago, ambiguo,* and *in-
comprensible.*[34] Similarly, Roget's *Thesaurus* has the following terms under *obscure*: *blinded, concealed, covered, dark, hard to understand, la-
tent.* With the word *darkness,* or any of its synonyms, and the vagueness
that it evokes, formlessness or chaos is represented. Within the myth the
word is very graphic, referring to what preceded the creation of the visible world, in which objects are distinguished from one another. The absence of darkness is precisely what makes this world visible. In these versions, the image of darkness performs the function of differentiating
between two moments: before and after the creation of the world, chaos
and order, and nothingness and being.

The intervention of Viracocha in the cosmogonic myth makes possible
the transition from one moment to the next and, as maker and creator of
all things, Viracocha separates one from the other. Therefore, the mere

mention of Viracocha as maker or creator implies a nonexistence before his presence even in the versions that do not mention a period of darkness. In all remaining variants, except those of Santacruz Pachacuti and Pedro Gutiérres de Santa Clara, Viracocha is mentioned as creator (Betanzos, Molina, Acosta, Cobo [I–IV]) or maker of all things (Las Casas, Cieza de León, Sarmiento de Gamboa [I and II]). The presence of the image of darkness in the five aforementioned versions does not contradict the other variants; it simply states what in the others is just implied.

Gutiérres de Santa Clara's rendition is very brief and appears to have been collected along the northern coast of Peru. In this version Viracocha is an extraordinary being who, having emerged from the sea, not only taught the Indians how to sail, but had also spent time with their ancestors "enseñándoles buena doctrina y pulicia" [teaching them good doctrine and civility]. This Viracocha shows no creative function, nor is there a mention of a time before creation, because of Gutiérres de Santa Clara's tendency to recontextualize this hero as one of Christ's disciples:

> Tiénese entendido por los españoles que debió ser algún discipulo de los discípulos del Señor, que pasó por aquí predicándoles. (Gutiérres de Santa Clara 245)

> [Spaniards believe that he must have been one of the disciples of our Lord, who came here to preach.]

Gutiérres de Santa Clara and others like him who attempt to assimilate an Andean hero into Christian tradition must necessarily reject any allusion to Viracocha's creative function in order to maintain the story's Christian coherence. Santacruz Pachacuti and Ramos Gavilán also purged their texts of any detail that could possibly deify the hero.[35] With the exception of these versions, all others allude, implicitly or explicitly, to a transformation from chaos/nonexistence/darkness to order/existence/light.

Viracocha Created Mankind, Animals, and All Things

In some renditions of the myth we can only infer an act of creation from the appellations assigned to Viracocha. Acosta mentions Viracocha Pachayachachic as "criador del cielo y tierra" [creator of heaven and earth] (219), and Calancha calls him "maestro i criador del mundo" [master and creator of the world]. Neither of these versions tells us which things were created or establishes when the creation occurred. But each version presents interesting aspects, if not about the myth itself, then about the way it was received and transcribed by the chroniclers.

The simplicity of Acosta's version does not necessarily reflect the version of the myth that was told to him; rather, it reveals the chronicler's attitude toward indigenous myths:

> Saber lo que los mismos indios suelen contar de sus principios y origen, no es cosa que importa mucho, pues más parecen sueños los que refieren, que historias. (Acosta 63)

> [It is not so important to know what the Indians themselves tell about their beginning and origin, because what they narrate are more like dreams than stories.]

That the Indians had a god named Viracocha, who created the heavens and the earth, was for Acosta part of a universal phenomenon which was common to all gentiles.

> Pues como sea verdad tan conforme a toda buena razón, haber un soberano señor y rey del cielo, lo cual los gentiles, con todas sus idolatrías e infidelidad, no negaron, como parece así en la filosofía del Timeo de Platón y de la Metafísica de Aristóteles y Asclepio de Trismegisto, como también en las poesías de Homero y de Virgilio. (220)

> [That there is a supreme lord and king of heaven is a clear truth to all sound reason; even the gentiles, with their idolatries and infidelity, did not deny it, as is evident in the philosophy of Plato's *Timaeus* and Aristotle's *Metaphysics* and Trismegistus's *Asclepius*, as well as in the poetry of Homer and Virgil.]

Even though the barbarians were ignorant of the true "Christian" God, Acosta believed that there was a ray of light that had been filtered through their understanding. By means of Viracocha the Christian missionaries could persuade the Indians of the existence of a supreme God, just like Saint Paul who had appropriated the *Ignoto Deo* of the Greeks in order to convert the gentiles.

Acosta's narrative becomes exemplary in the sense that it demonstrates clearly that the motives or elements of the myth that were preserved were only those that responded to existing European configurations. Only those elements that could fit into this frame of reference, whether by similarity or contrast, would eventually become part of the different versions. Thus reconfigured, the myths were either used as a "tool" in the conversion process or condemned as contemptible or diabolical during the extirpation campaigns. Therefore, every version of the myth of origin should be understood as a specular vision, wherein the image projected not only depends on the object that it reflects (the indigenous myth) but also on the magnitude and quality of the reflection (frames, contexts, points of view through which the myth is filtered). Everything located outside the reflective field (unintelligible or unacceptable to the chroniclers) could never form a part of the reflected image. Hence, the myths with which I am working are always partial visions of the Andean mythical world. Yet the variants among the myths allow one to focus on details that are either absent or not clear in some of the stories.

Las Casas states briefly that Condici Viracocha "había hecho el Cielo y la Tierra, y al Sol, y luna, y estrellas, y a todo el mundo" [had created the heavens and the earth, the sun, moon, stars, and the entire world], which explains why he was worshiped. He adds that Viracocha had an evil son, Taguapica Viracocha, who opposed his father in everything. If the father did good to man, his son did evil; if the father made the mountains, the son changed them into valleys. Unable to see the Janus aspect of the Andean deity, Las Casas transforms the myth into an exemplary tale, where Taguapica Viracocha is represented according to a Christian ethical code: an evil son who contradicts his father. These dichotomous characteristics are for Las Casas mutually exclusive and cannot exist in just one being, much less in a god who, in many respects, is similar to the Christian God.

Pedro Cieza de León includes in his version many details similar to those found in Las Casas, but without passing judgments that emanate from a Christian moral code. A different reading, then, becomes possible:

. . . queste varón [Viracocha] que así vieron tenía tan gran poder que de los cerros hacía llanuras y de las llanuras hacía cerros grandes, haciendo fuentes en piedras vivas; y como tal poder reconociesen llamábanle Hacedor de todas las cosas criadas, Principio dellas . . . (8)

[(They tell) that this man (Viracocha) had great power, that from hills he made plains and from plains high mountains, fountains from stones; and as such power was recognized they called him Maker of all things created, Beginning of all things . . .]

In this account Viracocha performs functions that could be considered antagonistic: both creative and destructive. Since opposite elements are united in him, Viracocha would be, like Lake Titicaca, the point of convergence for the opposites, which corresponds to the Aymara concept of the *taypi*. But this representation of Viracocha is coherent not only with this aspect of the Aymara mentality but also with what Mircea Eliade calls "*coincidentia oppositorum*" in his mythical model:

All these myths present us with a twofold revelation: they express on the one hand the diametrical opposition of two divine figures sprung from one and the same principle and destined, in many versions, to be reconciled at some *illud tempus* of eschatology, and on the other, the *coincidentia oppositorum* in the very nature of the divinity, which shows itself, by turns or even simultaneously, benevolent and terrible, creative and destructive, solar and serpentine, and so on (in other words, actual and potential). In this sense it is true to say that myth reveals more profoundly than any rational experience ever could, the actual structure of the divinity, which transcends all attributes and reconciles all contraries. (Eliade 1963, 419)

If we eliminate from the Las Casas version those parts that explicitly reflect a Christian moral code, and delete as well those words that denote evil and rebellion, his version and Cieza de León's would be almost identical were it not for the presence of two characters and the parental relationship between them in Las Casas's narratives. The presence of two different Viracochas could be interpreted as a necessary unfolding of a character in Manichean terms, given the moral code that informs it. However, Urbano's reading of Tunupa as someone who "a veces se confunde con Taguapaca y a veces con Pachayachachi, hecho éste que sugiere que, en realidad se trata del mismo héroe, con funciones semejantes a las dos caras del Viracocha principal y de Taguapaca" [sometimes is confused with Taguapaca and sometimes with Pachayachachi, suggests that it really is the same hero with similar functions to the two different faces of the main Viracocha and of Taguapaca] (Urbano 1981, xxxii) could be explained without requiring a doubling of the character. Viracocha or Tunupa would be the deification of the Aymara concept wherein two opposites are united. Thus, the different stories represent, through different characters, some of the attributes of the divinity. In this sense, the representation of the creation in the different versions varies in some narrative details, but not in essence.

Some variants mention the creation succinctly, and others specify what Viracocha created and how and when he did it. Betanzos (1551), Cieza de León (1553), and Sarmiento de Gamboa (I and II) (1572) suggest that mankind was created twice; once during the time of darkness, which he did not survive; and again, after the time of darkness.

According to one account, Con Ticsi Viracocha created a generation of men during "el tiempo de la escuridad" [the time of darkness] whom he later turned to stone because of their "disservice" to him (Betanzos 1551). Cieza de León also suggests the existence of men during the period of darkness, but makes no mention of a sin being committed. Instead, suffering from living in the darkness, these men rendered "votos e plegarias" ["vows and prayers"] to their gods, hoping they would provide the "light" they desperately needed. Cieza de León makes no reference to a punishment, nor does he mention the destruction of the first generation of men. Although the two versions compiled by Sarmiento de Gamboa do speak of two moments of creation, and the destruction of the first generation of men during the time of darkness, they differ in significant details from Betanzos's. In both versions, Sarmiento de Gamboa states that the "Criador" first made giants, and then later created men of normal stature. In the first account, he explains that the creation of the giants was to be a model, a trial run of sorts, for the subsequent creation of the human race. Considering it inappropriate, he destroyed the model and created men of normal stature:

> Y después de criado el mundo formó un género de gigantes disformes en grandeza, pintados o exculpidos, *para ver si sería bueno hacer los hombres de aquel tamaño.* Y como le pareciesen de muy mayor proporción que la suya, dijo: "No es bien que las gentes sean tan crecidas; mejor será que sean de mi tamaño". Y así crió, los hombres a su semejanza como los que agora son. Y vivían en oscuridad. (102)

> [And after creating the world he formed a type of giants of monstrous stature, he painted or sculpted them to see if it would be as good to make men of that size. And since they seemed to him of a larger proportion than his own, he said: "It is not good that people be so large; it would be better that they are of my size." So he created men in his image the way they are today. And they lived in darkness.]

In his second version, these giants, while not constituting a model, were also destroyed on account of their towering stature. Neither of Sarmiento de Gamboa's narratives attributes the destruction of the first creatures to their behavior, to their "disservice," as is the case in Betanzos's account, but rather to their unacceptable size. The inclusion on the part of some transcriptions of the "disservice" of the creatures with their corresponding punishment responds to an ethical code, but this interpretive filter is absent from Sarmiento de Gamboa and Cieza de León. Man's desire for light from God, as mentioned in Cieza de León, might be construed as his recognition of the creator's immense power. His power is both creative and destructive in Sarmiento de Gamboa's versions, which, as I have already indicated, is consistent with Viracocha's "double" function.

Turned to Stone: Transgression and Punishment, or the Birth of Lineages

Many of the stories coincide in their narration of the norms and precepts that Viracocha gave to his creatures, and in their subsequent punishment for disobeying the divinity. In the Betanzos version there is no explanation of the transgressive act which causes Viracocha to turn the first generation of men to stone. Cristóbal de Molina (1575) also narrates the transformation of the first men into stone as a punishment for their transgression. He recounts that after having created mankind, Tecsi Viracocha went to different villages in the mountains and

> que algunas naciones que halló rebeldes y que no habían cumplido su mandato, gran parte de ellos convirtió en piedras, en figuras de hombres y mujeres con el mismo traje que traían.
>
> Fue la conversión en piedras en los lugares siguientes: en Tiahuanacu, en Pucara y Jauja, donde dicen convirtió la huaca llamada Huarivilca en piedra, y en Pachacamac, en Cajamarca y en otras partes. (Molina 53)

> [that some nations were rebellious and had not followed his command, a great number of them were turned into stones, shaped as men and women with the dress they were wearing.
>
> The turning into stones occurred in the following places: Tiahuanacu, Pucara, and Jauja, where they say he converted into stone the *huaca* called Huarivilca, and in Pachacamac, in Cajamarca, and other places.]

Colonial sources indicate that the places which marked man's conversion into stone were principal sites of Indian worship. Bernabé Cobo, for instance, refers to both Tiawanacu and Pachacamac as a "santuario universal" [universal sanctuary] (194), and Cristóbal de Albornoz describes Huarivilca as "Guaca muy prencipal de los dichos ananguancas, es una piedra como indio" [a very important *huaca* of the aforementioned ananguancas, it is a stone shaped like an Indian] (Albornoz 183) and states that "Yanic Zuya [?], guaca de las más prencipales del reino de los yndios caxamalcas" [Yanic Zuya [?], the most important *huaca* in the kingdom of the Caxamalca Indians] was in Cajamarca (Albornoz 186).

The metamorphosis into stone in these versions is portrayed as divine punishment for an ethical transgression. More specifically, it is seen as a punishment with clear Christian resonances, since it echoes the punishment of Lot's wife for having transgressed against God (Gen. 19:15–26). This interpretation neglects to consider the episode within an Andean context. The Indians regarded the transformation of those first men into stone as the origin of the different lineages that later were to become the *huacas* that the different ethnic groups venerated:

> Cuentan más, que aquellos primeros hombres en aquellos mismos lugares, después de haber dejado sucesión se convirtieron, unos en piedras, otros en halcones, cóndores y otras aves y animales; y así son de diferentes figuras las guacas e ídolos que adoraban. (Cobo [1653] 1964, 151)

[Furthermore, they tell that the first men in those very places, after engendering their progeny, were converted, some into stones, others into falcons, condors, and other birds and animals; and that is why the *huacas* and idols they worship have different forms.]

The existing studies of these myths have failed to consider this notion of punishment as an infiltration of a Christian concept. By this I do not mean to suggest that the concept of punishment did not exist in these cultures. What seems to be clear, however, is that within the context of this myth the inclusion of the notion of punishment and transgression appears to be a superimposition. Having said this, and keeping in mind that in Andean culture stones or animals represented sacred origins for the Indians, we would have to regard the transformation of men into stone as the coming together of God, nature, and humankind. This type of "union" is particularly common among cultures in which ancestor worship is of primary importance.

The Flood: Punishment or Uno Pachacuti

In some of the variants of the Viracocha myth, the flood is mentioned in terms that are comparable to the conversion to stone, that is, as the consequence of a transgression. Sarmiento de Gamboa's first version (1572) situates the flood between the first and second creations of man. According to Cobo (I), after the creation there was a flood in which almost the entire human race perished; only a few survived and later multiplied. The same author's third version offers a small variation: one man and one woman survived the flood by floating on the water in a drum until the waters subsided. Calancha also mentions a flood before the earth was populated. In the other versions of the myth, the flood is not mentioned.

According to Bandelier and Bouysse Cassagne, the versions that include the flood exemplify a syncretic impulse, because some chroniclers' informants had already been exposed to the Christian religion for many years. What originally could have been a simple inundation was raised to the level of a Biblical flood because the Indians had assimilated the stories preached by the missionaries. Moreover, since different levels of water in the lake, the formation of the Island of Titicaca, changes in salinity, and other factors would have affected the lives of the different cultures throughout time, experiencing a phenomenon like a considerable rise of the water level in the lake would have remained in their collective memory, and its transmission from generation to generation would have become a legendary event. What Bouysse Cassagne can verify through geological data had already been perceived by Acosta ([1590] 1985):

Hay entre ellos comunmente gran noticia y mucha plática del diluvio; pero no se puede bien determinar si el diluvio que éstos refieren es el universal que cuenta la divina Escritura, o si fue algún otro diluvio o inundación particular de las regiones en que ellos moran, mas de que en aquestas tierras hombres expertos dicen que se ven señales claras de haber habido alguna grande inundación. Yo más me llego al parecer de los que sienten, que los rastros y señales que hay de diluvio no son del de Noé, sino de algún otro particular, como el que cuenta Platón, o el que los poetas can-tan de Deucalión. (63)

[There is among the Indians the memory of and a lot of talk about the flood; but one cannot determine clearly if the deluge to which they refer is the universal one narrated in the holy Scriptures, or if it was another del-uge or flood particular to the regions inhabited by them; in addition, ex-perts say that they see in these lands signs of a large flood. I am more in-clined to the opinion of those who feel that the traces and signs found are not from Noah's flood but of some other flood, like the one referred to by Plato or the one in which the poets sing about Deucalion.]

The representation of the flood in their myths could reflect either the in-formants' attempt to situate their stories within a newly learned frame of reference (the Biblical story) that would be understandable to their Euro-pean audiences, or the Spaniards' interpretation of the episode from within their own Christian context, the only frame of reference known to them.

Sarmiento de Gamboa informs us that the Indians called the universal flood *uno pachacuti*, which means "agua que trastornó la tierra" [wa-ter that disturbed the earth]. Imbelloni explains the term *pachacuti* as follows:

La frase *pacha kútin* o *pachan kútin* vale: "vuélvese o trastórnase la tierra", "vuélvese o trastórnase el tiempo". El verbo infinitivo pacha-kútin significa "revolucionarse" o "convulsionarse". El sustantivo (realmente verbo sustantivado) *pachakútiy* equivale a "el fin del mundo", significado (único) registrado por Torres Rubio. (Imbelloni 99)

[The phrase *pacha kútin* o *pachan kútin* means: "turning or disturbing of the earth," "turning or disturbing of time." The infinitive *pacha-kútin* means "revolutionize" or "convulse." The noun (really a substantivized verb) *pachakútiy* signifies "the end of the world," the sole meaning regis-tered by Torres Rubio.]

Thus, the flood in the myth is a representation of *uno pachacuti*, a cos-mic phenomenon (the destruction of the world) caused by Viracocha, a god with both destructive and creative attributes. A new creation (a second generation of men) follows this natural disaster. If the flood, when portrayed as a punishment, seems to be an assimilation of the Biblical flood motivated by mankind's decadence, the same flood, when seen as a *pachacuti*—that is, from an indigenous perspective—cannot be attributed to human failings. What is unquestionable is that both the Biblical flood and the *uno pachacuti* are great inundations, which explains their interchangeability in the different versions of the myth.

The application of the Christian interpretive framework imposed foreign and hence inapplicable categories upon the indigenous culture. The chroniclers' representation of *pachacuti*, which is informed by a moral code applicable only to human conduct, suffers from a westernization that obstructs any other possible meanings. Bouysse Cassagne focuses on the same problem from the perspective of temporal categories:

> Como demostraron los estudios de Imbelloni y más recientemente los de Harris, "pachacuti" no se puede traducir en términos humanos: y se refiere más bien a un acontecimiento cosmológico o, como sugiere Cobo al hablar del Inca Pachacuti, "le dieron el nombre de Pachacuti, porque por su gobierno tan acertado se mejoraron las cosas de tal manera que parecía haberse trocado los tiempos y dado la vuelta al mundo" (Cobo cap. XII, XII [*sic*]). He aquí, expresado en términos claros, el punto en que la historiografía occidental y la andina discrepan, y probablemente, el tope en el que la asociación por similitud (que no pudo realizarse) y la dimensión metafórica (siendo de hecho intraducible), de las dos culturas, pudiera combinarse la una con la otra. Efectivamente, en la concepción del tiempo aquí evocada, el instante fundador corresponde al momento en el que "se trocan los tiempos" o, expresado en términos espaciales, cuando se da "la vuelta el mundo"; mientras que la categoría de acontecimiento, que define la periodización, no corresponde obligatoriamente, en la historiografía occidental, a un acontecimiento cataclísmico, y cuando éste existe, no se lo vive obligatoriamente en términos de inversión, aún si a veces se lo identifica con "el castigo". (Bouysse Cassagne 1988, 13–14)

[As demonstrated by Imbelloni and more recently by Harris, "pachacuti" cannot be translated in human terms: and it refers rather to a cosmological event or, as Cobo suggests, speaking about Inca Pachacuti, "he was given the name Pachacuti, because he reigned so properly that it seemed that times had changed and the world had turned around" (Cobo ch. XII, 78). Here is expressed in clear terms the point in which the Western historiography and the Andean disagree, and, probably, the limit where association by similarity (which could not take place) and by the metaphoric dimension (which in fact was untranslatable), of the two cultures could combine the one with the other. In fact, in the conception of time mentioned here, the founding moment corresponds to the moment in which "times change" or, expressed in spatial terms, when "the world turns upside down"; while the categories of event, which define the periodization, do not correspond necessarily, in Western historiography, to a catastrophic event, and when such exists, is not experienced obligatorily in terms of inversion, even if at times it is identified with "punishment."]

The juxtaposition of categories is evident in the reference to both the flood and the divinity himself. One of the constants of this phenomenon seems to be the "filtration" of a Christian ethical code, along with a conscious or subconscious effort on the part of the transcribers to discover the Christian God within the Andean pantheon. If the Spanish chroniclers represented "the other" in terms of themselves, indigenous chroniclers, such as Guamán Poma and Santacruz Pachacuti, believed that this Europeanizing effort could go far beyond the mere representation of Andean concepts in European terms. These native chroniclers, like the Spaniards, availed themselves of European categories to represent the Andean world, but in doing so they also had recourse to Andean categories, the end result being a blending of both systems.

The reference to *pachacuti* in Guamán Poma's *El primer Nueva Corónica y Buen Gobierno* (1613) is very revealing because it turns on the notion of both punishment and miracle. In a Western context, all punishment and miracles are seen as negative and positive experiences, respectively. In the examples he extracts from Christian tradition, Guamán Poma combines positive and negative events. As he does this, he compares their contiguous existence with *pachacuti*, precisely because *pachacuti*—like the concept *taypi* and the god Viracocha—unites positive and negative elements that are able to "dar la vuelta al mundo" [turn the world around] and change its meaning. In the representation of *uno pachacuti*, a negative occurrence (humankind's destruction) paves the way to a positive event (a new creation):

> Gran juycio fue la caída de quel ángel con sus seguases tan prencipal y tan hermoso, la caída de todo el género humano por culpa de uno, el castigo de todo el mundo con las aguas del diluuio. Gran juycio fue la eleción de Jacop y la rreprouación de Saú y el desanparo de Judas Escariote y la bocación de San Pablo, la rreporbación del pueblo de los judíos, la elición de los gentiles y como otros milagros y castigos que pasan en los hijos de los hombres del mundo.
>
> Y ancí auido otros muchos milagros y castigos en el tienpo del Ynga. No se escrive cino son los testigos la caída de los serros y peñas derrunbadas.

Y ací se escrive toda la suma; por eso el castigo de Dios le llaman pacha-cuti, pacha ticra. (Guamán Poma 94)

[The fall of that angel, so important and so beautiful, with his followers, was a great justice; so was the fall of the entire humankind because of one, the punishment of the whole world with the waters of the deluge. A great justice was the election of Jacob and the reproof of Saul and the forsaking of Judas Iscariot and the vocation of Saint Paul, the reproval of the Jewish people, the election of the Gentiles and other miracles and punishments that happen to the children of men in the world.

And so have happened other miracles and punishments at the time of the Inca. They are not written, but the fallen mountains and rocks are the witnesses. To summarize, they call God's punishment *pachacuti, pacha ticra*.]

Divested of its Christian trappings, the flood or the *uno pachacuti* marks a moment, separating two cycles or ages, when Viracocha intervenes with his creative and destructive power.[36] In the second stage of the myth, Viracocha manifests his creative power once again in the Titicaca region.

Viracocha Created the Stars and Formed the Different Lineages

According to the different versions of the myth, the Island of Titicaca and Tiwanaku are the two sites where Viracocha creates the sun, the moon, the stars, and mankind. The predominance of one place over the other probably depends upon the place of origin or residence of the informants. Cobo notes that

sobre qué lugar haya sido éste hay tantas opiniones cuantas son las provincias y naciones deste reino, queriendo cada nación que haya sido en su tierra. Los moradores del Collao están divididos en dos pareceres: los unos afirman haber sido hecha la creación en Tiaguanaco, y los otros en la isla de Titicaca . . . (Cobo [1653] 1964, 150)

[there are as many opinions about where this place may be as there are provinces and nations in this kingdom. In fact, each nation wished to place creation somewhere within its own lands. The inhabitants of Collao are divided into two opposing views. Some hold that the creation happened in Tiaguanaco; others place it on the Island of Titicaca . . .] (1990, 12)

In almost all narratives, both Lake Titicaca or the Island of Titicaca and Tiwanaku are linked to the creation of the stars and mankind. The act of creation—whether single or double, antediluvian or post-diluvian—always entails a transformation: a change from chaos to order. Viracocha is the prime mover and Titicaca the focal point.

According to Betanzos, Con Tici Viracocha emerged from Lake Titicaca and proceeded to Tiwanaku, where he created the sun, the moon, and the stars. Before this, "esta tierra era toda noche" [this earth was in darkness]. By creating the sun, he also created the day. Nondifferentiation and darkness represent chaos, while segmentation and light illustrate order. This refers us once again to what we said in Chapter 1, namely, that to name is to segment, which is why this creation also represents the emergence of language. In this version, Viracocha creates man for the second time after creating the sun and the stars. The first creation differs clearly from the second in terms of differentiation and order.

While "en el tiempo de la escuridad [sic]" [in the time of darkness] Viracocha "hizo aquella gente" [made that people] whom he later turned into stone, the implications of which have been discussed, during the period of light his creation is much more precise:

> Que hizo de piedra cierto número de gentes y un principal que la gobernaba y señoreaba y muchas mujeres preñadas y otras paridas y que los niños tenían en cunas, según su uso, todo lo cual ansí hecho de piedra . . . (Betanzos 9)

> [He made from stone a number of people and a chief who governed and reigned, and many pregnant women and others having recently given birth and the children had cribs, according to their usage, all of which was made out of stone . . .]

In this new order people are distinguished by sex, by age, and through social hierarchies within each group. Furthermore, Viracocha organizes them spatially by sending them to different places where they would live and reproduce. He also gives them their respective names. We must note that Viracocha "speaks" for the first time in this story. He chose two individuals from among all of the people he created and ordered them to take the others to their respective places of origin,

> señalándoles y diciéndoles: "estos se llamarán los tales y saldrán de tal fuente en tal provincia, y poblarán ella, y allí serán aumentados; y éstos saldrán de tal cueva, y se nombrarán los fulanos, y poblarán tal parte . . ." (Betanzos 9)

> [pointing to them and saying: "these ones will be called such and will come out of such a stream and in such a province, and they will populate it and there they will reproduce; and these ones will be called so and so, and will inhabit such and such place . . ."]

The first creation story compiled by Sarmiento de Gamboa is very similar to the Betanzos variant, except that the second creation occurred after the flood. Chaos in Sarmiento de Gamboa's story is represented by both darkness and disaster. He writes:

> Pasando el diluvio y seca la tierra, determinó el Viracocha de poblarla se-
> gunda vez, y para *hacerlo con más perfección* determinó criar luminarias
> que diesen claridad. Y para lo hacer, fuése con sus criados a una gran la-
> guna, que está en Collao, y en la laguna está una isla llamada Titicaca.
> (105; my emphasis)

> [After the flood and once the land was dry, Viracocha determined to popu-
> late it a second time, and *to do it with more perfection* he decided to create
> stars that would give light. And to do that, he went with his servants to a
> great lake that is located in Collao, and in the lake there is an island called
> Titicaca.]

The order that Viracocha imposes upon his creation is represented here in terms of perfection. The creation of man and the beginning of the lineages echo Betanzos's account, but they lack its richness. One of the details that differs in this version is that Viracocha has two servants who originated in the first creation, and who were saved from the flood.

The second version compiled by Sarmiento de Gamboa differs in two ways. First, the creation takes place at Tiwanaku. Second, everyone spoke the same language before Viracocha sent them to their respective places of origin. Once at home each spoke their own particular language and

> en partiéndose variaron las lenguas, notándolos frases de fieras, tanto, que
> tornándose a topar después, no se entendían los que antes eran parientes y
> vecinos. (107–108)

> [when (the people) were separated the languages changed so much that
> when later they met they could not understand each other, even the ones
> that before had been relatives and neighbors.]

It is interesting to note that the emergence of different languages is represented, in this version, as a discordant element, which may echo an infiltration of the Biblical account of the Tower of Babel.

However, the reason for this version's deviation from the others can perhaps be linked to the political and social situation of the Lake Titicaca Indians at the time of the conquest and during the colonial period. The different languages spoken in the Kollao region during the sixteenth century contributed to the hierarchization of its inhabitants. For instance, at the highest level of society, the Kollas who had power during the Inca domination spoke both Quechua and Aymara. Within the lower levels, a marginalized group called the Uru spoke only in Uruquilla, while those who were a bit higher within the same group spoke Pukina or Aymara. It is possible that this discordant vision of the myth in terms of language reflects the sociopolitical problems that emerged with the Quechua domination of a mainly Aymara region.[37]

Cristóbal de Molina, "El Cusqueño," more or less follows the same story line as Betanzos and Sarmiento de Gamboa, while adding several valuable details. In this version, the creation takes place at Tiwanaku, and the two men who had appeared in other versions as Viracocha's servants are now his sons: Imaymana Viracocha and Tocapo Viracocha. Having created the different nations, Viracocha commands his sons to depart on different paths to each nation and to name all things. Imaymana Viracocha traverses the Andes while Tocapo Viracocha travels along the coastal plains:

> [Mandó a Imaymana] que fuese por el camino de los Andes y montañas de toda la tierra; y que *fuese dando y poniendo nombres* a todos los árboles grandes y pequeños, y a las flores y frutas que habían de tener, mostrando a las gentes las que eran para comer y las que no, y las que eran buenas para medicinas; y así mismo puso nombres a todas las yerbas y flores, y el tiempo en que habían de producir sus frutos y flores, y que éste mostró a las gentes las yerbas que tenían virtud para curar, y las que podían matar. Y al otro hijo llamado Tocapo Viracocha que . . . fuese por el camino de los llanos, visitando las gentes, y *poniendo nombres a los ríos y árboles que en ellos hubiese, y dándoles sus frutos y flores* por la dicha orden . . . (Molina 54; my emphasis)

> [(He ordered Imaymana) to go by way of the Andes and the mountains of the entire earth; and that he *would give names* to all trees, large and small, and to the flowers and fruits they had to bear, teaching the people which ones were edible and which ones not, and which ones were good as medicine, and to give names as well to all herbs and flowers, and the time in which they had to produce their fruits and flowers, and he taught people the herbs with curative properties, and the ones that could kill. To the other son, called Tocapo Viracocha, he gave an order to go by way of the plains, visiting the people, and *giving names to the rivers and trees that were found there, and giving to them their fruits and flowers* . . .]

In this version, language and creation are inseparable; things begin to exist as they are named. Once the plants have been named, their physical properties follow, their use, and the seasons in which they grow. Order is instituted through language.

My view differs from Henrique Urbano's, who assigns different "functions" to the three main characters in this story. What we have here is essentially one character, Viracocha, who unfolds into three to represent the synchronic creation in all directions. All three are depicted as basically the same:

> Tenían también estos indios, por muy cierto y averiguado que el Hacedor
> ni sus hijos no fueron nacidos de mujer y que eran inconmutables y que
> tampoco habían de tener fin. (Molina 55)

> [These Indians believed firmly that the Maker and his sons were not
> born of woman and that they were immutable and that they will have
> no end.]

Cieza de León's story of the creation of the sun is not as engaging as the others, though it also occurs on the Island of Titicaca. In his version, the change from chaos to order can only be inferred, since the men who lived in darkness suffered "gran trabajo" [great labors], and with the creation of the light came "el sol muy resplandeciente, con que todos se alegraron" [the shining sun, which made everyone happy].

Bernabé Cobo compiles several versions of the myth of creation and, because of their discrepancies, he concludes that the Indians "hablan muy confusamente, no distinguiendo la creación del mundo de su reparación después de pasado el diluvio" [speak very confusingly, not distinguishing between the creation of the world and its reparation after the great flood]. Cobo's first version adds nothing new. Perhaps the only detail worthy of mention is that the imposition of an order is represented precisely by the word *orden* [order]:

> [H]ubo un Hacedor del universo que crió el cielo y la tierra con las diver-
> sas naciones de hombres que la habitan; que pasó esto en Tiaguanaco, y
> que habiendo puesto *en orden y concierto* todas las cosas por él criadas,
> dando a cada una el lugar que le tocaba, se subió desde allí al cielo. (Cobo
> [1653] 1964, 150; my emphasis)

> [(T)here was a Creator of the Universe who created the sky and earth with
> the diverse nations of men that inhabit it. They say that after having put all
> the things he created in *order* and making sure that each one had its own
> proper place, he went from Tiaguanacu up to heaven.] (1990, 12)

Cobo's second version, since it does not take place in the Titicaca region, falls outside of the scope of this study. In his third variant, mankind was created before the flood, but everyone perished except for a man and a woman who floated inside a drum while the flood raged. The flood, according to this version, took place in a time of darkness, since the sun was hidden on the Island of Titicaca (the island was the first to appear when the waters receded). The drum which protected the couple that was destined to reestablish the human race landed at Tiahuanaku.

According to Bouysse Cassagne, the appearance of the island after the "flood" corresponds geologically to the final phase of the rising of the lake's waters. It marks a point of separation in the myth between the presolar and solar ages, and it also brings about a religious change:

> [L]a aparición del sol (o su corolario el fin del diluvio) señala el momento constitutivo de una nueva temporalidad y quizás podemos arriesgarnos a decir de una nueva divinidad ligada a la isla de Titicaca. (Bouysse Cassagne 1988, 109)

> [(T)he apparition of the sun (or its corollary, the end of the flood) points to the constitutive moment of a new temporality and, perhaps we could risk saying, of a new divinity linked to the island of Titicaca.]

Although Bouysse Cassagne's argument may be defensible, there is nothing in the myth under consideration that suggests the coming of a solar divinity. In the second narrative cycle, as we will see in Chapter 3, a solar divinity is the point of departure for the Inca narrative cycle.

Bernabé Cobo's fourth version is perhaps the most arresting of all the ones he compiled. In it, the creator gave shape after the flood to the peoples of nations with the clay of Tiwanaku, along with language, clothing, food, and songs. He then sent them underground so that they would emerge at different places, which they would later mark with their major *huacas* "por haber salido y empezado de allí su estirpe y linaje" [for having emerged and begun their lineage there]. This narrative includes the most important and distinctive aspects of the Andean world. According to Bouysse Cassagne, this myth represents the signs of cultural identity.

> Lo que enumera entonces el mito son los atributos simbólicos—vestido, lengua, canto, planta ceremonial, *huaca*—que constituyen los signos visibles de la identidad de cada grupo. Para aludir tan solo a la música, sabemos que aun en la época Inca, cuando en el centro ceremonial de la Isla del Sol se celebraba el Inti Raymi, cada grupo bailaba a su usanza. (Bouysse Cassagne 1987, 175)

> [What the myth enumerates are the symbolic attributes—dress, language, song, ceremonial plant, *huaca*—that constitute the visible signs of the identity of each group. To consider just music, we know that even in Inca times, when in the ceremonial center of the Island of the Sun the Inti Raymi was celebrated, each group danced according to its own custom.]

What Bouysse Cassagne calls "symbolic attributes" are modes of representation from different cultures, which result from political and social motives that the myth attributes to the creator himself. It should also be noted that in this version, as in all others, the establishment of order in the universe is represented by the command that Viracocha gave to the sun to rise in the heavens. Not one star or one cultural group is given priority over the others. Since Viracocha creates the sun, the moon, and the stars and makes all lineages at the same time, everything pertaining to the natural or social order exists on the same level. Everyone's relationship with the divine order is identical. As we will see in Chapter 3, where I discuss the Inca narrative cycle, this relationship is altered with the establishment of a social hierarchy which directly links one cultural group to the divine order.

Viracocha's Route: From the Mountains to the Coast

Five versions of the myth (Betanzos, Cieza de León, Sarmiento de Gamboa, Molina, and Santacruz Pachacuti) narrate Viracocha's pilgrimage through the Andes. The point of departure, not just in these but in all versions, is Lake Titicaca or the nearby Tiwanaku. The pilgrimage ends where the divinity disappears into the sea. During the journey he visits Cacha and Urcos (or Tambo Urcos) among many other places. The route that he follows goes from south to north, and from the high altitude of Lake Titicaca (3,815 meters) to sea level.

Let us consider first the Betanzos version of Viracocha's journey in order to contrast it later with the others. In order to populate the land Viracocha dispatches his two servants, one to the east and the other to the west, and himself embarks on a journey northward toward Cuzco. From the center, Lake Titicaca, the act of creation and differentiation radiates simultaneously in all directions. Viracocha travels from Titicaca to the north. One of the servants or sons goes toward the rising sun while the other travels toward the setting sun. Meanwhile Viracocha descends from the mountains to the coast, and the people are submerged below the earth to emerge later on the surface in their respective *pacarinas* (places of origin). The presence of two servants is a narrative ploy that allows the representation of the multidirectionality and synchrony of creation.

On his way to Cuzco, Viracocha arrives at Cacha, which, according to Betanzos, was eighteen leagues from Cuzco, and the place where the Cana Indians lived. Upon his arrival, the Cana Indians armed themselves with the intention of killing Viracocha, who, realizing their intentions, "de improviso hizo que cayese fuego del cielo y que veniese quemando una cordillera de un cerro hacia do los indios estaban" [suddenly made fire fall from heaven and the fire came burning the mountain range toward the direction of the Indians] (Betanzos 10). The terrified aggressors threw their weapons to the ground and prostrated themselves before Viracocha, who in turn proceeded to extinguish the fire with "dos o tres varazos" [two or three stampings of his staff]. Viracocha then revealed himself to the Indians as their creator. In memory of the rain of fire and in honor of Viracocha they built a "suntuosa guaca" [sumptuous temple] on this site.

Betanzos claims to have seen the scorched hill and rocks, which led him to inquire about them among the oldest villagers, who provided him with the information he later transcribed. Although Betanzos categorizes the event—the rain of fire—as a "miracle," he does not contextualize it within a Christian framework, as he had apparently done with the men-turned-to-stone episode. The rain of fire is not seen as divine punishment but as the manifestation of Viracocha's powers.[38]

Continuing on his journey northward, Viracocha arrived at Tambo de Urcos, where on some high rocks he created a new lineage. These new people made a "muy rica y suntuosa guaca" [rich and sumptuous *huaca*] on the rock where Viracocha had sat. According to this version, Viracocha gave the name "Cuzco" to the place where he created Alcaviza, a man whom Viracocha made responsible for the introduction, upon his departure, of the class of nobles known as the *orejones* (the Incas).

Betanzos mentions three specific places along Viracocha's route to the coast: Cacha, Urcos, and Cuzco. At each of these places Viracocha reveals himself directly to the people, and his presence makes these places sacred. As with any theophany, this sacralization is made evident by the establishment of *huacas*. Why are these three places privileged given that there are many others between Titicaca and Cuzco? Since in the myth the distribution of the different lineages and the act of populating places tended, as we have seen, toward a "universalization" of the events, one cannot but wonder what this "specificity" in Viracocha's journey may signify.

A possible explanation is to posit that the most important temples to Viracocha were found in those places. This is true in the case of Cuzco:

Había en la ciudad del Cuzco un templo llamado Quishuarcancha, dedicado al dios Viracocha, el cual le edificó Pachacutic, y por su mandado se puso en él una imagen de bulto deste dios, la cual era de figura humana, del tamaño de un muchacho de diez años, toda maciza de muy fino oro. Fuera désta había otra estatua del Viracocha en el templo de Coricancha. (Cobo [1653] 1964, 156)

[In the city of Cuzco there was a temple called Quishuarcancha, dedicated to the god Viracocha. The temple was built for him by Pachacutic, and on his orders a statue of Viracocha was put in this temple. The statue was in human form, about the size of a ten-year-old boy, and it was made entirely of solid gold of very high quality. In addition to this one, in the temple called Coricancha, which was dedicated to the Sun, there was another statue of Viracocha among the statues of the other gods.] (Cobo 1990, 23–24)

There was such a temple near Cacha or Urcos. Its ruins are near the present town of San Pedro de Cacha (Gisbert 1980, 38). In this connection, it is worth pondering why other *huacas* in the region, which other chronicles mention, do not enter into Betanzo's version of the myth.[39]

Betanzos also privileges two ethnic or cultural groups: the Canas and the "orejones" or noble class—in other words, the Incas. The Canas are represented negatively because they bear arms and fail to pay homage to Viracocha. The *orejones*, however, are mentioned in a positive light; Viracocha sends them Alcaviza, the man who would establish their lineage after his departure. Although the myth clearly states that Viracocha created all the lineages, the explicit mention of the Canas and the *orejones*, and of Cacha and Urcos, invites reflection. I will offer as a possible explanation that Betanzos's story is a local version of a pan-Andean myth.

Juan de Betanzos was married to the Inca princess Auximay Occllo, baptized as Doña Angelina Yupanqui, who had been the *pirviguarmi* (principal wife) of Atahuallpa and later Francisco Pizarro's concubine (Porras Barrenechea 309; Hemming 319; Villanueva Urteaga). Because of this, it would be reasonable to believe that Betanzos had as his informants Indians from the Cuzco region and the Incas themselves, which would explain the privileging of the Inca lineage in his version. Furthermore, the mention of the Canas may also be a reflection of historical circumstances involving both these Indians and the Incas.

Guamán Poma mentions the Canas, along with the Collas, the Charcas, and the Canchis, among the peoples of the Kollao region (Guamán Poma 31, 172, 183). The Canas and the Canchis resisted unsuccessfully the Inca expansion, which occurred during the reign of Inca Viracocha. The Incas defeated the Canchis and made a pact with the Canas (Millones 96). Thus, the brandishing of arms by the Canas along with their loss of power in the myth may very well have as its source this historical event.

Lastly, the fact that the god and the Inca ruler had the same name— Viracocha—could have also contributed to the mixing of historical characters and events in the myth. Guamán Poma also notes that the captains of the Canas fought during the reign of Guayna Capac (ca. 1493–1528) in the conquest of Tumi (Guamán Poma 172). The prostration of the Canas before the god Viracocha could correspond, then, to the historical alliance they made with the Inca Viracocha.

Cieza de León's version of Viracocha's journey is similar to that of Betanzos, but there are important differences that deserve special consideration. The major difference is that in the Cacha episode the divinity is not Viracocha, who had earlier disappeared, never to be heard from again. Cieza de León explains:

> [P]asados algunos tiempos volvieron a ver otro hombre semejable del questá dicho, el nombre del cual no cuentan . . . (19)

> [(A)fter some time they saw again another man similar to the one mentioned, whose name they do not tell . . .]

This unnamed character, like Viracocha, whom he replaces, performs great miracles: if Viracocha turned mountains into valleys, he healed the blind and cured the sick with his words. In Cacha, reacting to the Indians' intention to stone him, he knelt down, raising his hands to the heavens, "como que invocaba el favor divino para se librar del aprieto en que se veía" [as if invoking God's favor in order to be saved from the distressing circumstance in which he found himself]. Then his assailants, upon seeing a frightening fire in the heavens, recognized "el pecado que habían cometido en lo así querer apedrear" [the sin they had committed by wanting to stone him] and begged him for protection from the fire. He complied with their request by extinguishing the fire, leaving the burned rocks as testimony to the miraculous event (Cieza de León 20).

Unlike Betanzos's Viracocha, he does not have the power to create a rain of fire himself. He has to invoke a supernatural force, or a god, for the production of the fire, which is sent to protect him from an attack and not to show divine superiority, as is the case in Betanzos's version. He is thus portrayed as a miraculous Christian saint and not as a supernatural being. His portrayal within a Christian ethical code, which is substantiated by the references to "sin" and "punishment," suggests that the Indian myth has been recontextualized. More specifically, the elements of the story have been manipulated in order to have the myth fit the pattern of the well-established hagiographic tradition.

If the local renditions demonstrate a tendency on the part of the Indians to exalt cultural heroes by inserting them into their myths, exemplified in Betanzos's version, the recontextualization of Indian myths in Christian terms responds at best to an eagerness on the part of the

Spaniards to discover vestiges of Christianity in the New World or to the common practice of demonizing Indians' beliefs. It is clear that Cieza de León cannot bring himself to portray the divinity in this episode as a pagan god, or to represent the Inca Viracocha as a Christian saint. Only by stripping the divinity of a fixed identity and dissociating him from the Viracocha of the first part of the story can Cieza de León suggest a possible Christian connection. Although Cieza de León claims to have seen the idol that was later erected in memory of the event, and of which the Spaniards affirmed that "podría ser algún apóstol" [it could be one of the Apostles], he expresses doubt regarding the truth of the story and suggests it could have been the work of the Devil. In any event, his reaction to the idol and the stories it inspired matters little; the fact remains that Cieza de León, consciously or unconsciously, narrates a Christian fable.

Speaking about the Spaniards' perception of Inca religion, MacCormack explains:

> Initially, Spaniards had difficulty with the idea that Andeans knew nothing about Christianity, that the message which was to be proclaimed "to the ends of the earth" and which constituted one of the criteria of the unity of mankind, had somehow not been heard in the Andes. It thus seemed natural that Andean religious rituals and belief should enshrine some residue of that message. Yet these pious hopes were prone to being disappointed. Objects . . . , myths which apparently recalled Noah's flood and the preaching of the apostles, on closer inspection turned out to be so many illusions. What had at first been perceived as likenesses or resemblances, however distant, between Andean religion and Christianity became in due course, quite simply, so many indicators of Andean error. For, so the reasoning went, if Andeans had indeed in the past known of the true religion, it was obvious that they had forgotten or misrepresented it because the devil had imprinted their minds with illusory images such as had also proved to be a powerful means of demonic deception back in Europe. (1991, 52)

Cieza de León exemplifies simultaneously the two reactions exhibited by Spaniards toward indigenous religion.

Sarmiento de Gamboa's version shares elements with the stories by Betanzos and Cieza de León: Viracocha, creator of the universe, arrives at Cacha, where, reacting to the Indians' wish to kill him, he kneels and asks the heavens for protection, which comes in the form of a frightening fire. Begging for forgiveness, the Indians persuade Viracocha to extinguish the fire with his staff. This version, unlike the others, does not mention the Canas. Leaving Cacha, Viracocha arrives in Urcos, where the Indians make a *huaca*, to which "en los tiempos futuros los ingas ofrecieron muchas cosas ricas de oro y otros metales, . . . [que] cuando los españoles entraron en el Cuzco, hallaron y partieron entre sí, que valió diez y siete mil pesos; tomólo para sí por joya del general el marqués don Francisco Pizarro" [years later the Incas made offerings of gold and other metals . . . which the Spaniards, when they came to Cuzco, found and divided among themselves; it had a total value of seventeen thousand pesos] (109).

The *suntuosa huaca* to which Betanzos refers is appraised in Sarmiento de Gamboa's version; by speaking of it in monetary terms he deprives it of its religious meaning. Also noteworthy is the allusion to the Incas, who are not associated, as in Betanzos, with the mythical event. The religious importance of this *huaca* for the Incas will come later in relation to the establishment of the idol. Neither Sarmiento de Gamboa nor Cieza de León mentions Cuzco as one of the places which Viracocha visits.

Cristóbal de Molina does not narrate the kind of travelogue that is present in the other versions. His narrative about the creation only states that Tecsi Viracocha "vino por el camino de la sierra visitando y viendo *a todas las naciones*" [following the mountain route he visited and saw *all nations*] (53; my emphasis). It is in this variant that Viracocha unfolds into different beings: his sons, who travel along the mountains and the coast, respectively, pursuing their creative mission. The rain of fire happens spontaneously in Pucara rather than Cacha and not as a result of Viracocha's clear intervention. Some people who had not kept Viracocha's commandments were turned to stone. Molina notes that in many places, among them Tiwanacu and Pachacama, there were enormous stone statues that were taken to be those whom Viracocha had turned to stone.[40]

The Indian chronicler Santacruz Pachacuti offers the most detailed and complicated version of Viracocha's journey. If in Betanzos, Cieza de León, and Sarmiento de Gamboa the story was filtered through a European or Christian lens, in Santacruz Pachacuti's version such a superimposition is lacking. Instead, it displays an apparently indiscriminate mixture of codes and references that at times becomes difficult to unravel. To begin with, although this author assigns a variety of names to the deity (Tonapa o Tarapaca Viracochanpachayachicachan or Pacchacan and Bicchhaycamayoc Cunacuycamayoc), he opts for Tunupa (with several different spellings) throughout the narrative. If Santacruz Pachacuti represents the Collavine perspective, as Bouysse Cassagne asserts, this would confirm that Viracocha and Tunupa are the same deity. The name Tunupa would be the Collavine or Aymara counterpart to the Quechua

Viracocha. But to further complicate the matter of the name and the identity of the deity, Santacruz Pachacuti asks himself if "no será este hombre el glorioso apostol Sancto Thomas?" [I wonder if this man was not the glorious Saint Thomas the Apostle]. As we will see, Santacruz Pachacuti tries to reconcile the Christian and Andean traditions in those instances in which the categories are not mutually exclusive.

Despite being an Indian, Santacruz Pachacuti portrays himself as a faithful Christian:

> Yo Don Joan de Santacruz Pachacuti Yamqui Salcamaygua, *cristiano por la gracia de Dios Nuestro Señor*, natural de los pueblos de Sanctiago de Hananaguaygua de Orcusuyo, entre Canas y Canchis de Collasuyo, hijo legítimo de . . . todos caciques principales que fueron en la dicha prouinçia y *cristianos profesos en las cosas de nuestra santa fe católica.* (281; my emphasis)

> [I Don Joan de Santacruz Pachacuti Yamqui Salcamaygua, *Christian by the grace of God our Lord*, native of the town of Sanctiago de Hananaguaygua in Orcusuyo, between Canas and Canchis in Collasuyo, legitimate son of . . . principal lords of the said province and *professed Christians in all things of Our Holy Catholic faith.*]

That he wants to appear as an orthodox Christian may explain why he fails to mention that Tunupa (or Viracocha in most other versions) was worshiped as a god by the Indians. By not representing him as a god, Santacruz Pachacuti dissociates Viracocha from the creation of the universe.

Like Viracocha, Tunupa travels throughout the different regions of the Andes. In addition to Cacha, Urcos, and Cuzco, Santacruz Pachacuti mentions Apotambo, Cachapucara, Carabuco, Caravaya, Chacamarca, Tiquina, Tiwanaku, and Yamquesupa and adds that he traveled through "todas aquellas provincias de los Collasuyos" [all the provinces of Colla-suyo]. At least three of these places (Carabuco, Tiquina, and Tiwanaku) are within the Lake Titicaca region. It is likely that this account is a local, Aymara, rendition of the myth.

Santacruz Pachacuti's representation of Tunupa is continually informed by both Christian and Andean categories. Let us turn first to the Christian elements in the myth: Tunupa was "parlero" [articulate], he went from place to place "predicando" [preaching], "les enseñaba a los naturales con gran amor" [he taught the natives with great love] (283), and he performed miracles: "solamente con tocar a los enfermos los sanaba" [simply with his touch he healed the sick]. What he preached to them "caçi caçi era lo mandamiento de Dios" [was almost God's Commandments] (283); the only thing they lacked was Our Lord's name. On the shores of the lake at Carabuco, where he preached to the Indians, "dizen que fueron echados en la cabeza con agua" [it is said that they were poured water on their heads]. Because of his preaching, Tunupa was sent to prison, where he said to a fellow prisoner: "no tengas pena, que ya vengo a llamaros en nombre de la matrona que os está aguardando solo, el qual está para irse al lugar de hulguras." [Do not be afraid, I come to call you in the name of our mother, he is waiting to go to the place of comfort] (284). Tunupa was condemned to die, but before daybreak, he liberated his cellmate by only touching the rope that tied him, and they both departed to Titicaca. A strong wind destroyed all the idols as they left.

It is impossible not to notice the depiction of Tunupa as a Christ-like figure: sermons, miracles, healing by the laying on of hands, and baptism. And what Tunupa says to the other prisoner echoes Christ's words at Golgotha: "This day shalt thou be with me in Paradise." From this brief summation, one can see that Santacruz Pachacuti's version is an inversion of the others. If Betanzos and Cieza de León recontextualize Viracocha within a Christian framework, making of him one of the Apostles, Santacruz Pachacuti recontextualizes Christ's story within an Indian framework. It seems that the Viracocha stories narrated by the Spanish chroniclers mold the events in the Indian myths into a Christian narrative, while Santacruz Pachacuti molds the Christian story to the Indian myth.

Let us now turn to the Andean elements in the myth. Tunupa, who in Apotampo had denounced the errors of man "con amor afable" [with affable love], cursed the people when he arrived at Yamqueupa, and made the entire village disappear below the waters of the lake. The destructive aspect of the Andean deity is here evident, as it is in the episode at Cacha, where Tunupa destroys with fire an idol made in the figure of a woman: "y se abrasó el dicho cerro con el dicho ydolo, rrebentandoles y derretiendoles como una cera el dicho cerro" [the said mountain burned with the idol, bursting and melting as if it were made out of wax] (283–284). And those who ignored his preaching at a marriage feast in Quinamares, "fueron maldecidos, convirtiéndolos en piedra que hasta el día de oy se echa de ver; y lo mismo sucedió quél, en Pucara y otras partes" [were cursed and turned to stone; they can still be seen today. The same happened in Pucara and other places]. Subsequently, he was taken prisoner and escaped. The "punishments" inflicted by Tunupa upon mankind remand us to the flood sent by Viracocha, the rain of fire in Cacha, the transformation into stone of the original creation, and the marking of the origin of the lineages by the *huacas*. Santacruz Pachacuti writes a version of the myth that has both a Christian and an Andean meaning. It is a *mestiza* or hybrid version, as have been all cultural productions in this part of the Andes since colonial times, productions wherein two cultural veins coexist synchronically.

The last section of this segment of the myth does not vary substantially from the other versions. Viracocha or Tunupa arrives at the coast and goes into the sea—sailing on his robe, or walking on the waves, he disappears.

If one deletes from the various versions of the myth the extraneous elements, both the local and non-Andean ones, one is left with the following sketch of this segment of the myth: the power of the creator, Viracocha or Tunupa, was felt throughout the Andes. It spread out from north to south, from east to west, and from the highest mountains to the ocean. His creative and destructive attributes, manifested through fire or water, were cosmic.

THE KOLLA NARRATIVE CYCLE: FROM COSMIC CHAOS TO NATURAL ORDER

The sacred history of Lake Titicaca, as we have seen, may be constructed using stories that link the site to a divine manifestation. In the Kolla cycle, the first of three, the ancient Andean myths compiled by the sixteenth- and seventeenth-century chroniclers refer to a primordial moment when the creation of the universe, including mankind, takes place. After a careful consideration of the different versions, which allows the identification of foreign elements, one can say that the texts that have come down to us are "reflections" or "local versions" of the original myth. During this first age of the world, which was called *wari wira qucha runa* [primitive lords] or *purunpacha* [barren time/space] by Guamán Poma and Santacruz Pachacuti, respectively, a supreme being, called either Viracocha in Quechua or Tunupa in Aymara, appears at Lake Titicaca and imposes order on chaos.[41] The period of chaos, which had been a time of darkness when everything coexisted in an undifferentiated state, is represented in the myth by the absence of the stars. Bouysse Cassagne and Harris use the Aymara concept of *taypi* to refer to a time/place that allows the coexistence of opposing elements (e.g., fire and water) or in Aymara, *awqa*. The first age, then, is that of the *taypi*, a potential microcosm where all the *awqa* coexist, and from which all the different ethnic groups would originate.

Viracocha's (or Tunupa's) creative and destructive powers may also be understood in the light of the concept of *awqa*. His creative aspect (e.g., the creation of the stars, the plants, and man) coexists with his destructive nature (e.g., the transformation of men into stone, the flood, and the rain of fire that ignites the mountainside). He is also an ordering god who assigns each lineage a specific place of origin, a language, distinctive attire, and nourishment. He also brings order by naming the lineages, the plants, the animals, and all things, thus separating and segmenting the universe. The birth of language brings order to chaos. A pan-Andean god, he creates all Andean nations, and thus his founding mission is all-encompassing: it reaches the four cardinal points and covers all elevations from the highest mountain peaks to the ocean.

Viracocha emerges from Lake Titicaca, and it is from there that he organizes the universe. He commands the sun, the moon, and the stars to appear in the heavens and that night follow day. Lake Titicaca becomes the point of departure for his journey through the Andes. Like the appearance of any theophany in a given place, Viracocha's appearance at Lake Titicaca makes this site sacred.

In addition to the versions of the myth provided by sixteenth- and seventeenth-century chroniclers, stories from the first cycle have also been preserved within the oral tradition. However, these versions, whose study would require extensive fieldwork, fall beyond the scope of the present study.

3

The Inca Narrative Cycle

THE INCA EXPANSION INTO KOLLA LAND

In the *Historia del Tahuantinsuyu*, Maria Rostworowski uses archaeological evidence to show that the Inca expansion took place a century before the arrival of the Spaniards. The Incas moved southward from Cuzco, annexing the territory of Kollasuyu, which they named after the Kolla, the most important ethnic group in the region. The southern Andes then became part of the Inca Empire of Tahuantinsuyu.[42] The Kollasuyu was home to many ethnic groups or nations, of which the most important were the Lupacas, the Kollas, the Pacajes, and the Urus (Julien 9–62). They lived on the shores of Lake Titicaca and shared the same language—Aymara.[43] It appears that the Inca attempt to gain control of the region generated interethnic conflicts. Sometime in the fifteenth century, the Kollas attempted to dominate the region, and led by Zapana, launched a military campaign against the Lupacas, whom they believed were about to conquer several islands in Lake Titicaca (Meiklejohn 24; Cieza de León 148).

Although not much is known about the origins of the Lupacas, it is certain that they lived along the shores of the lake as early as the twelfth century (Meiklejohn 23). Around the fifteenth century their leader, Cari, tried to expand his power in the Lake Titicaca region and eventually precipitated their confrontation with the Kollas. The Incas appeared on the scene during this crucial period of instability.

Cieza de León recounts the expansionist ambitions of both the Incas and the Kollas:

> Estando Ynga Yupangue en el Cuzco *procurando de lo ennobleçer, determinó de yr a Collasuyo*, que son las provinçias que caen a la parte del Austro de la çibdad, porque tuvo aviso que los deçendientes de Çapana que señoreavan la parte de hatuncolla, eran ya muy poderosos y *estavan tan*

sobervios que hazían junta de gente para venir sobre el Cuzco, y así mandó aperéivir sus gentes. (Cieza de León 135; my emphasis)

[When Yahuar-Huacac (Ynga Yupangue) was in Cuzco engaged in ennobling the city, he decided to go to Colla-suyu, which are the provinces which lie to the south of the city, because word had been brought to him that the descendants of (a chief named) Zapana, who was lord of the region of Hatuncolla, had become very powerful and *were so haughty that they were assembling people to march against Cuzco, and he ordered his troops to make ready.*] (206)

Inca Yupanqui never carried out his intentions because the Chancas attacked Cuzco and killed the Inca. His son Viracocha was named his successor (Cieza de León 138–141). During the reign of Inca Viracocha, the Kolla chief, Zapana, sent a diplomatic mission to Cuzco to denounce the expansionist ambitions of the Lupacas (Cieza de León 148–151). On his way to the Kollao, Inca Viracocha conquered the Canas and the Canchis. Meanwhile, the Lupacas and the Kollas met in battle, and the former emerged victorious (Cieza de León 152–155). Since the Inca arrived in the Kollao after the conflict had been resolved, he did not become the unquestioned lord of the Kollao (Cieza de León 156–158). Nevertheless, Inca Viracocha and Cari, the Lupaca lord, formed an alliance, which marked the beginning of the Inca presence at Lake Titicaca.[44] As this brief summation indicates, internal conflicts within the Kollao facilitated the eventual Inca conquest of the region (Rostworowski 100; Millones 96).

According to Sarmiento de Gamboa (188), it was Viracocha's successor, Pachacuti Ynca Yupanqui, who in fact conquered the Kollao.[45] Inca domination of the region becomes a reality with him. Cieza de León explains:

Pasando adelante Ynga Yupangue, quentan que visitó los más pueblos que confinan con la gran laguna de Titicaca y que con su buena maña los atraxo todos a su serviçio, poniéndose en cada pueblo del traje que usavan los naturales, cosa de gran plazer para ellos y con que más se holgava[n]. Entró en la gran laguna de Titicaca y miró las yslas que en ella se hazen, mandando hazer en la mayor dellas tenplo del Sol y palaçios para él y sus deçendientes. (Cieza de León 1553, 186)

[Proceeding, the Inca is said to have visited most of the settlements bordering on the great lake of Titicaca, and with his great skill he won them over to his service, attiring himself in each village in the garb used by the natives, which was the thing that pleased them most. He went out on the

great lake of Titicaca, observed its islands, and ordered built on the largest
of them a temple to the sun and palaces for himself and his descendants.]
(Cieza de León 1979, 233)

The construction of the Temple of the Sun on the Island of Titicaca,
along with palaces for the Inca, marks the importance of the site for all of
Pachacuti's successors.

The religious importance of the Island of Titicaca predates, however,
the Inca expansion (Ramos Gavilán 20). The inhabitants of the region,
fearing that Titicaca would lose its religious importance, sent a priest
from Titicaca's famous sanctuary to Cuzco to solicit the Inca's protection
for this sacred place. The priest exaggerated the wonders of the sanctuary and its oracles in order to obtain the Inca's patronage, telling the Inca
that many had witnessed the Sun emerging from a rock on which the
birds dared not land. After having "ponderado las muchas y nunca vistas
maravillas" [praised the many and unheard marvels], he invited the Inca
to take possession of the sanctuary. Inca Yupanqui became the first in his
dynasty to visit the site.

> Cuando llegó a vista de la deseada peña no hizo menos que mocharla (que
> es lo que nosotros decimos adorarla). Como si viera a Dios en zarza, se
> descalzó, miró con atención y no viendo en la peña señal alguna, que
> mostrase haber asentado pájaro allí, la tuvo por tan misteriosa como le
> habían significado, y de tal suerte acreditó aquella romería, que cobró
> opinión de la más célebre de todo el reino que de la misma manera que en
> tiempos pasados acudían los Atenienses, y otras naciones al Templo de
> Apolo en Delfos, ...así acá en el Perú venían desde Quito, Pasto y Chile
> a esta isla Titicaca, a encomendarse al Sol. (Ramos Gavilán 21)

> [Arriving at the desired rock, he performed a *mocha* (which is what we call
> worship). He took his shoes off as if he were seeing God in a bush, he
> stared but not seeing any sign on the rock of a bird landing on it, regarded
> it as mysterious as they had told him, and in this way he gave credit to that
> pilgrimage, that became the most famous in all the kingdom, in a similar
> way that in old times the Athenians, and other nations went to the Temple
> of Apollo at Delphi, . . . here in Peru, they came to this island Titicaca
> from Quito, Pasto, and Chile to pray to the Sun].

Realizing that the sanctuary was the perfect place to promote the worship of the sun among his subjects, Inca Yupanqui had buildings and
temples built to complement the sanctuary, established an *acllawasi*
(monastery for Virgins of the Sun), built a *tambo* (hostel) for pilgrims,
and uprooted the majority of the lake's inhabitants in order to secure

control of the region. Tupac Yupanqui repopulated the area with people from forty-two different nations throughout the empire and placed the Incas at the head of the regional government (Ramos Gavilán 43–45).

We must remember that Lake Titicaca was a strategic location for exerting political control in the region. As a result of Inca domination, the Kollas suffered the most for having resisted the Incas in armed combat. Because of their alliance with the Incas, the Lupacas were better able to conserve their internal organization, their language, and their customs. In any case, the inhabitants of the Kollao lost their supremacy in the region and were subsequently marginalized. Nevertheless, some appear to have adapted to the new system: the principal Kolla lords, for instance, adopted the Quechua language, and Kolla contingents joined the Inca army during the northern campaigns (Guamán Poma 168).

The Incas respected the local cults in the territories they conquered and, in fact, adopted some local rituals and idols with the sole condition that the Sun be recognized as the supreme deity (MacCormack 1991, 148; Espinoza Soriano 446; Lara 46). Yet with regard to religion, the Kollas experienced inequality. They were not allowed to participate in the most important religious ceremonies, like the festivals of Inti Raymi and Capac Raymi, which were solemn celebrations honoring the Sun god. Ramos Gavilán explains that

> a esta gente Colla como a gente maldita y más desordenada en todos los vicios de la sensualidad, los tenía por particular decreto excluídos de aquellas sus mayores festividades. (Ramos Gavilán 93)

> [these Kolla people were regarded as damned and wild in the vices of sensuality and were excluded by decree from the major festivities.]

Rupture and disorder resulted from the Kolla's subordination to the Incas: their annexed nation could no longer exercise its autonomy. The language of their conquerors, Quechua, replaced Aymara as the language of the ruling classes, and their religious worship was restricted. Although the Inca presence, in the eyes of the Kollas, must have been seen as the advent of chaos, the Inca myths depict themselves as the organizing element in an already chaotic world. Furthermore, the myths of origin of the Inca ethnic group represent the Titicaca region as their place of origin, justifying their expansion and domination of the Kollao. The myths claim the region as rightfully Inca, and thus the Incas claimed that, with their conquest, they were returning to their own land, that is, reclaiming their roots. Through this recuperation of a past, their discourse attempts to establish a continuity that eliminates the cultural and psychological gaps their incursion into Kolla territory might have created.

LAKE TITICACA: THE INCA NARRATIVE CYCLE

For the analysis of the second narrative cycle of the hierophantic history of Lake Titicaca, I have considered sixteen different variants of the myth of origins of the Inca dynasty compiled between 1552 and 1653, which by no means constitute an exhaustive catalog of all versions collected at that time.[46] Although Henrique Urbano has compiled forty-one different variants of the Inca myth of origin, I have limited the corpus to sixteen following two criteria: first, the versions explicitly mentioning Lake Titicaca or Tiahuanaco as the place of origin of the Incas; and second, those that link the origin of the Inca dynasty to a divine order.

Following the same methodology used in the analysis of the first cycle, I isolate the elements that the majority of the versions share to construct a master narrative, which then permits the study of the variants in the Inca myth.

MASTER NARRATIVE: THE SUN AND THE ORIGIN OF THE INCAS

On the Island of Titicaca, the Sun—a resplendent personage in the form of a man—summoned the Incas and adopted them as his children. Since humankind was living in a state of barbarism, the Sun conferred a civilizing mission upon the Incas. These divine emissaries traveled to the north and emerged from the mouth of Pacaritambo, a cave near Cuzco. These original Incas, a brother and a sister or four brothers and four sisters, wore clothing richly adorned in gold and carried corn seeds. The men and women carried slings and metal utensils, respectively. One brother, Manco Capac, also carried a golden rod that would sink into the ground at the exact place where, according to the wishes of the Sun, they should settle. The rod was thrust into the ground at either Pacaritambo or Cuzco. Three of the original four brothers were turned into *huacas*. The remaining brother, Manco Capac, had a son with one of his sisters, thus becoming the progenitor of the Inca dynasty.

LAKE TITICACA: INCA PLACE OF ORIGIN AND
THE APPEARANCE OF A NEW HIEROPHANY

Inca myths of origin also mark Lake Titicaca as a sacred place. The myth of creation is usually narrated together with the Inca origin myth, as mentioned before. After the flood a new hierophany—the Sun god—appears in these myths. The Andean creator god, as Franklin Pease calls Viracocha (Pease 1973), disappears in order to allow a new manifestation of the sacred. From the more universal perspective of the history of religions, this new hierophany corresponds to a solarization of the supreme beings. According to Mircea Eliade, having completed the creative labor, the supreme beings give way to new hierophanies or religious forms that are more relevant to the daily lives of people in society. In his study of solar hierophanies, Eliade explains that all sun worship exhibits

> the solarization of Supreme Beings, the sun's connection with sovereignty, initiation and the élite, its ambivalence, its relations with the dead, with fertility and so on. But it is worth underlining the close connection between solar theology and the elite—whether of kings, initiates, heroes or philosophers. Unlike other nature hierophanies, sun hierophanies tend to become the privilege of a closed circle, of a minority of the elect. (Eliade 1963, 150)

This tendency is evident in the Inca myth in which these Indians, portrayed as the progeny of the Sun, are deified, and, as a result, their caste is placed above all others. Comparative studies of religion have determined that, once a celestial god ceases his creative labors, he becomes a *Deus otiosus* and plays a minimal role, or disappears entirely, from the religious rituals of a culture. The celestial god traditionally gives way to another deity whose functions are more immediately relevant to the lives of the people (Eliade 1963). For some scholars the myth of creation and the absence of specific rituals, as in the case of the Sun or the Pachamama, depict an otiose deity. Demarest (1981) argues that Viracocha and the Sun share an identity because of several overlapping functions, forms of address, rituals, and prayers. For these reasons he proposes that Viracocha is one facet of a complex Andean godhead (21). His interpretation does not contradict the notion of a pan-Andean creator derived from the first narrative cycle, where all creative and destructive powers coexist, but I believe that the Sun is an aspect or a representation of the Andean concept of the supernatural. While there are shared attributes, there is also an embedding of the underlying narrative cycles that I propose. In the narratives analyzed here, there is a time of darkness before the creation of the sun, and it is Viracocha who sends the sun to Titicaca. If Viracocha and the Sun were, in fact, identical, the implication is that the sun sends the sun, an impossible feat as Guardia Mayorga points out (145). Demarest solves the problem by noting that "it is consistent with the alternative possibility that the sun could be a separable part of itself" (21). From my point of view, however, Viracocha and the Sun are portrayed as separate personages in the discursive representations, each of them a hierophany of its own and, as such, share multiple characteristics and functions. This notwithstanding, each too is represented with different levels of specificity, as I will seek to demonstrate subsequently.

In most narratives of Inca origins the Sun is the new hierophany at Titicaca. Waldemar Espinoza Soriano explains:

El dios privativo de la etnia Inca era el Sol, del que se creían descender.
Conforme avanzaban sus conquistas, en cada *llacta* o centro administrativo
que fundaban hacíanle levantar un templo, pero sin tratar de imponerlo a
la fuerza en los pueblos anexados, a cuyos dioses locales respetaban. (446)

[The exclusive god of the Incas was the Sun, from whom they believed they
descended. As their conquest advanced, in each *llacta* or administrative
center they founded, they erected a temple (in the Sun's honor), but they
did not try to forcefully impose their cult on the annexed peoples, whose
local gods were respected.]

Clearly the state religion of the Tahuantinsuyu was centered around
sun worship. However, despite Espinoza Soriano's assertion, the Sun was
not "el dios privativo" [the exclusive god] of the Incas. While the Incas,
in order to justify their control over other ethnic groups, portrayed themselves in their myths as direct descendants of the divine order, there existed a solar cult in the region prior to the Incas (Bouysse Cassagne 1988,
70).[47] Ramos Gavilán's aforementioned story of the Kolla priest who requests Inca protection for the sanctuary of the Sun on the Island of Titicaca indicates that the solar divinity had already achieved some stature
among the inhabitants of the Kollao before the Inca expansion. It is also
worth mentioning here that the Kolla chief's appellation, *Capac Ca-
paapoyndichori*, meant, according to Betanzos, "rey y solo señor hijo del
sol" [king and only lord, son of the Sun], which would also imply that
the Kollas worshiped the sun and portrayed themselves as possessing a
divine heritage. The hymn of allegiance between the Kollas and the Incas,
transcribed by Santacruz Pachacuti, is also worth recalling:[48]

Tú el poderoso del Cuzco
yo el poderoso del Collao:
bebamos,
comamos
[y] convengamos
que ninguno [de nos] padezca
Yo aferrado a la plata
tú aferrado al oro
tú—adorador—de Huiracocha
el conservador del mundo,
yo
el adorador del Sol.

[You the powerful from Cuzco
I the powerful from Collao

let us drink,
let us eat
(and) let us agree
that neither of us suffer
I attached to silver
You attached to gold
You worshipper of Viracocha
the world preserver,
I
the worshipper of the Sun.]

Claiming divine origin from the Sun, already recognized as a god by the subjugated ethnic groups, was an effective political strategy on the part of the conquering Incas. The Incas at once lent their own solar cult a particular institutional character as they appropriated a local solar cult shared by prior cultures and other ethnic groups. Bouysse Cassagne suggests that the relationship between sun worship, the use of gold in its representation, and the finding of rich gold deposits in Peru points to the Inca arrogation of religious observances of other ethnic groups:[49]

> A este propósito, es importante notar que es precisamente después de la conquista de las dos más importantes provincias aúreas del Perú, que los Incas emprendieron la construcción de su mayor templo y que se constituyó la religión del Estado. . . . De este modo, las dos grandes provincias auríferas del Perú asequibles a la tecnología minera prehispánica, correspondieron al dominio de la influencia mochica y chimu, al norte, y colla, al sud; y es sólo por su integración al sistema religioso inca que éste, y el culto solar, cobraron la importancia que es conocida. (1988, 68–69)

> [For this purpose, it is important to notice that immediately after the conquest of the two most important auriferous provinces of Peru, the Incas started the construction of their main temple and that it constituted the State religion. . . . In this way, the two largest auriferous provinces of Peru accessible to the prehispanic mining technology corresponded to the Mochica and Chimu influence to the north, and to Colla to the south; it was only through its integration to the Inca religious system that gold and the solar cult gained their known importance.]

The importance of gold as a symbol of the Inca empire is also evident in Pedro Pizarro's version of the myth of origin, which fails to make a connection between the Incas and the sun:

> En esta laguna ay una ysla que se dize Titicaca, donde tenían por ydolo una muger, de la çinta arriua de oro y de la çinta auaxo de plata, de la

estatura de una muger mediana. Esta uide yo que la truxeron dallí, de quien dizen los yndios auían salido el primer señor deste rreyno. (46)

[In this lake there is an island called Titicaca, where they had an idol in the shape of a woman, from her waist up made out of gold, and from the waist down of silver, of the stature of a middle-sized woman. I saw it when they brought it from there, and the Indians say that the first lord of this kingdom was born of her.]

It is obvious from this passage that both gold and silver were important precious metals for the Indians. But gold, which appears on the upper portion of the statue, was more highly valued. For instance, the symbols of Inca power (e.g., the *mascaipacha*[50]) and social caste (e.g., golden earspools) were worn on the head. The idol described by Pedro Pizarro, in which silver is shown, literally and symbolically, as being inferior to gold, echoes the Kolla hymn: The Incas, "attached to gold," are placed at the head of political power to whom the Kollas, "attached to silver," are subservient.

It would seem, then, that the Inca myth of origin seeks to justify Inca political domination of the Titicaca region and their exploitation of the area's resources. What discursive modifications of the myth would promote the accomplishment of these objectives? If any myth is a manifestation of the collective thought of a given culture whose divine, social, and natural orders are redefined through time, we can see how the goals and objectives of the conquering Incas dictated comparable transformations in their etiological myth.

With respect to the divine, social, and natural orders, there are modifications of the Andean myths of creation in the Inca myths of origin which have implications on many different levels. In the myth of creation, Viracocha is the divine order from which the two others emanate: the natural order, represented by the hills, stars, plants, animals, and mankind, which in turn creates the social order with its different lineages and customs. These relationships among the integral elements of each order are horizontal; a hierarchy of lineages, stars, or plants does not exist. The Inca myth of origin introduces a modification that introduces hierarchies in each of the orders. If, in the myth of creation, the sun was just one of many elements of the natural order, in the Inca myth of origin the sun becomes a new hierophany, modifying both the divine and natural orders. A hierarchy of celestial bodies is established in which the Sun reigns above all other stars, which are also deified along with other natural phenomena.[51] This hierarchy within the divine order has its counterpart in the social order, where the Incas are at the top because of their association with the Sun. Inca rule is not only justified but, in this representation, almost axiomatic.

The Incas appear as "hijos del Sol" [children of the Sun] in six of the sixteen versions I use and in sixteen of the forty-one compiled by Henrique Urbano. At least eight more versions indicate some type of supernatural origin for the Incas, but not all accounts about their origins are mentioned in a religious context (see, for instance, Viceroy Toledo's reports, pp. 132–143). I will return to this omission in my discussion of the chronological extension of the Inca dynasty.[52] The genealogical connection between the Incas and the Sun god is generally followed by derogatory commentaries. Molina says that the Incas "empezaron a jactarse y llamarse Hijos del Sol" [began to boast and call themselves Children of the Sun] (50). Salinas y Córdova says that Manco Capac presents himself as "hijo natural del Sol" [the Sun's natural child] through "traça y arte del Demonio" [the design and art of the Devil] (Salinas y Córdova 14).[53] Vázquez de Espinosa observes that "Manco Capac . . . salió de la Laguna de Titicaca . . . por mandado del Sol su padre (según la patraña que ellos cuentan)" [Manco Capac . . . came forth from Lake Titicaca . . . following the command of the Sun, his father (according to the lies they tell)] (378). Bernabé Cobo introduces the different versions of the myth as a "variedad de desatinos," "otra fábula no menos ridícula," "otro desvarío," or "ficción" ["a kind of folly," "another ridiculous fable," "another delirium," or a "fiction"]. These commentaries by the compilers arise naturally from the fact that their versions are narrated from a Christian perspective for a Christian audience. Although the chroniclers might have distorted the myth, their compilations still provide information that enables us to understand the importance of the myth within Andean culture.

The only narratives devoid of derisive commentary about the possible supernatural origin of the Incas are those compiled by Inca Garcilaso de la Vega. It is interesting, however, that it is his uncle—his indigenous mother's brother—who is said to narrate the first version of the myth so that, as Garcilaso explains, "se sepa por las propias palabras que los Incas lo cuentan, que no por las de otros autores extraños" [it be better to have it as told in the very words of the Incas than in those of foreign authors] (41). At the end of the other versions of the myth he states: "Otros pasos de la una fábula y de la otra quieren semejar a los de la santa historia, que les parece que se semejan. Yo no me entremeto en cosas tan hondas; digo llanamente las fábulas historiales que en mis niñeces oí a los míos; tómelas cada uno como quisiese, y déles el alegoría que más le cuadrase" [Other parts of this legend and the other seem to point to those of Holy Writ, which they are thought to resemble. I do not venture on such profound matters: I simply repeat the fabulous accounts I used to hear my family tell in my childhood; let each take them as he wishes and apply whatever allegory he thinks most appropriate] (49). In all cases Inca Garcilaso never compromises himself; he imposes distance with respect to what he narrates, while at the same time narrowing the gap by representing the myth as a narrative arising from within the culture itself. By employing prosopopoeia, the Inca is able to narrate from both a Christian and an Andean perspective, as he writes for both a European and an Andean audience.

The justification for Inca domination in the Kollao region is not based solely on the supremacy of Inca lineage and its relationship with the God common to both ethnic groups. The myth also reclaims the sacred place, Lake Titicaca, as its own since ancient times.

Cuzco was historically the center of the Tahuantinsuyu, yet these versions of the Inca myth of origin establish Lake Titicaca as the dynasty's primordial seat. As MacCormack points out, the extant version of the Inca myths are narrated together with the myth of creation (1991, 100). In stories by Molina, Murúa, Garcilaso (II), and Cobo (II), the Incas make their appearance after the flood. Unlike the creation myth, where Viracocha creates all lineages without distinguishing one from the other, the combined versions make specific mention of the Incas.[54]

One may think that the mention of the Incas sets them apart as a chosen people in the same way that the Bible singles out Noah and his descendants as having been chosen to perpetuate the human race after the flood. However, if the myths are seen as separate entities, by cycles or by themes, as MacCormack proposes, in the creation story the Incas are but one ethnic group among many. Yet those versions that combine cycles or themes operate chiefly as a temporal marker, because they represent the origin of the Incas as ancient. Garcilaso de la Vega's first version, which according to him is the most authoritative because it originated directly from the Incas, while it fails to mention the flood does refer to a primordial moment in ancient times: "en los siglos antiguos . . ."

This representation of the origin of the Incas in ancient times has implications that transcend the chronological placement of this story. By expanding the temporal limits of Inca history and by situating its primordial seat at Titicaca, the myth portrays the conquest as a return to Inca patrimony rather than as an appropriation of a neighbor's territory. By so doing, the myth accomplishes two things: it justifies the conquest and subjugation of Kolla territories before the Spanish conquest; and, during the colonial period, when these versions were written, it attempts to legitimize Inca control of the region.

It must be taken into account that when these texts were transcribed, the legitimacy of Inca control was being questioned. Viceroy Toledo's government compiled many reports (1572–1575) depicting the Incas as arrogant, capricious, and cruel. One of the clear goals of Toledo's policies (1569–1581) was to provide evidence of the illegitimacy and tyranny of the Incas in order to justify the Spanish conquest, which would permit Toledo to declare the Inca territory a no-man's-land. His policies attempted to undermine Las Casas's reforms and impose political, social, and economic structures that would uphold the legitimacy and authority of the Spanish Crown.[55]

From the Andean perspective, the justification for Inca domination of the Kollao could not be based solely on the antiquity of Inca history, since the pan-Andean myth of creation represents the origin of *all* lineages. The Incas' relationship with the divinity and the establishment of a world hierarchy suggested by their myth of origin become vital parts of this justification. From the Spanish perspective, it is precisely the temporal aspect of the Inca myth of origin that legitimizes Inca preeminence over other ethnic groups, which in turn allowed the Incas to assume a privileged place in the new social order.

BARBARIC PEOPLE AND THE INCA CIVILIZING MISSION

The Inca myth establishes a hierarchy which privileges the Incas over other ethnic groups not solely on the basis of their "chosen" status as divine emissaries *ab initio*. According to most variants, social and political chaos reigned in the region before the coming of the Inca dynasty. The other ethnic groups are represented as engulfed in barbarism, political chaos, and continual interethnic wars which the Incas—by divine command and because of their unique organizational skills—were called upon to resolve.[56]

These unruly groups subjugated by the Incas were considered *behetrías*, a legal term that refers to a group of people who, having no natural lord, elect as their leader someone who is not of noble ancestry. Pedro Pizarro, for instance, states that before the Incas imposed their rule,

> hera todo behetrías, aunque auía algunos señores que tenían subjetos algunos pueblos pequeños cercanos a ellos, y éstos heran pocos; y así en las behetrías trayan guerras unos con otros. (45)

> [they were all *behetrías*, although there were some lords that had subjected a few nearby towns, but not many, so in the *behetrías* they waged war on one another.]

The concept of chaos that the native informants tried to transmit was transformed by the chroniclers into the notion of *behetría* just as in the earlier treatment of the creation a moral judgment was imposed on Viracocha's turning the people into stone. In both cases, ideas foreign to Andean thought permeate the myths.

In his *Tesoro de la Lengua Castellana o Española*, Covarrubias explains the term *behetría* in a way that is especially relevant to our context:

[E]n la behetría como no tienen cabeça a quien respetar, todos hablan a bulto. Y por esso donde quiera que dan vozes confusamente, dezimos ser behetría. . . . Behetrías es nombre corrompido de benefactrías en lugares adonde teniendo el rey algún dominio y ciertos derechos y tributos tomavan el señor que les parecía y lo dexavan cuando querían; porque la preeminencia de la behetría era mudar señor por sola su voluntad. [discutiendo el caso de España en el siglo XI]: Otras behetrías se dezían de entre parientes, por no poder tomar para señor suyo a quien quisiessen, sino que eran forçados a tomar señor de ciertos linages, que para cada lugar estavan ya conocidos y determinados. . . . Estando pues esto assí, la larga esperiencia mostró cómo esta libertad de mudar señores traía gran confusión y desconcierto en el govierno, tanto que dio lugar al proverbio castellano, el qual a una cosa muy sin orden y desbaratada, la llama cosa de behetría. También se entendió cómo esta preeminencia de las behetrías perjudicaba mucho con la confusión de las rentas del rey y a los derechos dellas. . . . Agora llaman behetrías, largo modo, a las villas eximidas de ciudades, que no están sujetas a ningún corregimiento por apelación ni por residencia, sino al Consejo y Chancillerías.

[(I)n a "behetría" since they do not have a head to respect, they all talk at the same time. And that is why we called them *behetrías* whenever they yelled confusingly. . . . *Behetría* is the corrupted form of *benefactría*, a name for places where the king had some dominion and certain rights and tributes, but where they took any lord that they wanted and dropped him at will; because the characteristic of the *behetría* was to change rulers at will. (discussing the case of Spain in the eleventh century): There were other *behetrías* among relatives, who—unable to take as their lord whoever they wanted, were forced to take one of a certain lineage, which for each place was already known and determined. . . . Being things as such, the long experience showed how this freedom of changing lords brought with it great confusion and disconcert in the government, so much so that it gave rise to the Castilian proverb, which calls a *behetría* anything without order and in disarray. It was also understood how this preeminence of the *behetrías* was harmful to the revenues of the king and to his rights . . . Now they call *behetrías*, in a wide sense, those villages far from the cities, that are not subject to any jurisdiction either by appellation or by residence, but by the Council and chanceries.]

The *behetría* forms part of a legal discourse that presupposes a political order led by an unquestionable ruler to whom obedience and tributes are rightly due. A *behetría* thus connotes chaos within an established order which is based on the principle of nobility and wealth as the basis of power.

The representation of the Inca domination from this frame of reference reveals two tendencies: one legitimizes its power, and the other seeks to subvert it. Both tendencies, however, derive from the same categories. The first distinguishes the Incas from all other groups categorized as *behetrías* and allows them to become the legitimate rulers and the embodiment of order. The Incas are thus represented as "los hombres más nobles, ricos y poderosos de todas las tierras" [the most noble, rich, and powerful in all the land] (Gómara 1552). Vázquez de Espinoza's account also favors the Incas:

> Mango Capac primero rey de los incas salió de la Laguna de Titicaca con su mujer y hermana la reina . . . predicando a aquellas bárbaras naciones la Ley natural, enseñadoles político modo de vivir como gentes, sacándolos del barbarismo en que como brutos irracionales vivían, . . . fundó la imperial ciudad, madre y patria de tantos reyes y emperadores de aquellas regiones, . . . sujetó a su obediencia con sus armas, y con sus leyes las mantuvo y sustentó por espacio de 500 años en paz y buen gobierno. (379)

> [Mango Capac, first king of the Incas, came from Lake Titicaca with his wife and sister, the queen . . . preaching natural law to all those barbaric nations, teaching them to live like people, taking them out of the barbarism in which they lived like irrational beasts, . . . founded the imperial city, mother and seat of so many kings and emperors of those regions . . . he subjected them to his obedience with his arms, and with his laws maintained and sustained his rule for a period of 500 years of peace and good government.]

In his different versions of the myth, Bernabé Cobo depicts the Incas as "hombres de prudencia y valor" [prudent and brave men] (Cobo [I]), whom the Sun god had sent so that they could "enseñasen a vivir como hombres de razón en policía y orden, estableciéndoles leyes con que fuesen mantenidos en paz y justicia" [teach (others) to live like men of reason, in order and civility, establishing laws by which peace and justice were maintained] (Cobo [IV]).

The second tendency is to consider the Incas one of the *behetrías*. Their government, which had been imposed by force and violence, was portrayed as illegitimate. Agustín de Zárate, one of the early chroniclers, takes this position and remarks:

> Estos ingas comenzaron a poblar la ciudad del Cuzco, y desde allí fueron
> sojuzgando toda la tierra y la hicieron tributaria; y de ahí adelante iba
> sucediendo en este señorío el que más poder y fuerza tenía sin guardar or-
> den legítima de sucesión, sino por vía de tiranía y violencia; de manera que
> su derecho estaba en las armas. (471)

> [These Incas founded the city of Cuzco, and from there they conquered all
> the land and made it its tributary; and from that time on in this dominion
> the one who had more power and strength succeeded without keeping an
> order of legitimate succession, but by way of tyranny and violence; there-
> fore his right was in weapons.]

Sarmiento de Gamboa (1572), Viceroy Toledo's official historian, observes that "Mango Capac y los demás hermanos [fueron] a buscar
tierras y tiranizar a los que mal no les hacían, ni les daban ocasión de
guerra, ni con otro derecho ni título más del dicho" [Manco Capac and
his brothers went in search of lands and to tyrannize those who were not
doing any harm to them, nor had given them a motive for war, without
any right or title other than the aforementioned] (120). Other reports
sent to Viceroy Toledo (1572–1575) make similar accusations.

For some, then, the Inca imposition of power in the Lake Titicaca region is rendered legitimate; for others it is portrayed as questionable. In
either case each perspective is an *a posteriori* one which interprets the information from a foreign viewpoint. Most versions attempt to serve the
interests of the Crown, especially those versions shaped by Toledo's ideology. However, even if the issue of the legitimacy or illegitimacy of the Inca
domination of the region is disregarded, because it is clearly a European
imposition, the issue of chaos and order remains and is incontrovertible.

Covarrubias's definition of the term *behetría* makes specific reference
to human discourse: "donde quiera que dan vozes confusamente, dezimos ser behetría" [a *behetría* occurs wherever people yell confusingly].
Many of the narratives I have analyzed are based on a discursive chaos
because, according to the chroniclers, the stories told by the natives fail
to coincide with each other. For instance, Murúa notes that:

> Varias y diuersas cosas y graciosas fábulas quentan los yndios del apareci-
> miento de los primeros Ingas y de la manera con que entraron en la ciudad
> del Cuzco y la conquistaron y poblaron, sin que en este casso pueda hauer
> cossa cierta ni determinada. (Murúa 21)

> [Several and diverse things and amusing fables are told by the Indians
> about the appearance of the first Incas and the way in which they entered,
> conquered, and populated the city of Cuzco, and in none of them can one
> find anything certain or definite.]

Garcilaso also makes a distinction between the story told by his uncle and the other versions in whose discourse "no se entiende la razón y orden" [there is neither sense nor order]. Garcilaso privileges the Inca discourse over all those originating in other ethnic groups, such as the Kollas and the northern Indians.

Told by his maternal uncle, Inca Garcilaso's first version describes the chaos a divine mandate ordered the Incas to correct:

Sabrás que en los siglos antiguos toda esta región de tierra que ves, eran unos grandes montes y breñales, y las gentes en aquellos tiempos vivían como fieras y animales brutos sin religión ni policía, sin pueblo ni casa, sin cultivar ni sembrar la tierra, sin vestir ni cubrir sus carnes, porque no sabían labrar algodón ni lana para hacer de vestir. Vivían de dos en dos, y de tres en tres, como acertaban a juntarse en las cuevas y resquicios de peñas y cavernas de la tierra. Comían como bestias yerbas del campo y raíces de árboles, y la fruta inculta que ellos daban de suyo, y carne humana. Cubrían sus carnes con hojas y cortezas de árboles, y pieles de animales; otros andaban en cueros. (Garcilaso [1609] 1976, 37)

[Know that in olden times the whole of this region before you was covered with brush and heath, and people lived in those times like wild beasts, with no religion or government and no towns or houses, and without tilling or sowing the soil, or clothing or covering their flesh, for they did not know how to weave cotton or wool to make clothes. They lived in twos and threes as chance brought them together in caves and holes in rocks and underground caverns. Like wild beasts they ate the herbs of the field and roots of trees and fruits growing wild and also human flesh. They covered their bodies with leaves and the bark of trees and animals' skins. Others went naked.] (1966, 42)

The "ancient" and "savage" times were characterized in this way because agriculture did not yet exist; the Indians were essentially gatherers. Industry had not yet appeared, houses were nonexistent, and social organizations had not developed, since regional divisions had not yet been established. Inca Garcilaso describes here what anthropologists call the formative period of primitive cultures. Guamán Poma's and Santacruz Pachacuti's explanations of the first ages of the Andean world coincide with Garcilaso's description of pre-Inca times. However, the Indian chroniclers introduce significant variants worthy of careful consideration.

Following quite closely the Judeo-Christian tradition, Guamán Poma depicts the ages of the world, beginning with Creation—as described in

Genesis—and ending with the arrival of the Spaniards in the Tahuan-tinsuyo. He then gives a parallel account of the history of the Andean peoples. According to him there were four generations of Indians.[57] The first, called *Uari Uiracocharuna*, lived in caves and in rocks and lacked manufacturing skills. Despite their "uncivilized" state, however, they possessed some knowledge of their creator and were not idolatrous. Dur-ing the second age, *Uariruna*, the Indians had not advanced much tech-nologically, as evidenced by the fact that they barely "edeficaron unas cacitas que parece horno que ellos les llaman pucullo y no savian hazer rropa cino que se bestian de cueros de animales" [built little houses that looked like ovens and that they called *pucullo* and that they did not know how to make clothes and dressed in animal skins] (54). As in the first age, the inhabitants of the second had knowledge of and worshiped a single god. Civilization seems to have advanced quite rapidly by the time of *Purunruna*, the period comprising the third age. People no longer dressed in animal skins since they wove *awasca* and *cumbi* cloth, and they had elegant clothing with feathers. Architecture and politics also de-veloped: their houses were built of stone with straw roofs, and they elected their legitimate rulers, whom they called *capac apo*. These rulers developed a just system of laws and set a good example for their sub-jects. They also seem to have been monotheistic. During the fourth age, *Aucaruna*, war appears and brings disorder with it: many deaths and bloody conflicts occurred; they took wives and children from each other, and pillaging and cruelty prevailed.

When the lineage of the first and "real" Inca, Capac Ynga Tocay Capac Pinau Capac, who appears during the *Aucaruna*, died out, Manco Capac, who "no tubo pueblo ni tierra ni chacara ni fortalesa ni casta ni parientes antigualla pacarimoc" [had no nation, no land, no pasture, no fortress, no caste, and no known ancestry], began his reign. During this era, idolatry entered Peru largely through the efforts of Manco Capac's mother, Mama Huaco, who is characterized as a "gran fingedora y ydu-latra hechisera" [great deceiver and idolatrous witch] (Guamán Poma 49–64).

Guamán Poma's vision of the ages of the Andean world, like Hesiod's of the Classical world, is one of a progressive spiritual decadence. Guamán Poma does not attribute technological and material progress to the Incas, which is evident in the architecture, irrigation channels, tex-tiles, and road construction. Not only does Guamán Poma deny the Incas a civilizing role, but he even portrays the divine envoy of the Sun, Manco Capac, as an outcast: Manco Capac is the offspring of a demonic union, and the instigator of idolatry in the land. According to this Indian chronicler, before the coming of the Incas, Andeans were not only paving the way for the advent of Christianity (a role also ascribed to the Incas by Garcilaso), but in fact might have been considered true and pious Christians had they only known Christ's name. Guamán Poma, as he evokes the devout sensibilities of the ancient Andean world, even exhorts European Christians to follow their example.

Santacruz Pachacuti also tells a tale about an ancient time when confusion reigned:

> Dicen que en tiempo de *purunpacha* todas las naciones de Tauantinsuyo beneiron de hacia arriba de Potossí, tres o cuatro exercitos en forma de guerra, y así los benieron poblando, tomando los lugares, quedandose cada uno de los compañías en los lugares baldíos; a este tiempo se llaman *ccallacpacha o tutayachacha.* . . . Passaron muchisimos años y al cabo, despues de aber estado ya poblados, abia gran falta de tierras y lugares, y como no abian tierras cadal dia abian guerras y discordias, que todos en general se ocupauan en hacer fortalezas, y así cadal dia en abido encuentros y batallas, sin haber la paz en este tiempo de tantos combates y guerras . . . en tiempos de *purupacha*, dizen que los *hapiñuños*[58] andauan bissiblemente en toda esta tierra, que no abian seguridad de andar en anocheziendo, porque a los hombres y mugeres y criaturas los llebauan arrebatandoles, como tiranos infernales y enemigos capitales del género humano. (282)

> [It is said that at the time of *purunpacha* all nations of the Tahuantinsuyo came from the north of Potosí, three or four warlike armies, and so they came populating and taking over the places, remaining each one of the companies in the empty places; this time is called *ccallacpacha* or *tutayachacha.* . . . A great many years had passed, and at the end, after having populated all around, land was scarce and there were few places, and since there was no more land, each day there were wars and disagreements, so most of them were busy making fortresses, and so each day there were clashes and battles, there was no peace at this time due to the many combats and wars . . . at the time of *purunpacha*, they say that the *hapiñuños* were visible all over the earth, there was no security when one walked at night, because they snatched men and women and children, like the infernal tyrants and capital enemies of human kind that they are.]

The Incas, who emerged during this chaotic period, assumed political control as stipulated by Tunupa's divine mandate. Later, Inca Apomancocapac "començó poner leyes morales para el buen gouierno de su gente, conquistandole a los ynobedientes muchas prouincias y naciones de los Tauantinsuyu" [began to make moral laws for the good government of his people, conquering the disobedient of many provinces and nations of the Tahuantinsuyu] (Santacruz Pachacuti 286).

Garcilaso and Santacruz Pachacuti portray the Inca intervention as an ordering principle in a chaotic social situation, while Guamán Poma judges it to be a source of social chaos. All three see the Inca mission as a response to a supernatural mandate that is either divine (Garcilaso, Santacruz Pachacuti) or diabolical (Guamán Poma). The supernatural intervention that imposes order on chaos is analogous to the same type of intervention in the Viracocha myth. Chaos is cosmic in the creation myth and social in the myth of origins. However, in both cases the organizing force, whether Viracocha or the Incas, emerges from Lake Titicaca. In the creation myth there are creative and destructive cycles. An initial creation is destroyed by the flood, which in turn leads to a new creation. The earlier lineages represented in stone give rise to the new lineages. This cyclicity also appears in Guamán Poma but in social rather than cosmic terms. Men in his version exist in a state of savagery during the first age. In the second, a civilizing process begins and reaches its culmination in the third. In the fourth and final age, however, civilization reverts back to a state of chaos and is marked by wars and idolatry. In addition, the cosmic *pachakuti* in the myth of creation finds as its counterpart a succession of social changes in the Inca myth of origin.

Another interesting parallel between the Creation and Inca narrative cycles lies in the juxtaposition of two opposites which correspond to the concept of *taypi*. In the myth of creation this is embodied in the figure of Viracocha, whose attributes are fire and water, destruction and creation, multidirectionality. These oppositions continue to separate and order themselves as part of the creative act. A *taypi*-like notion also manifests itself in Santacruz Pachacuti's version of the Inca myth of origin in the figures of the *hapiñuños*, who were "fantasmas o duendes que solían aparecerse con dos tetas largas que podían asir dellas" [ghosts or goblins that used to appear with two long hanging breasts] (Holguin). These ghosts, who belong to the realm of the dead, are present in the world of the living during the age of *purunpacha*. *Purunpacha* is related to the term *Puruma*, the period of darkness, that Bertonio defines in the following manner:

> Puruma, vel Cchama pacha: Tiempo antiquissimo, quanto no auia sol, segun imaginauan los indios, ni muchas cosas de las que ay agora. (178)

> [Puruma, or Cchama pacha: Ancient time, when there was no sun nor many of the things that one finds now, according to the Indians' imagination.]

Purunpacha is situated in the social order, and *puruma* corresponds to the period of darkness in the cosmic order of the Viracocha myth. The appearance of the Sun symbolizes the introduction of order to the worlds depicted in both versions. Viracocha creates the sun, and a new creation emerges from the light. The Sun god guides his offspring, the Incas, as they set out from Lake Titicaca on a civilizing mission under the guiding emblem of his light. The Inca origin myth thus duplicates the events of the cosmic period in the myth of creation.[59]

LAKE TITICACA — PACARITAMBO — CUZCO

Once they received the mandate from the Sun god, the Incas departed from Lake Titicaca toward the north, the same direction taken by the god Viracocha. All sixteen versions of the Inca myth concur in the point of departure and destination of the demiurges: Lake Titicaca and Cuzco. These two sites establish a territorial dividing line between north and south separating the two regions, the Urcosuyu in the north and the Umasuyu in the south.[60] The importance of these two points, south and north, Titicaca and Cuzco, is obvious in the two narrative cycles. The first cycle emphasizes Lake Titicaca because all creation radiates from that site; the second highlights Cuzco because civilization radiates from there. This opposition between north and south can be interpreted in Andean terms as a *pachakuti*: a change in time and space, "se da la vuelta el mundo", "se trastocan los tiempos" [the world turns upside down, time turns around and changes]. Prominence migrates from the south to the north, and barbarism gives way to civilization.

The Incas' journey from Titicaca to Cuzco is represented in the various narratives in two ways. They either travel underground and emerge from a cave at Pacaritambo, or they cross over the mountains to arrive at Cuzco. All versions also coincide in identifying two stages in the journey: the first from Titicaca to Pacaritambo, and the second from Pacaritambo to Cuzco.[61] The first stage of the journey establishes a strong link between Titicaca and the Incas, which not only justifies Inca domination in the Kollasuyo but also answers a need to maintain a link between the myth of origin and the myth of creation.

The motif depicting the subterranean journey of the Incas is found in three versions (Molina and Cobo [I and II]). In these the Maker confers his divine mandate on the Incas, who, having been saved from the flood, emerge from Pacaritambo at the moment that the Maker separates night from day. The continuity established by this part of the myth with the creation myth is explicit. Cristóbal de Molina adds that the Incas "vinieron a salir a la cueva de Pacaritambo, de donde se jactaban proceder, aunque de la dicha cueva dicen salieron otras naciones" [came forth from the cave of Pacaritambo, from where they boasted to have originated, although many other nations say they also emerged from the same cave] (52).

The act of emerging from the cave reminds us of the notion of *pachakuti*, for what was below the earth is now above it. From the darkness inside the earth, the Incas emerged onto the surface "al punto que el Sol" [at the same time as the Sun] (Molina 52). This *pachakuti* in the myth represents the beginning of a new era, the Inca era.

In the narratives in which the Incas travel from Titicaca to Cuzco overland, the new era is represented by changes introduced by the divine emissaries. As we will see, these transformations of civilization are essentially agricultural, industrial, and military and take place within a religious or ritualistic context laden with implications for the social order.

Before Manco Capac departed from Titicaca, the Sun god presented him with a golden rod to carry on his journey. According to the divinity's instructions, the Incas were to attempt to plant the rod in the earth every time they stopped to rest. If the rod easily penetrated the soil, this was the sign that they had reached their journey's end, an event which happens only with their arrival in the valley of Cuzco (Garcilaso [I] and Cobo [IV]).

The golden rod given by the divinity performs a double function. It serves first to symbolize the divine character of the Incas' mission, since the Sun god himself had bestowed it upon them, and it possesses magical or religious powers because it marks the land chosen to fulfill the Sun god's prophesy. In addition to its religious function, the rod also serves a more pragmatic and technical function: the attempts to plant the rod in the earth along the route of the journey may be interpreted as a form of soil testing intended to determine the land's suitability for cultivation and agriculture. Understandably, the rod would not penetrate the arid land of the high plateau extending from the lake toward the mountains surrounding Cuzco. This search for fertile land on which to settle is represented independent of a religious context in some of the narratives. For example, Murúa notes that "[los Incas] salieron . . . por hallar buena tierra" [they left . . . in search of good land] (21). Vázquez de Espinosa also notes that the Incas departed from Titicaca and arrived in places where they taught others how to "cultivar la tierra y sembrarla" [cultivate and sow the land] (379). These two functions, one magical/religious and the other agricultural, are inseparable in Inca culture. Waldemar Espinoza Soriano explains:

Las ideas mágico-religiosas tenían mucho vigor y tales creencias inter-
venían en todo. Para ellos, la religión ofrecía incluso la justificación del origen de la etnia Inca, del sapainca, del Estado y de la organización general;
. . . Pero donde se dejaba exteriorizar con más frecuencia es en las prácticas agropecuarias; y aun en este campo las más notorias constituían las
concernientes al maíz y las papas, como también los atinentes a la salud y
fecundidad del ganado, para lo cual ofrendaban e invocaban al Sol. (436)

[The magic-religious ideas had great value, and such beliefs were part of
everything. For them, religion offered even the justification of the origin
of the Inca ethnos, of the ruling Inca, of the State and its general organization; . . . But where it was more frequently exteriorized was in the agricultural practices; and even in this realm the most notable ones pertained to
corn and potatoes, as well as those concerned with the health and fertility
of the cattle, for which they made offerings and invoked the Sun.]

Since religion and agriculture are essential to the very fabric of Inca culture, they are interwoven into the textual representation of their journey
from Titicaca to Cuzco. Even those versions that attempt to diminish the
divine origin of the Incas cannot help but represent it within a religious
or supernatural context.

According to Guamán Poma, Manco Capac, the first Inca during the
second age of the world, had no father. He also tells us that his mother,
Mama Huaco, "fue gran fingedora y yudulatra hechisera el qual hablaua
con los demonios del ynfierno y hazia serimonias y hecheserias" [was
a great dissimulator and an idolatrous sorceress who spoke with the
demons from hell and performed ceremonies and cast spells] (81).
Guamán Poma thus suggests that the first Inca was the progeny of
a union between the Devil and Mama Huaco.[62] Both devised a plan
whereby they would announce to the people that the Sun's child would
emerge from the cave at Pacaritambo so that the infant would be revered
when Mama Huaco carried him forth from the cave. This, according to
Guamán Poma, explains how both the Inca dynasty and idolatry came
into being. The Indian chronicler affirms that Manco Capac "no le uenia
por derecho de dios ni de la justicia el ser rrey. . . . Y demonio no le biene
el derecho de ser señor y rrey" [did not have the right, either coming
from god or from justice, to be king. . . . But the right to be lord and king
came to him from the devil] (82). He establishes a connection between
Inca Manco Capac and the supernatural, just as he encodes this link in a
negative fashion.

Salinas y Córdova's version echoes Guamán Poma's. According to
Salinas, the Indians worshiped only one God during the first ages in Peru

until the devil introduced the Inca lineage "para reynar mas facilmente en cada uno dellos, y plantar la Idolatria en tan inmensa multitud de infieles" [in order to rule over each of them with ease, and implant idolatry in such an immense multitude of infidels] (14). To accomplish his objectives better, the Devil chose as his agent and accomplice the most beautiful woman, Mama Huaco. And because she was "deshonestissima, y lasciua con estremo hizose preñada con ayuda del Demonio, y auiendola industriado en lo que auia de hazer" [very dishonest, and lascivious in the extreme, she became pregnant with the help of the Devil, and had him instruct her in what she was to do] (Salinas y Córdova 14). As a result of the diabolical union, she bore Manco Capac. The representation of the supernatural as demonic, along with its association with sexual sin and lasciviousness, is doubtless the product of a Christian perspective that filters, interprets, and transforms the narrative.

Since an important stop on the Inca pilgrimage between Titicaca and Cuzco, Pacaritambo, may be considered a *taypi*, a point that unites opposites, it functions as a spatiotemporal sign marking the division between two times: between barbarism and civilization, between the darkness of the depths of the earth and the light of the sun, and between the divine and the human. With the appearance of the emissaries of the solar divinity at Pacaritambo, divine power is manifested and the place becomes sacred. Pacaritambo is transformed from a simple cave into one of the Inca's primary *huacas*.

There are other similarities between the myth of creation and the Inca origin myth. Just as Lake Titicaca is defined as the cosmic pan-Andean *taypi*, so too Pacaritambo is established as the social and individual *taypi* of the Incas. The destination on Viracocha's creative mission is the sea, just to the north of Puerto Viejo. In the Inca narrative, the Incas also reach the northern coast after their expansion. Sites along the path of Viracocha (e.g., Cacha and Urcos) became *huacas*, in the same fashion that Pacaritambo and Huanacauri were transformed into Inca *huacas*. Viracocha carried a staff, the symbol of his power, with which he extinguished the fire at Cacha. Manco Capac, likewise, carries a resplendent golden rod. In Santacruz Pachacuti's version, Tunupa's actual staff is carried by Manco Capac, since Tunupa had left it with Apotambo, an Inca ancestor.

Although correspondences or parallels between the myth of creation and the myth of origins abound, each cycle possesses a distinct focus. While creation in the one seems to be viewed through a wide-angle lens, the origins of the Incas in the other are seen through a much narrower perspective. The difference may also be understood as a movement from the general (cosmic or pan-Andean) to the specific (single or individual), a phenomenon that may be termed individuation. In the creation myth all lineages originate in mountains, caves, and rivers without the mention of specific names or places. In the myth of origin, however, a specific cave, Pacaritambo, is singled out among all possible caves. The Incas, likewise, are distinguished from among all the lineages emerging from caves in the mountain; and, within a certain caste of that ethnic group, one individual, Manco Capac, stands out.

GODS AND CULTURAL HEROES: THE BROTHERS AYAR AND INCA MANCO CAPAC

Who were the Incas, and how many of them departed from Pacaritambo on the mission that ultimately led them to Cuzco? The chroniclers provide three different answers to the question. In the first, one hero, generally Manco Capac, arrives at Cuzco at the head of his ethnic group (Gómara, Zárate, Pizarro, Molina, Cobo [I and III]). In the second, a couple, usually Manco Capac and Mama Ocllo, found the dynasty and mark the beginnings of Inca domination (Garcilaso de la Vega [I], Salinas y Córdova, Vázques de Espinoza, and Cobo [IV]). In the third group, four brothers and four sisters are the original pilgrims (Murúa, Garcilaso [III], Santacruz Pachacuti, Guamán Poma, Cobo [II]). The complexity of the narratives increases in direct proportion to the number of characters involved in the plots.

Francisco López de Gómara and Agustín de Zárate write that Zapalla, sometimes called Viracocha, was the one who led the Incas from Titicaca and established Cuzco as "la silla y corte de su imperio" [the seat and court of his empire] (Gómara 22); and it was from there that they "fueron sojuzgando toda la tierra" [conquered all the territory] (Zárate 470). The earlier chroniclers combined the myth of creation with the Inca myth of origin. Pedro Pizarro's narrative mentions one hero, though his version reveals more about the conquistador's obsessions (principally that of finding precious metals) than information about the myth. Pizarro fails to name the first Inca, but he gives a specific description of the gold and silver idol shaped like a woman, which, according to legend, gave birth to the hero.

Molinas's and Cobo's (III) renditions of the myth depict a single individual, Manco Capac. The fact that the latter combine events belonging to what appear to be two different narrative cycles distinguishes Molina's and Cobo's narratives from the others in this group. In both these texts, at the very moment when the Creator sends the Sun to the island of Titicaca, the solar divinity is personified and orders the Incas to go forth to "sujetar muchas naciones" [conquer many nations]. The creation cycle's protagonist is the Creator, and it ends with the placing of the sun, moon, and stars in the sky. With the Creator's personification, the solar divinity in turn becomes the main protagonist of the next cycle. Thus, the most important feature of these narratives is the appearance of a new hierophany, the Sun, and the origin of its worship, which permits the definition of two separate narrative cycles. As discussed earlier, the evolution of the divine order, with the introduction of the Sun god, has profound implications for the social and natural orders.

Cobo (I) tells how the Incas, "hombres de prudencia y valor" [prudent and brave men], traveled from Titicaca to Pacaritambo with Manco Capac as their leader. In this account the process of individuation takes place at two levels. The Incas are set apart from the other ethnic groups by their clothes and by the gold earspools. Manco Capac, in turn, stands out in this group because he wears sheets of silver on his chest and back—a tactic, Cobo (I) argues, designed to present himself as a divine emissary to the people of Cuzco. When the people of Cuzco come to greet Manco Capac, he stands at the top of a hill and is resplendent with rays of sunlight reflecting off his clothing. Upon seeing this, many are convinced of his divinity. It appears that in this narrative, as in many others, there is a constant effort by the chroniclers to recount the events in terms of the realm of the profane, or to historicize the myth while emptying it of its sacred or religious importance. As a result, most of the versions of the Andean myths which have come down often reveal more of the Western worldview that informs them than of the Andean world they set out to portray.[63] Perhaps for this reason, these six versions of the myth of origins represent the Incas, and particularly Manco Capac, as conquerors and vanquishers. Even in the best light, the Incas appear only as cultural heroes within their ethnic group, exhibiting no relation to the divine order, in spite of their attempts to prove otherwise in their quest for hegemony.

The next group of narratives focuses on the Inca's founding couple. According to Garcilaso (I) and Cobo (IV), the Sun god sent his two children, Manco Capac and Mama Ocllo Huaco, to teach the others how to worship the Sun, how to cultivate their land, and how to shepherd their flocks. Their mission in society was analogous to the function of the Sun in the cosmos: to provide light and heat, nurture plants and animals, and mark the order of time. They were thus to provide knowledge, protection, sustenance, and organization.

The knowledge they were to impart was basically of a religious nature. According to Garcilaso, the Sun sent his two children to the people "[para] que los doctrinasen en el conocimiento de nuestro padre el sol, para que lo adorasen y tuviesen por su dios" [so that they would teach them about our father the Sun, so that they would worship him and adopt him as their god] (42). In Huanacauri hill, where they first stopped on their journey from Titicaca, they gathered the people together, delivered the doctrine of the Sun, and built a temple in his honor. Everything in the messengers' mission in the narrative is subordinated to religion. All facets of the culture are ritualized and have a magical or religious meaning.

The founding couple was ordered to protect their followers from inclement weather as well as from their enemies. Garcilaso states that "porque la hambre no los volviese a derramar por los montes; [Manco Capac] mandó . . . hacer chozas y casas" [to prevent hunger from dispersing them again across the heaths . . . [Manco Capac] directed them to work on building huts and houses] (44). The queen "industriaba a las indias . . . a hilar y tejer algodón y lana, y hacer de vestir" [trained the Indian women . . . (in) spinning and weaving cotton and wool, and making clothes](45). As a result, in just a few years the Incas assembled a large group of people, and the Inca "tenía gente de guerra, armada e industriada para se defender de quien quisiese ofenderle" [had a force of men armed and equipped to defend themselves against any attackers] (46).

Everything the Incas did, including constructing houses and instructing in the art of weaving, was carried out in a religious context. Ramos Gavilán, in his chapter about "ritos y abusos que los indios tenian al tiempo de techar sus casas y levantar edificios" [rituals and abuses that Indians performed at the time of roofing their houses and building edifices], illustrates the point:[64]

> Es costumbre muy connaturalizada entre los Indios, al cubrir y techar sus casas, hacer junta de hechiceros para que . . . pronostiquen el bien o mal que les aguarda en aquella casa. Invocan los demonios en su favor, con cantares tristes, al son de tamboriles destemplados (para ellos suavísimos). (84)

> [It is a deeply rooted custom among Indians, that upon roofing their houses, they call a council of sorcerers to foretell the good or evil to be expected in that house. With sad songs, they invoke the devil to help them, playing dissonant drums (for them very sweet).]

Obviously Ramos Gavilán's censure of these practices as demonic is a Christian imposition, since for the faithful who performed the rituals their acts were deemed simply forms of religious piety.

Mama Ocllo, Garcilaso tells us, "industriaba a las indias . . . a hilar y tejer algodón y lana, y hacer de vestir." [trained the Indian women in all the feminine occupations: spinning and weaving cotton and wool, and making clothes . . .] (Garcilaso 45). Weaving, as all other daily activities, also possesses religious significance. In his discussion of the function of the hero Tocapo in the Viracocha myth, Henrique Urbano points out:

> Las funciones del tercer héroe . . . tienen algo que ver con la producción de tejidos finos, empleados sobre todo en las prácticas rituales, ya sea por los oficiantes encargados de ejecutar los ritos, ya sea en las ofrendas entregadas a las diferentes *wakas*. . . . De una manera o de otra, lo cierto es que el tejido tenía un significado ritual profundo y todas las ceremonias litúrgicas lo utilizaban en grandes cantidades. (1981, xxxiii)
>
> [The third hero's functions . . . have something to do with the production of fine weaving, used especially in ritual practices, by the officiant in charge to celebrate the rites, or as offerings to the different *wakas*. . . . In one way or another, what is clear is that weaving had a profound ritual meaning and all liturgical ceremonies utilized textiles in large quantities.]

Tocapo's weaving in the myth of creation finds its parallel in what Mama Ocllo does in the myth of origins. In the Inca Empire this function was commemorated by the Virgins of the Sun, women chosen for state and religious service who lived in the *acllawasi*, where they learned early on to weave the finest ceremonial cloth to be used in rituals (*cumbi*) to dress their idols as well as the reigning Inca (Ramos Gavilán 84). Through its designs and color combinations, the woven cloth is constituted as another vehicle for symbolic representation. Weaving becomes a pervasive theme in both mythic cycles and comprises an essential element in religious ceremonies. The quality and design of textiles were used to distinguish people, establish hierarchies, and divide the sacred from the profane. The Maker gave each ethnic group its distinctive clothing; later on, during the Empire, the Inca would rule that each group should maintain its original dress, and they would prohibit the use of any other clothing (Guamán Poma, Garcilaso, Cobo, among others). Only the Inca and their idols were permitted to use the most precious of all cloths, *cumbi*. The designs woven into the fabric, like the myth, represented symbols and concepts that formed part of the Andean world. Gisbert, Arze, and Cajías note that

> el tejido andino refleja de alguna manera no sólo el mundo religioso, sino el entorno espacial y ecológico . . . todas las piezas, y todos los grupos, distinguen la "pampa" del "pallai". La "pampa" tiene casi la misma acepción

que en su contexto geográfico, significa el mundo salvaje—no cultural—
semidesértico. . . . . La "pampa" en el tejido es el sector uniforme, carente
de decoración, en contraposición del "pallai" que es la parte decorada. . . . .
El "pallai" representa el mundo cultural con significado. Allí estaban la
representación de los dioses y linajes y allí también está el mundo circun-
dante. (16)[65]

[Andean weaving reflects in some way not only the religious world, but the
spatial and ecological environment . . . all the samples, and all the groups
distinguish the "pampa" from the "pallai." The "pampa" has almost the
same meaning as in the geographical context, meaning the savage world—
not civilized—semi-arid. . . . The "pampa" in the weaving is the uniform
sector, without any decoration, which contrasts with the "pallai," which is
the decorated part. . . . The "pallai" represents the civilized world with
meaning. There was the representation of the gods and lineages and there
was also the surrounding world.]

The life-giving sustenance provided by the Incas is represented in the
myth by the agricultural advantages the Incas conferred upon all other
ethnic groups. In order to fight the famine that Garcilaso suggests was
rampant among the scattered peoples prior to the arrival of the Incas,
Manco Capac taught "los oficios pertenecientes a varón, como romper y
cultivar la tierra y sembrar las mieses, semillas y legumbres que les
mostró que eran de comer y provechosas" ([1609] 1976, 40) [which
tasks were proper to men: breaking and tilling the land, sowing crops,
seeds, and vegetables which he showed to be good to eat and fruitful]
(1966, 45). In the Andean world there has always been a close relationship between agriculture and religion, as is evident in the fertility idols
that are part of Andean agricultural worship, in the ritual calendar, in the
ceremonies of sowing and harvesting, and in the agricultural products
which, because of their unusual appearance, are interpreted as divine
manifestations.[66]

   "Ninguna cosa de las que pertenecen a la vida humana dejaron nue-
stros príncipes de enseñar a sus primeros vasallos" (Garcilaso [1609]
1976, 40) [There was nothing relating to human life that our princes
failed to teach their first vassals] is the way in which Garcilaso claims his
uncle recounted the origins of the lineage. The organizational function of
the Incas encompasses the entire culture. Just as the Sun marks the separation between night and day, and just as its position determines the seasons of the year, the Inca presided over and initiated all aspects of social
life. If Manco Capac introduced agriculture, his successors ritually commemorated that primordial moment every year. Guamán Poma describes

Figure 5. The Inca Participates in Agricultural Labor

the Inca's participation in the agricultural rituals during *Chacra Yapuy Quilla* (August), the month when the ground was broken, and in one of his drawings he depicts the Inca plowing the earth (Guamán Poma, 250–251). (See Figure 5.)

In Garcilaso's version of the myth, weaving and agriculture are organized according to gender, and agriculture becomes the organizing principle in the division and conceptualization of space and territory. When Manco Capac and Mama Huaco take possession of Cuzco, they divide the place into two equal and complementary parts.

De esta manera se principió a poblar nuestra imperial ciudad, dividida en
dos medios que llamaron Hanan Cozco, . . . quiere decir Cozco el alto, y
Hurin Cozco que es Cozco el bajo. Los que atrajo el rey quiso que poblasen a Hanan Cozco, . . . y los que convocó la reina que poblasen a
Hurin Cozco. . . . . Esta división de ciudad no fué para que los de la una
mitad se aventajasen a los de la otra mitad en exenciones y preeminencias,
sino que todos fuesen iguales. (Garcilaso [1609] 1976, 40)

[Thus our imperial city began to be settled: it was divided into two halves
called Hanan Cuzco, . . . which means upper Cuzco, and Hurin Cuzco, or
lower Cuzco. The king wished those he had brought to people Hanan
Cuzco, . . . and those the queen had brought to people Hurin Cuzco. . . .
This distinction did not imply that the inhabitants of one half should excel
those of the other in privileges and exemptions. All were equal.] (Garcilaso
1966, 44)

This harmonious division of Cuzco corresponds to the Andean concept
of *yanantin* (or *yanani* in Aymara):[67] two equal but complementary elements that are always found together. Bouysse Cassagne and Harris discuss this notion in relation to marriage, where the union of a man and a
woman may be seen as an attempt to achieve the ideal harmony of the
yanantin: the achievement of simultaneous equality and complementar-
ity, reflecting an organic bilateralism like two eyes, two hands—in other
words, the union of "two halves of a single body." The *yanantin* tri-
umphs over the *auca*, where harmony is never achieved, because in the
latter the elements never coalesce and are in a constant state of discord
(Bouysse Cassagne and Harris 3–31).

The division of Cuzco aimed to achieve the harmony of the *yanantin*
for the benefit and prosperity of all. Garcilaso's account also mentions
that subsequently, using the primordial division of Cuzco as their model,
every region, every town, and every lineage was divided along the same
pattern, using the gender-marking terms *hanan* and *hurin*, masculine and
feminine, respectively.[68] If in the mythic cycle Viracocha established a
distinction between beings by creating man and woman, in the Inca myth
something analogous occurs, though in social terms: each gender becomes associated with a section of the territory and with a clearly established role in society.

Salinas y Córdova, whose narrative also contains a single couple, represents the origin of Manco Capac in demonic terms and characterizes
the latter's mother, Mama Huaco, as a prostitute. Similarly, clothing is
also extremely important in this account. Like Guamán Poma, Salinas y
Córdova narrates the origins of the Inca dynasty and depicts it as a farce

plotted by Manco Capac's mother and Pilcosisa, Mama Huaco's sister who was a renowned witch. Both women brought the heir to the top of the hill "engalana[n]do con ojotas de oro, y algodón . . . orejeras de oro, manta encarnada, y camiseta azul; y por corona una borla verde de algodón, que le cercaua las sienes, con otros dijes de oro, y plata" [dressed up . . . with golden sandals, cotton clothes and gold earspools, red shawl, blue shirt; and with a cotton green tassel as a crown, tied around his temples, where gold and silver pins were attached]. When the sun rose and struck the pins, they shone, and this was enough to trick the people into believing that this man was the child of the Sun. Although almost identical to Guamán Poma's account, this one is particularly noteworthy because of the manner in which Manco Capac is dressed. The garments and accessories correspond to what most chroniclers of the conquest describe as the royal garments and symbols of the Incas (Guamán Poma 87; Cobo 237–240; Anónima 162).

The third group of narratives is comprised of six versions that portray the origin of the Incas beginning with four pairs of siblings known as the Ayar (Martín de Murúa, Garcilaso [III], Santacruz Pachacuti, Guamán Poma [II], and Cobo [II]). Although they perform, to a greater or lesser degree, the same functions of Manco Capac and Mama Ocllo in the other narratives, the characters are represented with greater specificity and enjoy a more pronounced individuation. These narratives share an important feature with the versions of the story that combine the creation and the origins myths: these narratives seem to merge the more general myth of origins of the Inca ethnos with the more particular myth of the Ayar brothers. For this reason, this group of stories could conceivably form part of a subcycle of the Inca narrative cycle.

In the creation myth, the god Viracocha appears as a pan-Andean divinity who begets all the lineages in the Andes. *Huacas* that commemorate his journey to the north are found along the way from Tiawanaco to Cuzco. The second narrative cycle represents the origin of the Incas in terms of their being the children or the emissaries of the Sun god. The new hierophanies sacralize the places where they appear, and temples, such as the Sun Temple in Titicaca and Coricancha in Cuzco, are built in honor of the solar divinity. In the myth of the brothers Ayar, the new *huacas* are directly linked to Manco Capac's family. These narratives delineate the origin of the Penates or family gods of the royal *panaca* (the descendants of a ruling Inca).

The four pairs of siblings (four brothers—Manco Capac, Ayar Cache, Ayar Auca, and Ayar Uchu—and four sisters: Mama Huaco, Mama Ocllo, Mama Cora, and Mama Ragua) emerged from a window at

Pacaritambo.[69] This window, according to Cobo (II), was "la boca o respiradero de la dicha cueva" [the mouth or air passage of said cave] (62). Garcilaso (III), who tells of three windows inlaid with gold, explains that the brothers emerged from the middle window, which was encrusted with precious stones. After their emergence into the light, the brothers and sisters journeyed northward toward Cuzco from what may be thought of as a new point of departure. Garcilaso (I) tells us that Pacarec Tampu (or Pacaritambo) was "siete o ocho leguas al mediodía" [seven or eight leagues to the south] of Cuzco.[70] This south–north route of the pilgrimage appears to be a constant in all of the narrative cycles. The places in which the Ayar brothers stop during their journey later acquire religious significance. They sent Ayar Auca,[71] who behaved defiantly during the journey, back to Pacaritambo on the pretext that they had forgotten some golden cups and corn seeds. Although Murúa fails to explain why Ayar Auca was considered "defiant," other versions—Cieza de León's, for example—allude to the strength of his sling with which he could demolish mountains. When Ayar Auca reentered the cave to retrieve the forgotten objects, the others sealed the entrance, trapping him inside. This location became one of the fundamental *huacas* of the Incas, because it was the site from which the Ayar brothers initially emerged, and where one of the brothers remained trapped. In Pacaritambo, Cobo tells us, the Incas founded a town in which they built a palace and a magnificent temple. They also carved a window in stone at the entrance of the cave in memory of the heroes who had emerged from it (Cobo 64).

The three remaining brothers continued on their journey. From Huanacauri hill they saw a rainbow, a favorable sign that the world would never again be destroyed by flood. The rainbow symbolically represents the *uno pachakuti* in the creation myth.[72] Because he sat on a *huaca* in the form of a man at the base of the hill, near the village of Sano (Sañuc, according to Guamán Poma), Ayar Cache was captured and turned into stone by the *huaca*.[73] Ayar Cache had previously told his brothers that he would remain there, and asked them to make sacrifices and celebrate the *huarincho* in his memory. Ayar Cache's metamorphosis leads to a period of mourning in which the brothers lament incessantly. In this way, Huanacauri became one of the most important places of worship for the Incas. On the sixth ceque[74] of the Kollasuyo, the seventh *huaca* was Huanacauri,

la cual era de los más principales adoratorios de todo el reino, el más antiguo que tenían los Incas después de la ventana de Pacaritampa y donde más sacrificios se hicieron. Esta es un cerro que dista del Cuzco como dos

leguas y medio por este camino en que vamos de Collasuyo, en el cual
dicen que uno de los hermanos del primer Inca se volvió piedra. . . .
[H]acíanle muchas fiestas. (Cobo [1653] 1964, 181)

[it was among the most important shrines of the whole kingdom, the oldest
which the Incas had after the window [cave] of Pacaritampu, and where
the most sacrifices were made. This is a hill which is about two and a half
leagues distant from Cuzco by this Road of Collasuyu we are following.
On it they say that one of the brothers of the first Inca turned to stone. . . .
[T]he Incas held many festivals for it.] (1990, 74)

It is important to note that the brother (or brothers, depending on the
version used) was turned to stone for sitting on a preexisting *huaca*. The
myth thus dramatizes the appropriation of an already established form of
worship and the inauguration of a new one that is genealogically linked
with the Inca dynasty. There are, once again, clear parallels with the
myth of creation: the first men Viracocha created were also turned to
stone and became *huacas*—patron gods. In Huanacauri, according to
Garcilaso (I), Manco Capac's golden rod penetrated the soil. Pacaritambo is identified as the place to which the Sun god leads the Incas.
Huanacauri is portrayed as the foundational place divinely set apart by
the Sun god's prophesy, and a connection between the royal *panaca* and
their patron gods is specifically formed.

What follows demonstrates how the absence of the Ayar brothers,
or their conversion into stone, is ritually represented in Inca ceremony.
Garcilaso narrates the following:

La dicción *ayar* no tiene significación en la lengua general del Perú, en la
particular de los Incas la debía de tener; las otras dicciones son de la
lengua general: *cachi* quiere decir sal, la que comemos, y *uchu* es el condi-
mento que echan en sus guisados, que los españoles le llaman pimiento, no
tuvieron los indios del Perú otras especias. La otra dicción *sauca* quiere decir regocijo, contento y alegría . . . alegorizan la fábula diciendo que por la
sal, que es uno de los nombres, entienden la enseñaza que el Inca les hizo
de la vida natural, y por el pimiento, el gusto que de ella recibieron; y por
el nombre recocijo entienden el contento y alegría con que después
vivieron . . . lo dicen tan sin orden y concierto, que más se saca por conje-
turas de lo que querrán decir, que por el discurso y orden de sus palabras.
([1609] 1976, 43)

[The word *ayar* has no meaning in the ordinary tongue of Peru, though it
must have had one in the special language of the Incas. The other words
occur in the general language: *cachi* is the salt we eat; *uchu* is the condi-

ment they season dishes with, which the Spaniards call *pimiento* (the Peruvian Indians had no other spices). The other word, *sauca*, means "rejoicing," "satisfaction," or "delight" . . . (they) explained the fable by an allegory. Salt, which is one of the names, they declare to mean the teaching the Inca gave them about the natural life. The pepper is the relish they took in it, and the word "rejoicing" shows joy and contentment in which they afterwards lived . . . even this is told in such rambling, disjointed, and confused style that one understands what they mean by conjectures rather than by the sense and order of their words.] (1966, 48)

Ayar Cachi, if we accept Garcilaso's etymology, would represent the knowledge imparted by the Inca about "natural life." However, the connection between salt and the kind of knowledge involved in Garcilaso's interpretation remains unclear. The salt in the narrative could nevertheless bear specific associations to sexual knowledge in the Andean world. Salt from the Kollasuyo region is found in the great salt marshes of Uyuni or Coipasa, the high part of the cordillera. And here it is worth recalling that the entire territory of the Tahuantinsuyo was divided into two complementary parts: *Hanan* and *Hurin* (*urco* and *uma* in the Kollasuyo) which are respectively aligned with the masculine and the feminine. The mountains belonging to Urcosuyo are thought of as masculine. Thus, salt might also be symbolically associated with masculinity.

Garcilaso's discussion of *enseñanza* refers to the knowledge of natural law and not to any knowledge of gender. As in his *Commentaries of the Incas*, Garcilaso attempts here to ennoble the teachings of the Incas while avoiding raising questions regarding their morality. It is for this reason that he desexualizes the meaning of knowledge and emphasizes its civilizing mission. Ayar Uchu's name refers to the essential condiment in Andean food, *ají*, which may be linked to the feminine because it grows in the valleys. For Garcilaso, *uchu* stands metaphorically for the pleasure they received from that knowledge, and *sauca* for the joy it gave them. Following the interpretation of the other terms, this rejoicing could be associated symbolically with sexual pleasure. Partial confirmation of this conclusion may be derived from an analysis of how the myth is ritually enacted.

Guamán Poma describes in detail the *Capac Raimi*, the most important festival of the Inca calendar. It was celebrated during the entire month of January with offerings of many sacrifices to the *huacas* of Huanacauri and Pacaritambo. The natives wept at the temples, fasted, and abstained from sexual intercourse. Their fast consisted of refusing salt, *ají*, and sex (Ramos Gavilán 64). The celebration of *Capac Raimi* thus ritually reenacts the Ayar brothers' myth. During Manco's civilizing journey, Ayar Cachi, Ayar Uchu, and Ayar Sauca leave his company when they are converted into stone. In the ritual period, *Cachi* (salt), *Uchu* (*ají*) and *Sauca* (joy) are suspended from the natives' lives. In the myth they pass from one site to the other, and during the *Capac Raimi* the pilgrims repeat the journey by visiting the *huacas* erected in those places. And there the people weep in the way that Manco mourned his brothers. Guamán Poma's drawings support this interpretation. In several of his illustrations of Pacaritambo the idol—Huanacauri—is always depicted at the summit of the mountain (*hanan, urco,* up), a place associated with the masculine. Pacaritambo is represented below it, in the position of a valley (*hurin, uma,* down) and thus carries feminine connotations (see Figure 6). Moreover, the Huarincho ritual, which involved the initiation of young boys, was celebrated at the *Capac Raimi.* It is worth recalling that in the myth recounted by Guamán Poma, Ayar Cache asks his brothers to celebrate the *huarincho* in his memory. It was performed for the first time in the initiation of Cinchi Roca—the son of Manco Capac and Mama Ocllo or Mama Huaco—immediately after Ayar Auca was turned to stone. This ceremony is described by Ramos Gavilán:

El Inca o sus Gobernadores armaban caballeros a los mozos que en los juegos olímpicos se habían señalado y a todos los hijos de los nobles del Reyno, les daba insignias de nobleza vistiéndolos de camisetas y mantas curiosas de cumpi y en la cabeza les ponían una manera de borla y El Inca . . . les hacía una plática animándoles a que fuesen briosos, y se señalasen en las guerras, pues la nobleza los diferenciaba de los plebeyos. Poníanle entonces unos pañetes (que se llaman guaras) como si dijéramos calzones y a esta ceremonia llamaban Guarincho. (79)

[The Inca or his governors knighted the young men who in their olympic games had distinguished themselves and also all the sons of the nobility in the kingdom, they were given the signs of nobility by being dressed with shirts and fine *cumbi* shawls and on their heads they put a tassel and the Inca . . . gave them a talk encouraging them to be brave and to excel in war, because nobility is what separated them from the plebeians. They wore a kind of cloth (called *guaras*) similar to loincloths and this ceremony was called *Guarincho.*]

In these "olympic games" adolescent boys took part in certain competitions (e.g., a race to the top of a hill) to prove their strength and courage. Their feet, arms, and hands were whipped until they bled, and they smeared their faces with the blood to signify their willingness to shed

Figure 6. Huanacauri and Pacaritambo

blood in the service of the Inca. The winners of the race were honored by
"enviándolos a las guerras para que allí más descubriesen su valor; y a
los que habían sido flojos, los ocupaban en cosas humildes" [sending
them to war so that they could discover their courage; and those that had
been lazy, were occupied in humble tasks]. The entire ceremony marked
the fact that "habia llegado el tiempo que como varones se habían de
ocupar en cosas tocantes al servicio de su comunidad" [the time had
come when they, as men, had to take care of things relating to the service
of the community] (Ramos Gavilán 76). Only the Inca nobility partici-

pated in these ceremonies, and the particularity of the Inca myth is made evident by their exclusive participation in the ritual. Furthermore, on a symbolic level, the ceremony duplicates the civilizing mission of the Incas. The young men begin their participation in the organization of the state and pass from carefree adolescence into responsible adulthood. This progression parallels the passage from barbarism to civilization depicted in the age of *puruma*. The boys' personal development is analogous to the cosmic *pachakuti*. During the ceremony, material objects, of which *cumbi* was the most evident sign, symbolize their entry into a state of civilization. Some versions emphasize that at this point they were also ready for military service, as required by Manco Capac's imperial mission.

The sacrifices of the *capac cocha* were also associated with Huanacauri.[75] These sacrifices, together with the rites of initiation, stress the importance of biological reproduction in the perpetuation of civilization. According to Sarmiento de Gamboa, "[se] instituyó el sacrificio llamado *capa cocha*, que es sacrificar dos niños, macho y hembra, al ídolo Guanacauri, para cuando los ingas se fuesen [a] armar caballeros" [the sacrifice called *capa cocha* was instituted for when the Incas were knighted: it consists of sacrificing two children, male and female, to the Guanacauri idol] (129).

The sexual connotations of this rite are clear. Sexual reproduction in the Inca origin myth is represented by the union of Manco Capac with one of his sisters. The *huarincho* first performed on their son, Sinchi Roca, commemorates that union.

At the end of the Ayar myth of origin, the only remaining brother, Manco Capac, accompanied by his sisters, continues the journey until they arrive at Cuzco, where their civilizing mission begins.[76]

AGRICULTURE, INDUSTRY, AND WAR

The various versions of the Inca myth of origin agree in that the mission delegated to the Incas by the Sun god encompasses three fundamental aspects of culture: agriculture, industry, and war. These cultural features, which have political and religious significance, are reflected in the ritual life of society.

The civilizing order imposed by the Incas through agriculture is represented primarily in their search for fertile land, which led the Incas on the pilgrimage from Titicaca to the valleys of Cuzco. The often invoked corn seeds they carried symbolize agriculture's importance in the civilizing scheme.[77] Inca achievements in the field of agriculture are well known: the extensive development of cultivation on terraces, the vast irrigation systems, and a clear understanding of the different ecosystems at the different geographical elevations are among the most celebrated. The distribution of property was also of utmost importance in the Inca agricultural organization. Land, a highly valued commodity in Tahuantinsuyo according to most chronicles, was divided into three types: (1) that which belonged to the Inca, (2) that which belonged to the Sun, and (3) that which belonged to the rest of the people. This division is a necessary oversimplification of an infinitely more complex social phenomenon.[78]

The religious dimension of agriculture may be detected in the number of rites associated with it and in the many gods and idols that were dedicated to fertility in the Andean world. Of these the Pachamama was perhaps the most popular. Rostworowski explains that "en el ámbito andino cada huaca por pequeña que fuese [tenía] . . . tierra, cuyo usufructo [servía] para las ofrendas, y sobre todo para la preparación de bebidas para los asistentes a las celebraciones" [in the Andean region each *huaca*, no matter how little, (possessed) . . . land and its profit (was used) for the offerings, especially for the preparation of drinks for the officiants at the celebrations] (145). The Inca ritual libation, *chicha*, was made of corn, which in agriculture is considered a life-giving symbol. Coca, which was also used in religious ceremonies, "era de las más estimadas ofrendas que ellos tenían" [was one of the most esteemed offerings they could give] (Cobo 191).

Their golden cups, elaborate clothing, dwellings, palaces, temples, roads, bridges, pottery, and a number of plowing instruments represent their industrial production. The Incas structured society hierarchically so that each group had certain occupations and responsibilities (Rostworowski 181–233), and there is a strong link between industry and religion, as evidenced in the previously mentioned rites performed during the construction of temples and houses and in the religious significance of their textiles. The golden cups were reserved for ritual practices, and the use of gold as a sacrificial offering was common in the worship of the most important *huacas*.

Among the Incas' most important divine mandates was the one to conquer and subjugate other people. The sling, which appears in several narratives, was considered one of their most important weapons. And, although bellicose, the Incas conquered territory through bilateral agreements as well as in battle.[79] The versions of the myth that affirm the divine ancestry of the Incas, however (e.g., Garcilaso), discuss only their peaceful conquests. The accounts that seek to subvert the notion of a divine connection (e.g., Guamán Poma and Zárate), on the other hand, refer to their use of force in acquiring mastery over others. Religion and war were thought of as inseparable because the divine mission called for the use of military force. Religion also appears in the *huarincho* and later ritual practices of a military nature.[80]

FROM MYTH TO HISTORY: OF GODS AND CULTURAL HEROES

The parallels between the Andean myth of creation and the myths of origin of the Incas and the Inca royal family reveal a common structure in all of the narratives. The divine, natural, and social orders are clearly represented in all of them. Each narrative cycle redefines, or modifies, the divine order and by extension alters the other orders as well. This does not mean, however, that a narrative cycle may be completely divorced from the one whose divine order it modifies. It merely indicates that the modification "implants" itself in the earlier vision of divine order. In each, there is a movement away from the general and the cosmic toward the specific and the individual. This phenomenon may best be described as a *mise-en-abîme*, whereby the internal narratives progressively make the components of the creation myth more specific. The myth serves as the context from which the other, more specific narrative cycles emerge, and thereby provides continuity among the cycles. Figure 7 illustrates the relationship among the different narrative cycles.

In this concentric movement toward specificity, the primary characters in the more general narratives pave the way for characters who will assume key roles in the later narrative cycles. The steps involved in the mythical cycle of the creation are ordered as follows: Viracocha's creation of the sun, moon, stars, plants, animals, and man; his placement of each creation in its natural place; his regulation of the cosmic forces; and his separation of the human race into two genders.

In the mythical cycle of the origin of the Incas, the Sun assumes the position of prominence that Viracocha had occupied in the narratives of the first cycle. The Sun's importance increases, though his functions are progressively more restricted than Viracocha's. The Sun protects life, marks time, and chooses to favor one ethnic group—the Incas. From among the Incas he selects two individuals, Manco Capac and Mama Ocllo. In this cycle, man and woman bear specific names and are closely identified with key productive functions carried out in the culture (Manco Capac—agriculture; Mama Ocllo—weaving), just as each is associated with a discrete part of the city or territory.

The deification and worship of the Sun in no way eradicates the cult of Viracocha.[81] The individuals chosen by the Sun god become the protagonists in the subcycle of narratives of the brothers Ayar. Although the Solar divinity is "present" in the epithet referring to the Incas as *hijos del*

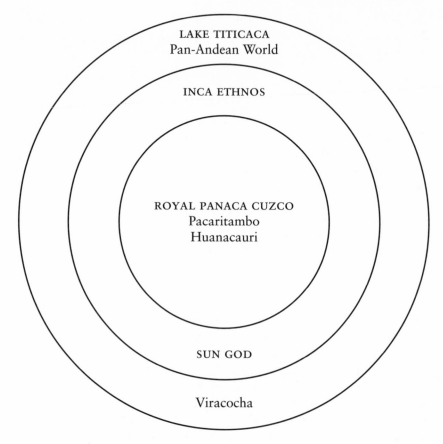

Figure 7. Andean Narrative Cycles

Sol, the brothers Ayar remain the principal protagonists of the plot. As in previous cycles, the importance of the individual characters increases just as their functions become even more restricted: their power and influence exist only within the scope of the family. The petrified brothers become the patron gods to the Inca's family, and their sexual symbolism points to the formation of a couple, the basic unit of the family (*uchu-ají-*femininity; *cachi-*salt-masculinity; *sauca-*rejoicing-sexual union).

In the myth of the Ayar, three brothers are deified when they are turned to stone. Later they become the primary dynastic *huacas.* Manco Capac, who, with his sisters, continues on the quest, is transformed into the main character of the next narrative cycle. His importance increases, but his functions are significantly limited in Inca history. Unlike his brothers, he is not a *huaca;* and his divine nature stems only from his relationship with the Sun. Manco Capac constitutes a cultural hero who originates a dynasty that remains in power until the arrival of the Spaniards. The achievements of this hero and of his descendants, the conquests, laws, and structures that mark a century of domination in the Andes, are recounted in many of the versions of the history of the Incas.

Manco Capac's descendants inherit his divine origin during the Inca empire. In the various accounts of the Inca myth of origin, Manco Capac is simultaneously depicted as a mythical figure and as a historical hero.[82] It is in the figure of Manco Capac that history and myth coalesce. He is, as well, also the link that signals the "juncture" between the Inca narrative cycle and the narrative cycle of the creation myth.

FROM POLITICAL CHAOS TO CIVIL ORDER

The history of the origin of the Incas in the region of Titicaca must not be understood solely as an Inca effort to legitimize Inca control of the Kollao. It may also be seen as the Incas' attempt to interject their past into an even more remote past, thereby claiming the latter to justify the expansion of the temporal limits of the Inca empire. As a result of the continuity established between Inca history and the pan-Andean myth of creation, Titicaca emerges as the common sacred space in both cycles. If Lake Titicaca maintains its sacredness in the Inca narrative cycle, it does so within new cultural contexts, with new meanings and new intentions. New narratives modify the elements of the divine order in the first narrative cycle in order to establish a direct relationship between the existing order and the new dynasty as the stories focus on Inca hegemony in the region.

The attempt on the part of many colonial chroniclers and some contemporary scholars to establish a linear (i.e., chronological) connection between the different narratives corresponding to the various cycles obstructs, in my view, the intelligibility of the stories, which form a vast interlocking text. This may explain why many chroniclers, believing the stories to be the products of feeble or deranged minds, attempted to give them "coherence" by invariably altering them. This is the case with several sixteenth-century Christian writers who, guided by the symbolism of the Holy Trinity, sought to impose a triangular structure on Andean figures.[83] Upon close examination, however, it is clear that these narrative cycles occur simultaneously and that they refer to different instances of a shared reality—cosmic, social, and familial (see Figure 8).

Manco Capac is portrayed as both a mythical and a historical hero. The mythical hero, who is also a divine messenger and the son of the Sun, is transformed into a historical hero, the founder of a dynasty. He

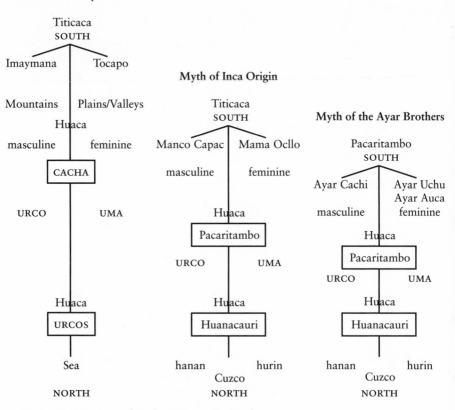

Figure 8. Structure of Andean Narrative Cycles

functions as the "juncture" between the primeval and prehistoric times of the Kolla cycle and the moment just prior to the conquest of America. In addition to constituting the link between these two moments, Manco Capac also performs a civilizing function. His mission, and that of his descendants, is to impose order on political and social (not cosmic) chaos in the times just before the arrival of the Incas. While the Inca expansion signaled great rifts and crises for other ethnic groups, the stories in this cycle depict the establishment of order and insist on marking a cultural continuity throughout time. Yet in the eyes of the conquered, the Inca myth of origin becomes a discourse of domination. During the period in which these narratives were compiled, however, the myth would have been understood as a discourse of resistance against the disempowering discourse of Spanish, specifically Toledan, politics.

4

The Christian Narrative Cycle:
Christ's Apostle and the Virgin of Copacabana

ARRIVAL OF THE SPANIARDS AT LAKE TITICACA

Soon after the Spaniards defeated the Incas at Cajamarca in 1532, Francisco Pizarro sent two of his soldiers on a reconnaissance mission to Cuzco. These two men were the first Christians to enter the region of Lake Titicaca. Their mission was twofold: to gather intelligence on the Inca Empire and to search for gold (Meiklejohn 25). Later, in 1535, Diego de Almagro traversed the Andean highlands en route to Chile. Almagro had requested the protection of Manco Inca II, who sent his brother Paullu and the high priest, Villac Umu, to accompany him (Hemming 177). Throughout his journey, Almagro left a path of destruction, forcing people in different villages to surrender clothing, food, and animals. He also used many Indians to carry his equipment as if they were beasts of burden, persecuting all those who refused to obey him and even burning alive several Indian leaders who resisted his commands (Hemming 178–179; Meiklejohn 25).

In 1538, after Diego de Almagro's defeat and execution in the "War of Salinas," Hernando and Gonzalo Pizarro, Francisco's brothers, mounted an expedition into the Kollao region. Inca Paullu and his Indian military troops accompanied the Pizarro brothers (Bouysse Cassagne 1987, 28). Perhaps remembering their earlier experience with Almagro (Meiklejohn 25) or commanded by Inca Manco II to resist the Spaniards (Murúa 215), the inhabitants of the region attacked the Pizarros when they entered Lupaca territory. Failing to stop them, the Indians then sought to prevent the Spaniards from crossing the Desaguadero river. However, the Spanish managed to cross the river on improvised rafts (Hemming 243). Hernando Pizarro returned to Cuzco, and his brother Gonzalo continued to press on toward Cochabamba, where local Indians waged a long, protracted resistance against the Spaniards (Bouysse Cassagne 1987, 29).[84]

Gonzalo Pizarro was forced to send to Cuzco for reinforcements. Six months later the fresh Spanish troops arrived. One by one the different ethnic groups were compelled to surrender, and the Spaniards began to divide up the conquered territories.[85] After this pacification of the Kollao, Francisco Pizarro visited the newly conquered lands and "determinó que la provincia de Chucuito quedase reservada para el mismo Rey" [determined that the province of Chucuito should be reserved for the King himself] (Meiklejohn 26). Since the distant King was the only sovereign of these new lands, both the King and the Indians were systematically robbed and cheated by the territorial administrators (Meiklejohn 27).

Kolla, Lupaca, and Inca aspirations to dominate the Titicaca region were forever frustrated. From this moment on, the inhabitants of the Lake Titicaca region were subjected to Spanish colonial rule. After the discovery of the incredible wealth at Potosí in 1545, the Indians of the Kollao region were also forced to work in the mines. The Spanish demands for forced labor were enormous, especially after the institution of Viceroy Toledo's harsh ordinances.[86]

CHRISTIAN RELIGION AT LAKE TITICACA

During the first decade after the conquest of the Kollao, there were no efforts by missionaries to christianize the Titicaca region. The civil war between the Almagro and Pizarro factions (1544–1548) and the uprising of Inca Manco II (1538) had unsettled the countryside in a way that made any evangelizing campaign almost impossible.

Pizarro finally appointed a priest, Francisco Ruiz, to take Christian doctrine into this region. Evidence indicates that Francisco Ruiz arrived at Chucuito between 1542 and 1544 (Meiklejohn 43). Soon thereafter, in 1547, the Dominicans were the first religious order to settle in the area and build churches in the larger villages such as Copacabana (Elías 62). The Dominicans ruled the area with a free hand, since they did not have to compete with any *encomenderos*[87] and the civil government did not interfere in their affairs. It seems that they not only took charge of the spiritual life of the peoples under their care but also imposed their will on merchants, caciques, and even royal authorities. When they were accused of corruption, their evangelizing mission finally came under scrutiny by the viceregal authorities (Meiklejohn 28–62).

Examples of this heightened surveillance include a letter written by the *factor* Bernardino Romani to the Council of the Indies accusing Viceroy Cañete of innumerable abuses. This letter prompted the Crown to request the Audience in Lima to organize a visit to the Chucuito province, around 1567, to determine whether the Lupacas might be able to pay higher taxes. Licentiate Castro, president of the Audience, sent a *visita* to Chucuito to investigate several aspects of the Province. As inspector, Castro appointed Garci Diez, who then spent the entire year of 1567 gathering data about life in the province. The report of his *Visita* provided the necessary information about the Lupacas' resources and whether they could indeed shoulder more burdens or not. The report also highlighted certain irregularities regarding the Christianization of the Indians and the Dominicans' missionary efforts. Responding to Garci Diez's reports, in 1573 Viceroy Toledo sent his private secretary, Gutiérrez Flores, on another *Visita* to the Chucuito province. Gutiérrez Flores's account led to an increase in the tributary rate (tax) as well as to the expulsion of the Dominicans (Meiklejohn 28). The reports of both *visitas* presented a poor picture of the Dominicans and concurred that

> Eran tan poderosos en la provincia que ningún indígena se atrevía a oponérseles . . . el temor era del todo auténtico ya que los frailes ejercían el poder total. Inflingían severos castigos a voluntad, incluso por ofensas que no tenían nada que ver con la doctrina, ante la aparente indiferencia, o al menos timidez, de los funcionarios civiles. También tenían costumbre de imponer multas en dinero, lana o llamas, las cuales . . . alcanzaban la cantidad de miles de pesos en toda la provincia . . . aparte del gran número de indígenas empleados por los frailes como fiscales y alguaciles, sirvientes y cantores, los que por este motivo estaban exentos de impuestos y de mita, había también varios nativos, cuya mita consistía en servir a los frailes . . . obligaban con frecuencia a los nativos a abandonar su trabajo y familia para llevar mensajes y diversos productos al Cuzco, Arequipa y La Paz. Todos éstos eran trabajos que los indígenas realizaban sin percibir remuneración de ninguna clase. (Meiklejohn 51)

> [They were so powerful in the province that no Indian dared offer any opposition . . . their fear was completely justified because the friars had complete power. In the face of the apparent indifference or timidity of civil officials, Dominicans inflicted severe punishments on the Indians whenever they wanted, even for offenses that had nothing to do with doctrine. They also had the habit of imposing fines to be paid in money, wool, or llamas, which . . . amounted to thousands of pesos throughout the entire province . . . besides the large number of Indians employed by the Friars as lay assistants, constables, servants, and cantors, all of whom were exempt from taxes and from going to the *mita*, there were several natives whose *mita* was to serve the friars . . . who often obliged them to abandon their

work and their families to take messages and products to Cuzco, Arequipa, and La Paz. All of these jobs were done by the Indians without any remuneration].

Following Viceroy Toledo's expulsion order, the Dominicans retired to Pomata, the only convent that remained under their control.

Once the Dominicans left, the secular clergy took charge of Chucuito's *doctrina* (ecclesiastical district). Two priests, D. Antonio de Almeida and Licentiate Montoro, administered the church at Copacabana (Ramos Gavilán 143).[88] During this period, when Copacabana's *doctrina* was directed by the secular clergy, the miraculous image of the Virgin of Copacabana became Lake Titicaca's new hierophany.

Father Montoro, "hombre solo y de edad mayor, no podía acudir a sus obligaciones de cura, y a la ocupación en que los peregrinos le ponían" [being alone and old, could not attend to his priestly obligations nor to the demands imposed on him by the pilgrims], because each day more and more parishioners arrived at the church as a result of the Virgin of Copacabana's enthronement (Ramos Gavilán 143). At this point, in 1589, the Augustinians arrived at Copacabana to take over the *doctrina* of the increasingly burdened and lucrative church.

THE RELIGIOUS CLIMATE IN THE PERUVIAN VICEROYALTY

It is no secret that the conquest of the New World was realized through the agency of both the cross and the sword. From the beginning of the conquest, the conversion of the Indians to Christianity was one of the Crown's primary goals, executed by both the civil and ecclesiastical authorities in the Indies. As I have already said, the evangelizing mission was carried out only superficially in Peru from 1532 until the end of the civil wars among the Spaniards (1548). Missionaries were sent into different areas, and friars and priests baptized thousands of Indians. Nevertheless, these practices had not produced the results desired by the ecclesiastical and political authorities. The viceregal Church thought that the constitutions adopted during the Councils at Lima would expedite the Christianizing process and the abolition of idolatry.[89] However, in 1609 the Jesuit Francisco de Ávila wrote a letter to the rector of the Society of Jesus explaining that, in spite of the Church's efforts, Christianity among the Indians was a facade that veiled the persistence of ancient beliefs.[90] Later, he took his allegations to Archbishop Lobo Guerrero, accusing the Indians of apostasy because they had instituted a clandestine system of worship that continued their ancient practices. The evidence he presented convinced Lobo Guerrero and resulted in an initiative to search for new ways to achieve their evangelical goals.[91]

The ecclesiastical authorities commissioned Francisco de Ávila and the Jesuits to inaugurate a new campaign to extirpate idolatry; as a result they established the *Visitas de Idolatría* (Duviols 1977, 182–190). Ávila was appointed *Inspector General de Idolatría* (general overseer). He began this great crusade against Andean religions with incredible zeal: all provinces were inspected, many people were accused, interrogated, and punished. Clearly encouraged by the civil government in Peru and by the Crown, Ávila's men destroyed the *huacas* and burned the *malquis*[92] as their campaign engulfed the entire territory of the Viceroyalty of Peru.

In 1612 Archbishop Lobo Guerrero called for an ecclesiastical inquiry to discuss the problem of idolatry. The *Constituciones* which were adopted by this synod detailed the different features which constituted a *Visita de Idolatría*. In order to soften their repressive nature, the Archbishop ordered that each inspection should commence with a proclamation of the *"Edicto de Gracia,"* which gave the Indians several days of grace to confess their idolatrous behavior and to surrender their idols. If they complied with the order they were absolved; if they did not, repressive measures soon followed. The Viceroy, don Francisco de Borja, prince of Esquilache, openly supported the campaign, and the extirpation of idolatry became an institutionalized practice (Duviols 1977, 185–188).

Five years later, around 1618, the problem of continuing idolatry had not yet been solved. In 1616, Francisco de Ávila drafted a report at the request of the Viceroy, declaring that idolatry was common in all of the visited provinces and proposing measures to enhance the effectiveness of the extirpation campaign.[93] This proposal called for an emphasis on preaching, additional efforts in the battle against drunkenness, suppression of the villages that had not yet been reduced, exile of the "maestros" (teachers) of idolatry, the learning of native languages (obligatory for priests of Indian parishes), the foundation of schools for the children of the Indian leaders, and finally, specific punishments to be meted out to persistent idolaters (Duviols 1977, 191).

The ecclesiastical and civil authorities drafted documents based on Ávila's *"Parecer."* The first one, the *Carta de Edicto,* signed on 30 August 1617 by Archbishop Lobo Guerrero, was relayed to all of the ecclesiastical authorities in the rural regions. This letter described the punishments that those convicted of idolatrous practices would suffer, as well as a series of incentives for those who provided information about the forbidden rites and customs. The Indians were ordered to gather in front of the church every month and have the letter publicly read to them. A second measure, entitled *"Ordenanza,"* was signed on 2 September 1617 and sent by the viceroy to the magistrates of the villages. This Ordinance compelled the authorities to comply with what the Edict demanded. The Viceroy also ordered the demolition of ancient villages and forbade the sale of wine to the Indians.

After the publication of these official documents, the extirpation campaign moved forward vigorously. By 1619, 25,000 cases of idolatry had been examined. Thousands of *huacas, malquis,* and idols had been destroyed. The guilty Indians were disciplined: many were imprisoned, others had their possessions confiscated, and still others saw their houses burned to the ground. The *Visitas de Idolatría* continued through the mid-nineteenth century, and the harshness of the *Visitas* eased only intermittently.[94]

Many civilians and clergy applauded the *Visitas* and their repression of idolatry, yet there were also many who opposed this extirpation policy. Numerous priests in the Indian villages had established a *modus vivendi* with their Indian parishioners and were inclined to overlook incidents that would have been officially sanctioned as idolatrous. Ávila and the *Visitas* were criticized for exaggerating the problem and were accused of being motivated by Ávila's desire to achieve personal prominence and power.

By the time Archbishop Lobo Guerrero and the Prince of Esquilache returned to Spain, critics of the extirpation of idolatry had grown in number and had begun to mount a public outcry. The Augustinians and the Dominicans even wrote to the King asserting that idolatry no longer existed in the Indian villages and settlements under their care.[95]

THE CHRISTIAN NARRATIVE CYCLE

Along with the Spanish conquerors and Christian missionaries, a new avatar of sacredness appeared at Lake Titicaca. With this new hierophany as well as an appropriation of indigenous stories there emerged a Christian narrative cycle which can be divided into two subcycles: the first subcycle comprised stories that refer to an Andean Christianization that preceded the arrival of the Spaniards in the New World, and the second consists of a series of narratives about the miracles of the Virgin of Copacabana.

Although many chroniclers had alluded to possible Christian meanings in Andean rites and myths, none asserted the existence of a Christian missionary effort before the conquest as explicitly as Ramos Gavilán and Antonio de la Calancha. Both of these *criollo*[96] writers were Augustinian friars, and their texts appear at a key point in the history of the evangelization process in colonial Peru: in an environment that was both ideologically and politically charged with concerns about idolatry. It is in this context that their texts can be interpreted as subversive, because they proposed an alternative to the official policy of extirpation promoted by the Jesuits and other Spaniards. In this narrative cycle only their versions will be considered as representative examples of that particular position.

MASTER NARRATIVE: CHRIST'S APOSTLE AT LAKE TITICACA

The Indians told of a time long ago when a tall white man with blond hair and a beard traveled through the villages and mountains with a disciple and preached the doctrine of one universal and true God. In their sermons they condemned the Indians' idolatry, their terrible drunken debaucheries, and their lascivious and incestuous behavior. To attract the Indians to their faith, the bearded man performed miracles and wonders. Along his path he left his footprints in stone. His mere presence in those places silenced the ancient oracles, and the *huacas* ceased communicating with the Indians. The Devil incited the Indians' anger, telling them that this extraordinary man was to blame for the silence of their gods. For these reasons, in many places the Indians attempted to kill the white man, but providence protected him from harm. In Cacha, they failed to accept his message and, tired of his reproofs, stoned him. However, a divine authority interceded and avenged their sacrilegious attempt on his life by sending down a rain of fire.

From Cacha this man traveled to the Island of Titicaca, where he spent time with the people and sought to correct their intemperance and to teach them his doctrine. However, neither his preaching nor his miracles could sway the Indians. In Carabuco he raised a miraculous cross that later became a relic of the celebrated traveler's journey despite the Indians' many attempts to destroy it, burn it, or submerge it in the lake.

In Carabuco they killed his disciple by driving a stake through his body, which they then placed on a raft and launched into the lake. Providence sent a strong wind which carried the raft through the rushes and cattails at a high speed. The supposed origins of the Desaguadero River would be traced to the path opened by this raft, which traveled all the way to Aullagas, where the body of the disciple came to its final resting place. Since then, at the same time each year, a green palm grows in Aullagas to commemorate the appearance of this protomartyr. The white man himself was led off by a beautiful woman who carried him away on a raft to the sea, where he sailed away on his cloak.

Extending Christian Tradition in the Andes:
Saint Thomas and His Disciple

Ramos Gavilán tells us that the Peruvian Indians, especially the ones who lived in the mountains, knew an extraordinary story about a white man who passed through these lands. For him, the events in the story had to have transpired 1,500 years before he wrote his text, because he was convinced that the miraculous man was one of Christ's disciples (Ramos Gavilán 27).

Calancha extends Ramos Gavilán's Andean story to many different places in America. Evidence corroborating the story, according to Calancha, had been found from Mexico to Brazil, and clergymen from all the different orders had discovered crosses marking the Apostle's path. Furthermore, he claims that additional evidence emerges in the Indian belief in a god who was "infinito, invisible i todo poderoso" [infinite, invisible, and all powerful], a mother who served as an intermediary between God and mankind (Islas de Varlovento), and a Holy Trinity (Calancha 714–717). Calancha gives credence to these testimonies by citing information from canonical chroniclers such as Pedro Mártir, Gómara, and Bartolomé de Las Casas. José de Acosta had also noticed similarities between certain indigenous and Christian beliefs and rites, but he attributes them to the Devil, who continually attempts to imitate God ([1590] 1985, 265–267).[97] Interestingly enough, Acosta is the source for Calancha's assertion about the Indians' knowledge of the Trinity prior to the Discovery, and, although he is willing to agree about diabolical intervention, Calancha claims that the influence of the Devil appeared only after the Apostle had preached in these lands. Acosta, however, clearly expresses his disbelief in stories of a pre-Hispanic evangelization:

> Pues lo que creen algunos que en tiempos lejanos sonó en estas regiones la trompeta del evangelio, aduciendo el testimonio del profeta, que trae San Pablo: "Por toda la tierra se extendió el sonido de ellos, y hasta los confines del orbe sus palabras", no me parece convincente, puesto que San Agustín afirma de su tiempo que en algunas partes de Africa era desconocido el nombre de Cristo, y ni siquiera la fama del imperio romano había llegado a ellas. ([1590] 1952, 56)

> [The belief held by some, that in earlier times the trumpet of the gospel resonated in this region, claiming testimony of the prophet quoted by Saint Paul: "The sound of them extended throughout the earth, his words reached to all corners of the orb," is not convincing, since Saint Augustine affirms that in his time the name of Christ was unknown in some parts of Africa, where not even the name of the Roman Empire had reached.]

Calancha and Ramos Gavilán, however, both maintain that the Gospel was preached in America before the arrival of the Spaniards. Calancha is certain of the identity and exact path of the apostle who preached in the

New World. The Augustinians' narratives include a second character, the Apostle's disciple, and are full of details about the sermons and relics they left behind. Calancha describes the two evangelists as "tall, one older than the other, white, bearded, one with blue eyes, both with white tunics to their ankles" (728).

This description of the Apostle and his companion coincides with the portrait of Viracocha in the creation myth related by many chroniclers. But it also coincides with Ramos Gavilán's description of the first Inca, Manco Capac, who, he says, was both white and blond, a physical description, we may recall, which had served to induce the Indians to believe he was the progeny of the Sun.

The physical characteristics attributed to the Apostle clearly distinguish him from the Andean phenotype. He is blond, tall, blue-eyed, and bearded, characteristics that correspond to European iconographic representations of the Apostles. This traditional Western representation of Christ's disciples clearly ignores the fact that the Apostles were semitic.

The episode of the raising of the cross in Carabuco facilitates the recontextualization of Andean narratives into a Christian frame of reference. The Augustinians support their interpretation of the story by basing it on the last chapter of the Gospel of Saint Matthew, where Christ sends his Apostles to all nations to preach the Gospel:

> And when they saw him, they worshipped him: but some doubted. And Jesus came and spake unto them, saying, All power is given unto me in heaven and in earth. Go ye therefore, and teach all nations, baptizing them in the name of the Father, and of the Son, and of the Holy Ghost: Teaching them to observe all things whatsoever I have commanded you: and lo, I am with you always, even unto the end of the world. (Matt. 28: 17–20)

Following standard exegetical practice, it was clear to both Calancha and Ramos Gavilán that when Christ sent his Apostles to preach, he specified all places on earth, even those unknown to the Old World. Furthermore, Calancha emphasizes several allusions to cardinal geographical points in the Bible; the great importance given there to the southwest, according to him, prefigures the prominence held by the New World in God's eyes since Creation. After citing different parts of the Old Testament which mention the southwest regions of the world, Calancha arrives at the following conclusion:

> Pecó Adán, encendiose Dios de furor, llenose de indignación, aguardó a que corriese el Sur para tratar del castigo, dando a entender que ya venía tenplado, más frío i menos riguroso. ¿Porqué de todo esto no aré yo conse-

quencia? que pues para mostrar piedad se vino por el Paraíso paseando, i venía mirando azia estas tierras, i porque le dava el ayre Sur, dio a entender que llegava tenplado, i sin el devido rigor; diré yo que desde el principio del mundo se estremó Dios en mirar piadoso a este Perú donde está ese viento Sur, i nace desta parte Meridional, mitigando su enojo con que destos Reynos le adorarían a millones y se salvarían a millares. (703)

[Adam sinned, and God's anger was ignited. Filled with indignation, He waited for the south wind before inflicting his punishment, thus suggesting that he became even tempered, cooler, and less rigorous. How can I interpret all this? To show his mercy he came walking through Paradise and gazed upon these lands; the south wind blowing meant he had cooled down, and was less severe; so I say that from the beginning of the world God looked mercifully upon this Peru where, born in this southern region, the south wind blows; God mitigated his anger knowing that in these kingdoms millions would worship him and thousands would be saved.]

A minor but revealing detail that confirms Calancha's American point of view appears in his reference to the southern wind that cooled God's fury. In South America the southern wind is cold because of the Austral currents, while in the northern hemisphere the cold wind, called *mistral*, originates in the north; since the southern winds warm up as they sweep across the deserts, therefore following Calancha's logic, they would have increased God's anger.

Spanish authors like Acosta, Arriaga, Sahagún, and Albornoz interpreted the circumstances differently; they believed that the Devil had reigned from the beginning of time among the indigenous peoples and that their redemption was possible only because the Spaniards had arrived. This proposition countered the position taken by Las Casas, who felt that the inhabitants of the New World had a fundamental prelapsarian knowledge of the truths upon which Christianity was based (Las Casas [1550] 1909, passim).

If Spanish authors based their denial of a Christian's presence in the New World before Columbus's crossing on patristic authorities, Calancha retorts by asserting that Saint Thomas fulfilled an apostolic mission to the Andes; he corroborates his conclusion by citing equally sanctioned patristic authorities. Because Saint John Chrysostom had written in his Homily 61 that Thomas was the Apostle who traveled most in the world, it must have been Thomas who—transported by angels or other divine powers—came to the Andes to spread Christ's doctrine (Calancha 718; Ramos Gavilán 27).

Calancha collapses many local versions of the myth into a single story which serves to elucidate the identity of the Apostle. While the onomastics and toponymies vary, the Augustinian writer always finds a way to interpret his name as some variation of "Thomas." He attributes these differences to the disparate pronunciation of the inhabitants in the region, which deformed the original name Thomas. The transformation of the name, according to Calancha, occurred as a part of a divine plan which, by anagramatically altering the order of the letters, gave the name a new and more profound meaning.[98]

While Calancha identifies this character as Saint Thomas, Santa Cruz Pachacuti, in his narrative about Viracocha, asks himself, referring to Tonapa Viracochapacachan, "if this man was not the glorious Apostle Saint Thomas?" (283). Guamán Poma, on the other hand, associates this character with Saint Bartholomew, and Ramos Gavilán, without doubting that he was one of Christ's Apostles, refers to him only with the appellative by which he was known locally: Tunupa.

The controversy surrounding a pre-Hispanic evangelization was not new in the sixteenth century. A Dutch publication of 1508 spoke of a Christian presence in the New World before the arrival of the Spanish.[99] Authors like Oviedo, Las Casas, Cieza de León, and Betanzos made allusions to a possible pre-Hispanic Christian presence (Duviols 1977, 55–63). Duviols comments:

> La cuestión de la evangelización prehispánica del Continente Americano—
> y muy especialmente del Perú—estará vinculada, por una parte a la más
> general de las relaciones históricas y bíblicas entre Nuevo y el Viejo Mundo,
> y por la otra, determinará el criterio que la Iglesia debe adoptar frente a la
> idolatría de los indígenas. (1977, 55)

> [The issue of the prehispanic evangelization in the American Continent—
> and especially in Peru—is on the one hand linked to the most general his-
> torical and biblical relationships between New and Old World, and on the
> other, determines the criterion that the Church had to adopt toward Indian
> idolatry.]

Had the Indians truly known of Christ before the arrival of the Spanish, they could be considered apostates, but not if they were simply unaware of Christianity. These debates not only questioned orthodox theological considerations but also had other repercussions. According to some theologians, either situation would constitute a fair justification of conquest, or, if the Indians were apostates and had denied the faith, they would fall under the jurisdiction of the Inquisition.[100] Had the Indians been subjected to the Inquisition, it would have created great political and economic problems. It should be recalled that at one time some 25,000 accusations were referred to the courts of the Inquisition. According to Ávila, this indicated that idolatry was a general practice in Peru. If the Inquisition found the accused guilty and acted with the same fervor shown to other Christians accused of apostasy, the entire Indian population, which had already suffered from sickness and war, would have been decimated, thereby leaving the land without laborers to work it.[101]

For this reason, the First Council of Lima (1551) rejected the legend of a pre-Conquest Christianization and declared the Indians to be neophytes in the faith. In a letter from Charles V, the Crown also officially rejected the legend's legitimacy on theological grounds (Duviols 1977, 68). An absolute silence ensued during the decades following the First Council on the subject of an earlier evangelization of the New World; the subject only reemerges after the arrival of Viceroy Toledo:

> No fue casualidad que en 1572, después de un largo silencio resurgiera el mito del apóstol, bajo la pluma de un turiferario de Toledo quien, como se sabe, reclamó la Inquisición para los indios con una constancia e insistencia excepcionales. No fue tampoco por azar que los grandes extirpadores y predicadores del siglo XVII, Hernando de Avedaño y Francisco de Avila, por un lado afirmaran el mito y lo utilizaran en sus sermones, para inculcar a los indígenas un profundo sentimiento de culpabilidad, y por otro, amenazaran a esos mismos indígenas, no obstante la legislación en vigor, con las hogueras de la Inquisición. (Duviols 1977, 69)

> [Through the writings of a fawn of Toledo, who—as we know—advocated insistently and constantly that the Inquisition have jurisdiction over the Indians, the myth of the Apostle reemerged in 1572 after a long silence. This was not a coincidence. Neither was it coincidental that Hernando de Avedaño and Francisco de Ávila, the great extirpators and preachers of the seventeenth century, used the myth in their sermons to inculcate a profound feeling of guilt in the Indians, on the one hand, and on the other, to threaten the same Indians, notwithstanding the legislation in effect, with the fire of the Inquisition.]

Accusing the Indians of apostasy benefited Toledo's delegitimization policy. However, the versions analyzed here not only fail to participate in this accusatory fervor but actually stand in opposition to this policy. Seen in this light, Duviols's analysis of the Ramos Gavilán and Calancha texts appears hasty because it ignores the significance which a more detailed analysis reveals. Duviols's reading denies any importance to these texts:

> A comienzos del siglo XVII, un grupo de monjes eruditos, a los que se conoce como "cronistas de convento", se apoderan de la leyenda del apóstol con espíritu apologético. La beatería edificante excluye desde entonces

todo espíritu crítico. Un agustino, fray Alonso Ramos Gavilán se ocupa del apóstol en varios capítulos de su *Historia de Nuestra Señora de Copacabana* . . . sigue luego otro agustino, fray Antonio de la Calancha sobre el tema mucho más que sus predecesores.

Lo primero que se observa es la definida tendencia a una erudición seudocientífica, y la renovada importancia que se concede a las reliquias, que un poco por todas partes, van descubriéndose en esos momentos, y a las que los autores confieren valor de prueba científica al mismo tiempo que las milagrosas virtudes de las santas reliquias. (1977, 63–64)

[At the beginning of the seventeenth century, a group of erudite monks, known as "convent chroniclers," appropriated the legend of the Apostle in an apologetic manner. Their edifying overpiousness excludes all critical possibilities. An Augustinian, Fr. Alonso Ramos Gavilán, deals with the apostle in several chapters of his *Historia de Nuestra Señora de Copacabana* . . . followed later by another Augustinian, Fr. Alonso de la Calancha, who continues with the same subject even further than his predecessors.

What is evident is the definite aspiration to a pseudoscientific erudition, and the renewed importance given to the relics, which kept appearing everywhere. These two authors simultaneously assign the value of both scientific evidence and miraculous virtues.]

Duviols, furthermore, believes that the narratives which confirm the existence of Christian relics in Peru and construct a plot centered on a journey of Christ's Apostle to these lands are a "desaforado regionalismo" [excessive regionalism]. Unfortunately, his analysis insists upon the historic referentiality of these texts and overlooks the exemplary and pragmatic intentions which inform them.

The Apostle's Pilgrimage through the Andes

The Apostle traveled through the Andes preaching, first from north to south, then back to the north. Ramos Gavilán narrates the events of the Apostle's pilgrimage, beginning with his visit to Cacha, a few leagues from Cuzco. He later refers to the Apostle's visit to the Kollao and his arrival at Lake Titicaca, after which he departs once again for the coast.

Calancha's story, more ambitious and detailed than Ramos Gavilán's, narrates a longer journey, which he describes in more specific terms. Calancha constructs, or, as he says, "reconstructs" the route of the Apostle using the testimony of nine places where he left his "footprints" during his pilgrimage. The journey covers 1,500 leagues, beginning in Brazil, continuing through Paraguay, covering almost the entire territorial expanse of the central Andes, and ending at the Pacific coast, where the man spreads his cloak over the sea and floats out of sight into the distance. Both versions coincide in the Apostle's many visits to different villages during his trip through the Andes. At each of these places, extraordinary events occurred to reveal his supernatural powers. The Augustinian chroniclers believed that his miracles offered proof that he was Christ's emissary.

The intentions evident in these narratives are clearly more than apologetic. This is not a cursed land, the Devil's dominion, but instead one which God himself had viewed with benevolence. Christ sent one of his Apostles to preach here, and he did so with love and gentleness. This is the evangelizing model that they would like followed, and not the one endorsed by the extirpation of idolatry. The Augustinians' evangelization model was more attuned to Las Casas's belief as expressed in *The Only Way to Draw All People to a Living Faith*:[102]

> Vemos . . . la forma que Cristo prescribió a sus apóstoles y a los que habían de sucederles en su misión, para invitar a los hombres a la religión verdadera. Cuán benigna fue, cuán suave, cuán pacífica y razonable; cuán inculpable, ejemplar y amable, cuán llena de mansedumbre y de paciencia; de clemencia. . . . Se refiere lo dicho a la forma que Cristo instituyó en la primera misión cuando envió a los santos apóstoles y a los discípulos a doctrinar. (1975, 200)

> [(We) see . . . the form Christ fixed for preaching the gospel truth, for inviting, for drawing people to a living faith, fixed for His apostles and for those called to fill their places. It is remarkably kind, gentle, peaceable, sensible, faultless, edifying, lovable. It is suffused with compassion. . . . We say this of the form Christ set the first time He sent His holy apostles and disciples out.] (1992, 80)

One cannot fail to see that the route followed by the Apostle is the same one followed by Viracocha in the creation myth and by Manco Capac in the Inca origin myth. The similarities between the pan-Andean myth of creation and the Apostle's history are evident, yet Calancha states that they are two independent stories. To support his position, Calancha imputes Fr. Gregorio García for mistakingly ascribing the name Viracocha to the Apostle, because that name corresponded to a man who, after the great flood, came to inhabit the region; and that, of course, was another story. Despite Calancha's claims, it is obvious that ancient myths have been appropriated, interpreted, and then recontextualized within a Christian frame of reference.

The Apostle's Mission: To Teach the Faith and Reform Morals

The Apostle preached "la creencia y el culto debido a un solo Dios universal" [the belief and cult of a single and universal God] and at the same time reproached "ásperamente su mal modo de vivir" [harshly their licentious living] (Ramos Gavilán 30). As on other occasions when Ramos Gavilán speaks of "mal vivir" [licentious living], he refers principally to the Indians' sexual morals and behavior:

> [El Apóstol] los exhortaba a que no tuviesen concubinas, mas de una sola mujer; afeándoles el vicio de la embriaguez y sensualidad. (40)

> [(The Apostle) exhorted them not to have more than one wife and no concubines; showing them how ugly the vice of drunkenness and sensuality was.]

If Viracocha's objective had been to impose order in the cosmic chaos, and if Manco's goal had been to build a social order, then the mission of the Apostle was to provide an ethical order based on Christian morals and principles.

The ethical problems depicted in Ramos Gavilán's text are not represented as stereotypically and exclusively Andean. Certainly there is virtue to be found among the Indians. For instance, he praises the Virgins of the Sun and also commends the Indians for their government and for some of their marriage customs. However, he also focuses on several aspects of their culture which he condemns: polygamy, incest, and, in particular, human sacrifices. At the same time, he also criticizes the Spaniards and castigates their lack of religiosity, explicitly accusing them of greediness and a lack of charity:

> No dejaré de condenar toda mi vida la crueldad con que tratan a estos miserable Indios, casi a una mano todos los ministros, y sobreestantes de los ingenios . . ., la que los españoles tienen en el tratamiento de estos pobres Naturales, haciéndoles trabajar de día, y de noche, doblándoles molestísimas tareas, que cuando la codicia hace oficio de obrero, no hay peón tan alentado que no parezca lerdo, ni diligencia que no parezca sorna. (Ramos Gavilán 198)

> [I will never cease to condemn the cruelty with which these poor Indians are treated by ministers and administrators alike . . ., the cruelty with which Spaniards treat these poor natives, make them work day and night, and double the most odious tasks, shows that when greed becomes a laborer, the fastest peon would seem slow and diligence a joke.]

For Ramos Gavilán humankind's sins are part and parcel of the human condition, the outcome of the Fall. If the Indians refused to accept "the true faith" that the Apostle sought to introduce, it was only because the Devil deceived them. When the Indians ventured to harm the Apostle, it was at the Devil's behest. The Devil was always an external motivating force.

Calancha's position is quite similar to Ramos Gavilán's. A belief in the natural inferiority of the Indians—an idea advocated by many writers in the sixteenth and seventeenth centuries—is not what informs Calancha's *Crónica*. MacCormack notes that, according to Calancha,

> Cualquier tipo de gobierno y toda clase de características de comportamiento individual son . . . manifestaciones de la condición humana que no merecen por sí mismas alabanza o reprobación; no pueden ofrecer ningún fundamento para la clasificación de las personas como mejor o peor capacitadas para ejercer el dominio y la autoridad. (MacCormack 1982, 75)

> [All types of government and all kinds of characteristics of individual behavior are . . . manifestations of the human condition undeserving in themselves of any praise or reproof; they cannot offer any foundation for the classification of people as better or less capable of exercising dominion and authority.]

When Ramos Gavilán informs his reader about the despicable customs of the Indians, he always balances these with similar examples of reprehensible conduct in the Old World. In a passage dealing with human sacrifice among indigenous peoples, for instance, he invokes the following analogies to classical antiquity and the Bible:

> En los sacrificios de Saturno, se hacía muchos de hombres hechos pedazos. Abominado el Santo Profeta David, sacrificios tan crueles y espantosos, dice de ellos: Ofrecieron en sacrificio sus hijos y hijas a los demonios, derramando la inocente sangre. El Profeta Isaias, tambien hace mención de estos sacrificios: "Inmolantes párvulos in torrentibus subter eminentes petras." (Ramos Gavilán 25)

> [In the sacrifices offered to Saturn, many men were cut to pieces. The Holy Prophet David, abhorring these cruel and terrible sacrifices, says: They sacrificed their sons and daughters to the demons, spilling innocent blood. The Prophet Isaiah also mentions these sacrifices: "Inmolantes parvulos in torrentibus subter eminentes petras."]

In this context, any condemnations of Indian behavior are indictments of pervasive historical events and circumstances that all peoples have experienced: they are denunciations of humanity's faults and fall within a universal vision of history as defined by Judeo-Christian tradition. In this sense, Calancha's and Ramos Gavilán's ample historical imaginations greatly surpass the "desaforado regionalismo" [excessive regionalism] Duviols perceives in them.

Miracles and Marvels of the Apostle

The Apostle showed the power of his doctrine by performing miracles and great wonders (Ramos Gavilán 39). On one occasion there was a terrible storm that frightened many Indians, during which the holy man knelt down and prayed, raising his hands to the heavens. With this gesture, he immediately "serenó los aires; porque nunca Dios es sordo a los ruegos de sus justos" [calmed the winds; because God always hears the calling of the just] (Ramos Gavilán 39–40). In Cacha, when the Indians attempted to kill him, Providence sent a rain of fire, as it "quiso vengar tan atrevida desvergüenza y tamaña demasía" [wanted to avenge such daring insolence and such boldness] (29).

In the same manner that Viracocha's and the Apostle's pilgrimages coincide, the transgressions and consequent punishments that occurred in Cacha concur in both stories. The only difference is that in the creation myth Viracocha himself controls the cosmic phenomena, while in the Christian story the Apostle must pray to God to exert his power. This recontextualization of the myth of creation may be viewed in many different ways. Duviols's reference to it as a "beatería edificante" [edifying overpiousness] constitutes one interpretation. The Apostle's story may also be viewed as the construction of a preamble to the larger evangelizing mission, which had pragmatic intentions and lead to a new conception of the New World's position within universal history.

Numerous colonial authors, among them Ramos Gavilán, Garcilaso de la Vega, Guamán Poma, and Calancha, observed certain beliefs and ceremonies in Andean culture which could be called proto-Christian. They intuited that these beliefs and rites might facilitate the Indians' conversion to Christianity. Of all these chroniclers, Calancha is generally the one who most explicitly found Christian meanings in indigenous religious practices and beliefs:

> De más de las estatuas de piedra i oro que digimos, en que davan a entender tenían noticia del misterio inefable de la santísima Trinidad, les quedó noticia del santísimo Sacramento del Altar, de la adoración de la Cruz, de la confesión de pecador al oído del Sacerdote, del agua bendita y las ceremonias del bautismo. Creían la inmortalidad del ánima, i que avía premios

i castigos para los malos i buenos después desta vida, i diferentes sillas i lugares para las ánimas en el otro siglo. Observaban el orar por los muertos,
i tenían por virtud el ofrendar por los difuntos. Ayunavan. (769)

[In addition to the stone and gold statues that we mentioned, which implied they had some knowledge of the ineffable mystery of the Holy Trinity, among them was also some knowledge about the Holy Sacrament, of
the veneration of the Cross, of the confession of sins to a priest, of holy water, and of the ceremony of baptism. They believed in the immortality of
the soul and that after this life there were rewards and punishments for the
just and the sinners, and different places and seats for the souls in the next
world. They observed the prayers for the dead, and giving offerings to the
dead was considered a virtue. They also fasted.]

Other authors, including Acosta, thought the Indians were capable of
understanding the true religion, despite never having been evangelized
before the discovery. The natives' belief in a supreme being, creator of
heaven and earth, made it easy for the evangelizers to "persuadirles que
hay un supremo Dios y Señor de todo" [persuade them that there was a
supreme God and Lord of everything] (Acosta [1590] 1985, 219).

Garcilaso, on the other hand, divided Peruvian idolatry into two distinct periods. The first, before the Incas, was marked by barbarism, and
there the gods were "conforme a las demás simplicidades y bajezas de las
cosas que adoraban . . . no había animal tan vil ni sucio que no lo tuviesen por dios . . ." ([1609] 1976, 29) [(in accordance with) the simplicity and stupidity of the times, . . . there was no beast too vile and filthy
for them to worship as a god . . .] (1966, 30–31). The second period began with Manco Capac and was marked by the belief in one visible and
one invisible god—the Sun and Pachacámac. They were the soul and
body of one sacred entity. According to Garcilaso, "tuvieron al Pachacámac en mayor veneración que al Sol" [they regarded the Pachacámac
with greater veneration than the Sun], and he refuted Fr. Gerónimo
Román's assertion that Pachacámac was the Devil (Garcilaso [1609]
1976, 69). Instead, Garcilaso believed that Pachacámac resembled the
Christian god. Confirming Cieza de León's remarks about Pachacámac,
he says:

El cual, en decir que el Dios de los cristianos y el Pachacámac era todo
uno, dijo verdad, porque la intención de aquellos indios fue dar este nombre al sumo Dios, que da vida y ser al universo. ([1609] 1976, 63)

[(He) was right in saying that the God of the Christians and the Pachacámac were one and the same, for the intention of the Indians was to give the

name to the Most High God who gives life and being to the universe.]
(1966, 71)

It was this belief, together with many other Inca virtues, that, according
to Garcilaso, prepared the path for a Christian conversion.[103]
Those beliefs and rituals, whether interpreted as vestiges of an earlier
Christianizing effort or as diabolical mimicry, had to be replaced by or
channeled to true Catholic ones. Christian confession, for instance, had
to replace the ritual of confessions inherited from the Indians' fore-
fathers. The recognition and reverence shown to the Andean deities had
to be relocated within a Christian scheme. Native myths and legends
were also included in this scheme of exchange. Ramos Gavilán believed
that, through the substitution of Christian elements for ancient ones,
these narratives would become part of the Christian tradition and support the new evangelical initiatives. Not only could content and meaning
be molded to fit that tradition but, through efforts like his own, the
ephemeral and malleable orality could achieve permanence through
writing.[104]
Ramos Gavilán and Calancha repeatedly lament the loss of important
information about Indian ancient history which resulted from the Indians' lack of writing. Had there been a system of writing, many more details about the Apostle's presence might have been known, and there
would have been fewer discordant opinions about him. Writing assures
permanence and ensures against a faulty memory. Ramos Gavilán, aware
of the preeminence of the Temple of the Sun at Titicaca, interestingly remarks that its importance and meaning "durara cuanto durare la que estos Naturales tienen de su principio" [will remain as long as these natives
remember their origin] (12). Yet in spite of the Temple's physical permanence, by writing the myth of Viracocha in terms of the Apostle, Ramos
Gavilán and Calancha attempt to inscribe into the sacred history of the
area a Christian narrative that would finally prevail over the ancient one.
Writing, particularly the writings of chroniclers like Calancha and
Ramos Gavilán, plays an important role not only in the evangelizing enterprise but also in the formation of an Andean cultural identity. Thus, it
becomes clear that texts like theirs should not be judged solely on their
historical referentiality but rather on their larger cultural value. While it
is also true that the Spanish chroniclers transcribed the different Andean
myths and guaranteed their preservation, their versions portrayed the
stories as ridiculous and incoherent fables. In contrast to Ramos Gavilán
and Calancha, who strive to inscribe the Andean past into the history of
Christianity with a more or less equal standing, the Spanish chroniclers,

by referring to the myths pejoratively, dismiss them and reveal their own patronizing attitude toward everything Andean. This attitude is a constant in their colonizing discourse.

Relics of the Apostle and the Martyrdom of His Disciple[105]

The Apostle left signs along the path of his pilgrimage. The itinerary, reconstructed by Calancha, connected the Apostle's footprints marked in stone in nine different places: Brazil, Calango, Chachapoyas, Chile, Chunchos, Frías, Paraguay, Santa Cruz de la Sierra, and Tarija. The prints consist of two or three impressions left by the Apostle's knees as he prayed; the third mark was the impression left by his staff. The last print left by the Apostle before he departed was, according to Calancha, near Calango, a few leagues from the city of Lima. Unlike the other "relics," this one exhibits certain peculiarities (see Figure 9):

> [S]eys varas i media tiene de largo, i de ancho quatro i media; está figurada e inpresa una planta de un pie izquierdo de más de doze puntos, i por encima unas señales o letras a XX, como pondré en la figura; más abajo están unos círculos, i otras como llaves. . . . Las dos llaves una mayor que otra, no las conocieron, ni usaron los Indios en sus casas, ni asta que vinieron Españoles vieron anclas, ni supieron caracteres ni letras; el áncora fue en las naciones Ebreas i Latinas símbolo de la esperança, como la llamó san Pablo. . . . Si acaso quiso significar, que en los venideros tienpos entrarían las llaves de la Iglesia de san Pedro en estas tierras, donde él dejó sus pisadas, i no pudo introducirse su Fe. (Calancha 741–743)

> [It is six *varas*[106] long and four and a half wide; a footprint of the left foot is depicted and printed, and above it some signs or letters like XX, as I will show in the drawing; below there are some circles, and other figures like keys. . . . The two keys, one larger than the other, were not known nor used by the Indians in their houses; until the coming of the Spaniards they had never seen anchors, nor did they know letters or characters; in the Hebrew and Latin nations, the anchor was a symbol of hope, as Saint Paul called it. . . . Maybe it meant that in future times the keys of the Church of Saint Peter would open these lands, where he left his footprints but could not introduce his Faith.]

Besides giving his interpretation of the meanings inscribed in the stone, Calancha states that the Indians identified this stone as the *Coyllor Sayana*, which means "donde se paraba la estrella" [where the star fell]. The Indians called it by this name because "aviéndose subido sobre la piedra un Indio i una India al acto venéreo, i estando mirando al cielo,

Figure 9. The Prints of the Apostle

cayó una estrella i los confundió entranbos" [two Indians, a man and a woman, were engaged in the venereal act on the stone, and while they were looking at the sky, a star fell and fused them together] (Calancha 741–742). This fusion of a copulating man and woman was, according to Calancha, divine punishment for the profanation of the Apostle's foot-prints. The stone appears to have been destroyed upon the orders of the *visitador* Duarte Fernández, who had discovered that the Indians wor-shiped it. Calancha, however, laments the destruction of the stone he calls a relic (743). How could it be possible that Calancha did not recog-nize *huacas*? Is it possible that his determination to prove the presence of the Apostle in the Andes led him to interpret signs in a way opposite to the extirpators'? If we take into account Calancha's historical perspec-tive, what stands out is his regret that the Spaniards were destroying the landmarks of Andean history, a history that the Augustinian was trying to graft onto the history of Christianity.[107]

The stone relics of the footprints of the Apostle correspond to the stone *huacas* in the myth of creation and the Inca myth of origin. What we have here is a recontextualization or appropriation of the landmarks of ancient cultures, so that, grafted onto Christian forms of representa-tion, they might become cultural cornerstones shared by all Americans:

Indians, *criollos*, and *mestizos*. Perhaps Calancha was even attempting to save cultural relics from the irrepressible zeal of the extirpators by garbing them as Christian relics.

In the myth of creation Viracocha unfolds into three characters. So too, in the narrative about the Apostle, there is an unfolding of characters for particular representational purposes.[108] Ramos Gavilán's version follows a very tortuous story line full of digressions that take the reader into different time frames, as, for instance, when the author diverges to narrate the contemporary discovery of some of the relics, or when he narrates parallel events separated by a millennium and a half. In his story, the names of Tunupa and Taapac merge and separate, giving sometimes the impression of one character and at others of two. Calancha, although he bases his story mostly on Ramos Gavilán's, solves the problem by clearly distinguishing two characters: the Apostle Thomas and a disciple, known by the natives as Tunupa and Taapac, respectively. Both men share characteristics with Christ and with the Apostles. The Apostle quite closely follows the traditional apostolic mission: to preach Christ's divinity and teach about his death, give them the light of the Gospel, and build churches (Calancha 745). After some time in the land, the Apostle leaves and goes to India, where he dies. The disciple, who at first accompanies the Apostle, remains behind to continue the evangelical mission. Like the Apostle, the disciple tries to teach the Indians the true religion, reproves their faults, and builds churches. But he also performs many miracles, cures the sick, calms threatening storms, and exorcises demons. At Lake Titicaca (Calancha), or more precisely in Carabuco (Ramos Gavilán), the disciple raises a cross and continues his efforts at converting the Indians to the true faith and trying to correct their abhorrent behavior. The Indians, infuriated not because he has vituperated their gods, but because he has criticized their customs, insult him, slap and hit him, and finally kill him by skewering him with a palm tree stick. The Indians place his body on a raft which is taken across the lake to a final resting place, where ever since a palm grows on Easter. The similarities with Christ are not only obvious but are underlined by Calancha himself as he draws parallels between the life of this disciple and that of Christ himself. For instance, referring to the Indians' reaction after being reproved by the disciple, Calancha says that "they resembled the Jews and Pharisees, who, having rancor against Christ because He reprehended their customs, proclaimed their anger not because He condemned their lives, but because He did not keep the sabbath" (764).

By unfolding the character, the narrative fulfills several purposes. The presence of Saint Thomas becomes a testimony of God's benevolence to the New World and inscribes these lands as part of the Christian history from its beginning. The gentle and loving ways they used to teach their doctrine to the Indians become the model for the future evangelizing mission. Perhaps a parallel is implied with the African Apples chosen to take care of the cult of the Virgin of Copacabana: the Augustinians had been the ones selected to lead the new mission. In the same way that an apple was instrumental to the Fall and the African Apples in the redemption, the first attempt to Christianize the Indians was not able to plant lasting roots, but the Augustinians' efforts were sure to yield plenty of fruits. Calancha's chronicle recounts the entire history of the Augustinians in the Viceroyalty of Peru and is full of innumerable examples of their great success in converting the Indians. Furthermore, the immolation of the disciple at Carabuco not only echoes Christ's temptation, because like him the disciple refuses all the riches and power offered by the Indians if he is willing to accept their idols as gods; it also becomes both an exemplary tale of what the Christianizing mission should mean as well as a veiled condemnation of priests and orders that were accused of profiting from their positions. In addition to all of this, the disciple becomes an American protomartyr whose relics—like his sandals and the indestructible cross preserved for centuries in Carabuco—are said to have performed countless miracles.

Duviols comments about the Apostle:

Así pues, Tunapa-Santo Tomás, queda consagrado en su triple papel de fundador de la Iglesia peruana, protomártir del Perú y campeón de la lucha contra la idolatría. (1977, 65)

[In this way, Tunapa–Saint Thomas is consecrated in his triple role as founder of the Peruvian Church, protomartyr of Peru, and champion in the fight against idolatry.]

Duviols makes this dismissive statement because the evidence presented by the Augustinian writers seems to him pseudoscientific—it lacks empirical truth and therefore is only indicative of their religious fanaticism. Apparently, to serve the demands of an anachronistic empirical imperative, Duviols insists that Ramos Gavilán and Calancha fit his criteria of history. Yet, the historical truth of the events narrated by the Augustinians is, in fact, irrelevant. It is, rather, the moral truth in which they seek to dress Andean history which is of primary importance in their writings. The function of the truth within their culture is the key element of their tales. Throughout them they sought to provide a model for preaching that would guide the evangelical enterprise and establish evidence that God always viewed the Indians with benevolence.

SAINT BARTHOLOMEW IN PERU: GUAMÁN POMA'S VERSION

Bartholomew, and not Thomas, was, according to Guamán Poma, the Apostle sent by God to these kingdoms (94). But like Thomas (Viracocha or Tunupa), Saint Bartholomew made it rain fire when the Indians tried to kill him in Cacha, and like Taapac, he raised a cross in Carabuco. Guamán Poma's story deserves attention not because of onomastic changes but because it includes some arresting elements. While Calancha and Ramos Gavilán merely tell us that the presence of the Apostle silenced the oracles, in Guamán Poma the silencing of the *huacas* is treated in more detail. The Apostle was traveling through the Kollao, and on one occasion, to protect himself from the cold, he entered a cave at the precise moment when a sorcerer was speaking with his idol. Saint Bartholomew's presence silenced the idol. The disconcerted Indian could not understand why the oracle was not responding to him, until the Devil spoke to him in his dreams and explained that, despite all his knowledge, this man was more powerful than he. After this revelation, the Indian followed the man, begged for his mercy and forgiveness, and became a faithful follower of Bartholomew. The Indian was baptized and received the new name of Anti Vira Cocha.[109] It was to commemorate this event that the cross at Carabuco was raised. This episode can be understood as a representation of the power that Christianity had over the local beliefs. In this way, a silencing occurs in the very writing of the text.

While in Ramos Gavilán and Calancha the silent oracles are also a way of representing the triumph of Christianity, it is the voice of the hegemonic religion which, from the perspective of the Andean religions, signifies the impossibility of realizing one's own discourse. Thus, Guamán Poma, Santa Cruz Pachacuti, and Garcilaso searched for a way to accommodate Andean religious elements within the Christian European discourse, because the Indians no longer possessed a voice. The Andeans also sought alternative ways to represent their beliefs, through dance, architecture, and painting.[110]

Guamán Poma's story also recontextualizes the Viracocha myth when it interjects the figure of Saint Bartholomew. The legend of Saint Bartholomew actually fits more easily into a Christian reinterpretation of the Viracocha myth than does the legend of Saint Thomas. According to the hagiography compiled by Jacobus de Voragine, Saint Bartholomew traveled to India.[111] There he entered a temple where the idol of Astaroth stood. When he entered into its presence, the idol was silenced. After the people discovered the reason why the idol became silent, they went in search of the man described by the idol as having a light complexion, big

Figure 10. Saint Bartholomew according to Guamán Poma

eyes, straight nose, and medium height and as bearded and dressed in a
white tunic. This description coincides with that of Viracocha in almost
all the versions, and Guamán Poma, although he does not write about his
appearance, depicts him in this way in his drawing (Figure 10). Bartholomew later converts more people and subjugates more idols. Like the disciple Taapac at Titicaca, Bartholomew was also martyred.

Guamán Poma's adaptation of the Saint Bartholomew legend was
much more direct and did not need long exegetical explanations like
Calancha's to arrive at Saint Thomas's story. Furthermore, Guamán

Poma's version is solely centered upon the destruction of idolatry, while in Calancha's and Ramos Gavilán's not only idolatry but also morals are the targets of the apostolic mission. Guamán Poma, in diametrical opposition to Garcilaso, blames the Incas for the introduction of idolatry and diabolical practices. According to him, prior to the establishment of their power, all Indians were monotheistic and had high moral values. In fact, in his text he insistently tries to demonstrate that the Andeans were almost Christians *avant la lettre* or at least followed Christian values from the beginning of time (50–82).

PRE-HISPANIC CHRISTIANITY WITHIN UNIVERSAL HISTORY

Through the recontextualization of the myth of creation and its reformulation as a Christian narrative, the sacred history of the Titicaca region was grafted onto the history of Christianity from its beginning. The history of Christianity in the sixteenth century was limited exclusively to the history of the Old World. This is significant especially if we see these new stories as the production of a discourse generated in America by Americans. This discourse differs from those produced by the majority of Spanish authors, who evaluated the narratives they found in America as chaotic, nonsensical, or enigmatic, arising from a separate world completely segregated from the European milieu.

The fact that *criollo*, *mestizo*, and native writers defended these narratives and that most Spaniards rejected them reveals the fervent desire of many writers to participate in the construction of the American portion of a universal history. This desire may also be viewed as a way of denying the Spanish claim to have been the first to introduce Christianity to the Indians. From the perspective of these early narratives, Spain and America would be placed on an equal plane, since Christianity spread to both simultaneously. Both traditions would introduce an Apostle who taught the Christian doctrine: either James or Paul found fertile ground in Spain, while in America Thomas's teachings on the existence of one invisible and omnipotent god were firmly ensconced in the beliefs of the Andean people. Calancha affirms that during the Apostle's first mission he converted some of the Indians and then emphasizes the patristic authorities who confirm James's conversion of only seven souls (743–775).

The logic behind the historical grafting carried out by the American authors is more consequential than a mere chronological sequencing of early Christianity in both hemispheres. Several additional parallels are drawn. For instance, with the invasion of the Moors, the Church lost its hegemony in Spain for many centuries; so too, as after the martyrdom of the disciple at Titicaca, the Devil beguiled the Indians and became the master of Andean religions. The year marking the final victory of the Spanish reconquest also marked the beginning of America's religious reconquest. The post-Columbian evangelization is linked to the earlier evangelizing mission and continues the earlier mission by fulfilling a promise to return.

The presence of the Apostle at Titicaca and the fact that he had been sent by Christ himself establish the site as a Christian hierophany *ab initio*. Within this context, Titicaca's past is transformed into a prelude to the evangelizing mission proposed by the Augustinians. By interpreting the legend through the prism of an early Andean Christianization, not only do Ramos Gavilán and Calancha unite two isolated moments during Titicaca's past, but they also project that past onto the very origins of the universal history of Christianity. The Augustinians attempt to historicize what is not susceptible to historicization. This process was intended to erase the rupture with the past that the Spanish conquest had forged within Indian consciousness. Through a discourse of recontexualization, the idolatrous period interposed between these two temporal points is recast as the consequence of a demonic intervention. This is how Ramos Gavilán and Calancha attempt to revindicate America's position in the annals of Christian discourse. Indeed, their discourse is conciliatory and restitutive, proposing both to fill the historical gaps precipitated in Andean consciousness by the arrival of the Spaniards and to counterbalance the violence which was generated by the campaigns to extirpate idolatry.

FROM MORAL CHAOS TO CHRISTIAN ORDER

In Ramos Gavilán's and Calancha's stories, the mission of the divine emissaries is, like Viracocha's and Manco Capac's, to impose order on chaos. However, the chaos thwarted by the Apostle and his disciple is neither cosmic nor political—it is moral. The Apostle has divested himself of his mythic qualities and carries out his evangelizing labor within a clearly delineated historical period. Calancha and Ramos Gavilán comment that the extraordinary nature of the events surrounding his pilgrimage facilitated the preservation of the narrative for more than 1,500 years. The reinstitution of the evangelizing mission transforms the events associated with both the first pre-Columbian and post-Conquest evangelizations into historical material.

Seeds had been sown by the first evangelizers in the Andes, but they did not take root; therefore, moral chaos and idolatry continued for centuries. The *Visitas de Idolatría* sought to rectify the moral chaos by invoking catechetical precepts along with the eradication of all idols and the institution of punitive measures. Ramos Gavilán and Calancha agreed that idolatry needed to be eliminated, but they also searched for ways to establish continuity between the Andean culture and the Christian world. Moral order and a sincere religious transformation would create a Christian republic after the manner of Saint Augustine's *City of God*. Thus, Ramos Gavilán heralds the advent of this new order by recounting the miracles of the Virgin of Copacabana.

DEVOTION TO THE VIRGIN WITHIN CHRISTIAN TRADITION

Toward the middle of the thirteenth century, the cult of the Virgin Mary grew significantly throughout Europe. Until then, only the worship of a distant, justice-seeking, fear inspiring God was prevalent. Because she represented a gentler and nonthreatening figure, many of the faithful were inclined to worship the Virgin; by the thirteenth century, Mary had become an integral part of Christian worship.[112]

The emergence of feudal patrons who sponsored the construction of churches, hermitages, and monasteries in honor of the Virgin followed in the wake of this devotion. Worship of feminine pagan deities partially lay below the surface of the cult of the Virgin, and attributes of Ares, Diana, Isis, and Rhea were assigned to Mary.[113] The Church expanded the festivals honoring her in order to commemorate the different events of her life. Many of the miracles attributed to the Virgin or her image circulated in the form of narratives. These narratives endeavored to humanize the same doctrine that formal theology had dehumanized by presenting her as a mediator between God and humanity (Bland 1928).

The rise of the cult of the Virgin prompted the appearance of Latin and vernacular collections of her miracles in the thirteenth century. These anthologies began to form a genre of their own, though initially the miracles appeared as appendages to hagiographies (Bland; Warner). The miracles performed by the saints differed from those associated with the Virgin in that the former were cast as models of conduct, or *imitatio*. The miracles of the Virgin, in contrast, perform the function of *laudatio* and existed to inspire reverence and feelings of admiration in those who heard or read them. Their purpose was to "[recuperar] desde ese momento al oyente o lector para el servicio de Maria" [retrieve the listener or reader from that moment on to the service of Mary] (Montoya Martínez 52).

Collections of miracles circulated widely in the vernacular. An analysis of these reveals that the texts traced their origins to the earlier Latin collections and that they shared a common intention and design. The laudatory objective of the vernacular texts remains obvious. However, their intentions were also practical: they were often used in sermons in a manner similar to *exempla*. The collections of vernacular miracles aspired to proselytize the unbelievers and heighten the belief of the faithful.

In his research on "the literary miracle," Montoya Martínez analyzes three early collections of vernacular miracles compiled by Berceo, Coinci, and Alfonso X. His study demonstrates that all of the miracles recounted by these three authors may be reduced to one basic model which appears to have endured throughout the Renaissance and Baroque periods.[114]

The Collection of Miracles Concerning the Virgin of Copacabana

The narratives of the miracles of the Virgin of Copacabana unquestionably reflect the well-established tradition of the European model.[115] However, tracing the origins and discovering the models that inspired the miracles of the Virgin of Copacabana reveal little about the distinctiveness of these American texts.

The unique and complex features presented in Ramos Gavilán's collection of miracles demand an appropriate analytical perspective in order to reveal the political and religious climate that motivated it. Although subscribing to European models, the stories provide abundant, explicit, and unique information pertaining to the Andean world and allow a better understanding of the role religion played in that culture.

Ramos Gavilán's rendition of the miracles shares a laudatory aspect and a didactic function with traditional models. A unique peculiarity of his text, however, is a chronicle of the pre-Columbian Andean world that precedes the collection of miracles. The relevance of Ramos Gavilán's work arises not only from the specific content of the narratives, which emerge from a cultural and historical context particular to the Andean region, but from the interpretation of those narratives in a dialogical relation to the chronicle which frames them. Although part of a well-established European tradition, Ramos Gavilán's rendition varies enough from it to conclude that, along with introducing an example of pious literature to America, his text constitutes, as I will show later, a significant segment of a larger cultural project.

The Miracles of the Virgin of Copacabana

The Virgin of Copacabana is the most recent hierophany in the sacred history of Lake Titicaca. The origin of her image and worship, as outlined in Chapter 1, may be traced back to 1583. According to Ramos Gavilán's *Historia*, the image had thaumaturgic powers and performed wondrous and faith-promoting miracles from the very moment it came to the village of Copacabana. Longstanding Christians and recently baptized Indians were inspired by these astonishing events.

Ramos Gavilán compiled 132 miracles attributed to the image. According to him, the collection represents only a selection, because he decided to narrate only those miracles that he considered the most moving and the more liable to awaken devotion to the Virgin (127). The series of miracles, together with the narrative of the Apostle, should be understood as complementary components of the evangelical design which underlies his text. Both parts have pragmatic purposes: the Apostle's narrative proposes a model for peaceful evangelization, whereas the miracles are meant as exemplary narratives for the sermons to the Indians and for religious instruction. Beyond these practical aspects, the presence of the Virgin of Copacabana and the diffusion of her miracles in narrative form within local culture served as links of continuity at religious, cultural, and political levels: religious because they attested the permanence of the sacred at Lake Titicaca, cultural because they tried to smooth the transition between the Andean past and the new Christian order, and political because they allowed for the continuation of certain Andean political structures.

The Missional Methods to Convert the Indians and the Miracles of the Virgin of Copacabana

The earliest document to refer to the Christianization of the Indians dates from Columbus's first voyage. On 12 October 1492, the very first day that the Admiral sees the people in Guanahani, he assures the Monarchs that they will quickly become good Christians (Colón 31). The optimistic predictions of Columbus were not quite fulfilled, and during the next couple of centuries the evangelization of the Indians stumbled over many obstacles. The Crown, the Church, and the religious orders were all committed to the evangelical mission, and all were engaged at various times in serious discussions about how to put into effect their apostolic ideal. From early on there were centralized efforts to collect information about the nature of the Indians and their beliefs, recognizing that knowledge was essential to carrying out their missionary endeavors (Borges 27–52). Until the end of the sixteenth century the methods used in the evangelization were constantly revised, based on the degrees of success or failure of those previously employed and on the assessment they made about the Indians (Borges passim).[116] During that period a large number of regal and ecclesiastical documents dealing with the issues about the Christianization of the natives were composed. Many individual authors also wrote about the Indians' religious practices and offered their views on how to accomplish the mission.

In the Viceroyalty of Peru the Constitutions of the Council of Lima and

Acosta's *De Procuranda Indorum Salute* gave precise instructions on how to convert the Indians. These instructional texts addressed the methods of persuasion to be used in the Christianization of the Indians. The Third Council of Lima (1582–1583) proposed the preparation of pedagogical literature in three languages (Spanish, Quechua, and Aymara) in order to instruct the Indians, including a catechism, a confessor's manual, and a book of sermons (Duviols 1977, 173). The 1613 Synod explicitly stated that the Indians should be taught in their own language, and it required parish priests to pass an examination in native languages before being commissioned for the cure of souls (Duviols 1977, 339–340). The catechism was used to teach the principles of the faith, while the confessor's manual guided priests in their interactions with the Indians. Books of sermons contained many different homilies dedicated to proving the falseness of the ancient Andean religions through the use of examples (Duviols 1977, 341–369). All of these methods of persuasion presumed that the Indians were passive repositories of principles and aimed at proving to the Indians the superiority of the Christian religion.

In the same spirit, Ramos Gavilán sought to make his own contribution to these methods of persuasion and therefore compiled his miracles. Clearly, these miracles circulated because of their use in sermons and proselytizing sessions attended by the Indians. Many authors, such as Ávila and Molina, had compiled Indian myths and researched their beliefs in order to use them as part of sermons for the purpose of disproving or demonizing them. Opposing these methods of persuasion, Ramos Gavilán's collection of miracles represents the Indians not only as the repositories of doctrine but also as the protagonists of the narratives in more than half of the miracles. The majority of these protagonists lived in the Titicaca region. Thus, many of these miracles purport to narrate events which were firsthand positive Christian experiences of inhabitants in the region.

The representation of the Andean world contained in these narratives must have been immediately recognizable to the Indians. These miracles spoke more clearly to the Indians than abstract, foreign dogma and the precepts dictated by the ecclesiastical constitutions. They gave them examples to emulate rather than a diabolical image of themselves. Representation of the Indians as protagonists in the miracles allowed them to participate actively in the conquering religion. In addition, the Indians experienced a different religious situation within the narratives since the Virgin always interceded on their behalf, healing them, bringing them back to life, freeing them, or making their lives more bearable. The miracles compiled by Ramos Gavilán do not emphasize the Indians' ques-

Figure 11. The Virgin of Copacabana in the High Altar of the Basilica

tioning of the faith, nor do they underscore immoral behavior on the part of the Indians. They call attention to the divine mercy and protection offered them by the Virgin of Copacabana. To be sure, as early as the beginning of the seventeenth century, the Indians referred lovingly to the Virgin of Copacabana as *Mamanchic*, or mother of all. In fact, to this day, they refer to her as "Mamita de Copacabana" (see Figure 11).

The following miracle illustrates the significance of these narratives to the Indians. Ramos Gavilán tells the story of a couple who traveled from Copacabana to the mines in Potosí. During the journey, one of their llamas died. Distraught over the loss, they decided to tie the *medida*[117] from the Virgin of Copacabana around the animal's neck. The llama was immediately brought back to life in the presence of many witnesses.

This story doubtless had a powerful meaning for the Indian population. The demands imposed by Toledo's reforms were becoming more and more burdensome.[118] State intervention in the form of taxes and other duties had left the Indians in destitute circumstances. In addition, the Indian gods no longer communicated with them. The llama's death, therefore, attains a heightened significance within the context of the *mita*, or the state-imposed tributary forced labor.

The implications of a llama's death in Andean culture extended well beyond the mere loss of a material possession and tacitly signaled the presence of the state and the tensions between it and the indigenous population. The couple's journey to Potosí is portrayed within the context of fulfilling an obligation placed upon them by the state, the *mita*. Indeed, if they failed to obey the command to go and work in the mines at Potosí, the repercussions would have been severe, not only for them specifically but also for the entire province in which they lived. The audience of the miracle would have understood that the couple had been forced to traverse the Andean highlands on foot for nearly 800 kilometers from Copacabana to Potosí. They would have known, too, that llamas carried food, clothing, and the Indians' scant personal belongings. In short, they would have understood that the journey would have been impossible without the animal. The couple's loss would have placed them in a life-or-death situation.

The didactic function of the miracles complemented the exemplary function found in the narrative that presented the Apostle as an evangelizing model. The Apostle's narrative functioned as an illustration of the most efficacious missionary model, while the collections of miracles served to portray the active, exemplary presence of the Indians themselves and the protection and favors received as they became eager practitioners in the Christian precepts they were assimilating.

SILENCE VERSUS THE POSSIBILITY OF DISCOURSE

In the legend about the Apostle, the idols are silenced by one of Christ's vicars, in the person of either Thomas or Bartholomew. The quelling of the idols' voices symbolizes the victory of Christianity over the Andean religions. Throughout post-Conquest Andean discourse, this silence also represents the chaos and confusion doubtless created by the imposed colonial, cultural, and ideological structures. In one of Ramos Gavilán's miracles, an Indian becomes mute as a result of demonic intervention and recovers his voice due to the intercession of the Virgin of Copacabana. The message is clear: Indians will regain their voices only when they participate in a Christian discourse and ultimately become advocates of the faith. Although this story initially portrays a rejection of Andean religions, its conclusion represents a happy and exemplary circumstance which diverges significantly from the type of solutions proposed by the official policy of extirpation.

An event that occurred in 1609 illustrates the difference between the method of evangelization proposed by Ramos Gavilán and the exemplary lesson given to the Indians by the campaigns against idolatry. On 20 December 1609, an "Auto de Fe" was conducted on the Plaza Mayor in Lima. Since the Indians did not fall under the direct jurisdiction of the Inquisition, because Archbishop Lobo Guerrero had declared them to be ignorant of the faith rather than heretics, they could not be burned at the stake. However, their *malquis* and their idols were fuel for the fire. Hernán Páucar, an Indian from Ávila's parish in Huarochirí, was accused of being a sorcerer. Páucar was forced to confess publicly, received 200 lashes, and was shaved—a most degrading punishment from the Andean perspective. According to Duviols, this event

> señalaría, tanto en la pompa excepcional en que estuvo rodeado, como por su contenido, la voluntad, existente ya en las esferas civiles y religiosas, de poner en práctica una nueva política, de inspiración draconiana, contra la idolatría. (1977, 184)

> [because of the exceptional pomp with which it was surrounded and because of its content, would point to the will with which the civil and religious establishment had to put into practice a new policy, draconian in essence, against idolatry.]

Although burning the Indians' mummies and idols was categorically better than burning the Indians themselves, it is important to bear in mind that their *malquis* and the *huacas* represented their link with the gods, the universe, nature, and the past, as has been illustrated in the earlier discussion of the myth of creation and the Inca origin myth. The "Auto de fe" of 1609 must have been viewed as a cultural dismemberment since, much like the representation of the myth of Incarrí, it left the Indians without a body, without an identity, indeed without a history.[119] The displacement produced by these events must have been equal to, or worse than, the martyrdom they might personally have suffered at the stake. Calancha, by attempting to preserve the "relics of the Apostle," was trying to avoid this form of cultural mutilation.

Ramos Gavilán, in the miracle about the mute Indian, presents a totally different perspective than that of the *Auto*. Domingo Calisaya, a twenty-three-year-old youth, traveled to Yungas de Larecaja where the Indians grew coca, ají, fruit, and cotton. While in Yungas, Domingo was told by an old sorcerer that the idols had revealed that he had been chosen to attend the service of the *huacas*. As a result, the "satanic" teacher initiated him in the rites and ceremonies of the *huacas*, ordained him a minister, and showed him the places where the *huacas* were worshiped. The Devil possessed the young man and "thankfully" crippled and silenced him. When Domingo's mother learned what had happened to her son, she had him taken to Copacabana. After Father Montoro discovered the boy was not ill but possessed by a demon, he advised that a mass be observed at the altar of the Virgin of Copacabana so that she could intercede for the boy. They carried Domingo to the church in a sheet. The mass had no effect on his condition, so they requested a second mass. During the second mass, they gave Domingo a candle and noticed incredible signs of suffering on his face as he held the light in his hand. At the end of the mass, they carried him to the church door and set him on the ground so as to get a better grip on the sheet in which they carried him. Domingo stood up and began to walk and then related the story of his visit to Yungas. These events took place in the presence of a huge crowd, which was immediately filled with reverence and devotion for the Virgin of Copacabana. The news of this miracle spread quickly throughout the region, and with it spread a new enthusiasm for and devotion to the Virgin (Ramos Gavilán 133–135).

Ramos Gavilán's narrative inverts the role of the priest presented in Hernán Paúcar's story. It is the Devil and not the priest who confers bodily punishment upon the Indian, and it is the priest, the vicar of the Church, who conveys Domingo to the altar at Copacabana and becomes the instrument of the Virgin's miraculous cure. The miracle symbolizes the impossibility of the Andeans' sustaining the ancient discourses of their native religions. At the level of the physical, Domingo's paralysis represents the inability to function in everyday society. As it restores his freedom of movement, the miracle of the Virgin gives Domingo a voice which doubtless corresponds to Christian discourse. However, at the same time, the story captures the Indian's own discourse, since Domingo himself is the one who recounts what happened to him before the miracle occurred.

Ramos Gavilán's text emphasizes the fact that the Indians function not only as the protagonists of the miracles but also as their narrators: they become the spokespersons for the new religion and the forms of piety which it advocates. In yet another example, another paralyzed Indian, healed by a miracle of the Virgin of Copacabana, could not stop talking about the marvels of the Virgin, exhorting everyone to come to serve her, because she consoled them in their labors and came to the help of those who called her (Ramos Gavilán 192).

Ramos Gavilán represents the Indians as producers of a discourse that, although originally belonging only to the European tradition, gradually took root in the Andean culture and became one of its discursive possibilities for the notion of the sacred. Ramos Gavilán was aware that the appropriation of Christian discourse on the part of the Indians represented the possibility of recuperating the coherence and order lost with the Conquest.

"FROM THE INCA SUN GOD TO THE VIRGIN OF COPACABANA":[120] POLITICAL CONTINUITY

The transformation of preexisting power structures in the Kollao at the time of the Inca political expansion was discussed in Chapter 3. The advent of the Inca state religion modified social and political structures in the Titicaca region. The original inhabitants of the Island of Titicaca were removed and replaced by ministers in the worship of the Sun. Copacabana had always been one of the most important landmarks for the constant pilgrimages to the sanctuary at Titicaca. Pilgrims who journeyed there had to perform certain rites of purification before entering the *sanctum sanctorum* on the Island of Titicaca.

Copacabana had been repopulated by forty-two different nations of *mitimaes*,[121] and within these the Incas represented imperial power. The presence of these *mitimaes* prompted the restructuring of the previous social order and in fact inverted the established system. Sabine MacCormack explains that

> in Copacabana and Carabuco, on the east shore of the lake, it was the newcomers who were classified as Ananasaya (Upper), making the indigenous people Urinsaya (Lower), whereas according to the traditional Andean pattern—observable both among the Incas and elsewhere—the indigenous people constituted Anansaya, and the newcomers, the less privileged, were Urinsaya. This reversal of Andean social organization, which was caused by Inca patronage of the cult of the Sun on the island, matched the social organization of Cuzco, where also the newcomers, that is, the Incas, had become Anansaya, thus displacing the indigenous people, who became Urinsaya. (1984, 45)

The selection of the Virgin of the Candlemas as the patroness of Copacabana corresponded to the preservation of the power structures established by the Incas when they came to the area. The Anansaya from Copacabana sought to preserve their power during the colonial period, while the Urinsaya tried to recuperate it.

In 1582 a frost threatened to destroy the crops and, as mentioned in Chapter 1, the Indians decided to place their fate in the hands of their patron saint. Let us recall that the Anansayas insisted that the Virgin of the Candlemas was the appropriate patron saint, since Tito Yupanqui had already sculpted her image while the Urinsayas wanted Saint Bartholomew to be the intercessor. The Anansayas' wishes were imposed in both the enthronement of the Virgin of Copacabana and the foundation of a brotherhood. Don Alonso Viracocha Inca directed the negotiations with the archbishop and oversaw the entire process by which Tito Yupanqui sculpted the image of the Virgin. Don Alonso Viracocha was the grandson of Paullu Inca, who had accompanied Almagro in the conquest of the Kollao.

Yet, the Virgin was also the patron of the Spanish conquerors, having reportedly inspired them on the hill above Cuzco in 1536. In reference to this, MacCormack writes:

> The Virgin as patron of Copacabana could be connected with the Virgin who had miraculously intervened at the siege of Cuzco on behalf of the Spaniards and their allies, among whom could be counted the Incas of Copacabana. The Virgin whom Anansaya wanted for Copacabana, then was the Virgin who had brought the Spaniards victory, just as the Sun had brought victory to the Incas. In this way, one may view the Incas of Copacabana integrating themselves into the new ruling class. They did this by using a time-honored Inca method: seeing that the Sun could no longer be an imperial deity, the victorious Virgin of Cuzco succeeded the Sun in this role, and in this way became the Sun's successor at Copacabana. (1984, 49)

In terms of local politics, the Virgin of Copacabana became the unifying link between pre-Conquest power structures and a new social order.

RAMOS GAVILÁN'S *HISTORIA:* THE EXEMPLARY HISTORY OF MISSIONARY WORK IN THE LAKE TITICACA REGION

The 132 miracles compiled by Ramos Gavilán may be seen as individual narratives used to illustrate doctrinal points that were being taught. However, when analyzed as a complete series, it is possible to detect an evolution and a qualitative difference between the first miracles and the later ones.

The miracles cover a period of more than three decades: the first occurred around 1582, and the last ones date from 1618. The first miraculous event attributed by Ramos Gavilán to the Image of the Virgin occurs during the festival of the Candlemas, on 2 February, the very day that the image entered the village of Copacabana, after Bishop Granero had accepted it as a sacred object.[122] Ramos Gavilán suggests that this miracle provided the opportunity for the initiation of a series of miraculous events that sparked the devotion of the Indians to the new image. Although he does not discount the possibility that the cross was poorly mounted and that the incident might have been purely accidental, he interprets it as a Providential sign (Ramos Gavilán 124). The absence of injury to the Corregidor was deemed a sign of gratitude from the Virgin. The incident also confirmed that she was pleased with the place they had chosen to enthrone her.[123] In this way, a new hierophany was able to appropriate the ancient sacred place.

The second miracle was performed on the Image itself. Ramos Gavilán reveals that, although everyone admired the beauty of her face, Father Montoro discovered that the image had a physical defect:

> El niño estaba tan levantado sobre el pecho de la Madre, que poniéndole la corona cubría gran parte del rostro de la Virgen, de manera que impedía su vista, y no podían verla. Daba esto una cuidadosa pena, y cuidado muy penoso al P. Montoro, el cual llamando al Escultor con alguna aspereza, le mandó, enmendar aquella falta. Afligiole mucho el pecho aquel apretado precepto, no hallando orden para reparar la falta. (129)

> [The babe was so high up on the Mother's chest that his crown covered most of the Virgin's face, making it impossible to see it. Saddened by this, Fr. Montoro called the sculptor, whom he sternly ordered to amend the fault. The sculptor, not knowing how he could repair the mistake, felt very distressed.]

Tito Yupanqui appealed to the Virgin for help with the problem, and the following day Father Montoro noticed that the figure of the Child had reclined so as to make the Virgin's face completely visible. This convinced Montoro of the Image's miraculous nature and its determination to reign in Copacabana.[124]

The next miracle occurred in 1583. A severe drought was threatening the lives of the Indians, when a cloud materialized in the midst of a clear sky, and it began to rain on the fields of the Anansaya. As in the miracle of the falling cross, the Image appeared to express gratitude to those who had sculpted it and placed it on the altar. This miracle functioned as an excellent means of persuasion because the Urinsaya saw the blessings bestowed upon their rivals, and as a result, they decided to offer a mass at the altar of the Virgin. After the mass, the rain came and soaked the fields of both groups.

This miracle's message seems to have been that the Virgin of Copacabana would help all her devotees without discriminating among them. While the solar divinity had provided a place of distinction only for the

Anansaya, within the new religion all social and class divisions would be erased by the Virgin. The achievement of a more equal society seemed to have been one of the aims of Ramos Gavilán's project, and this goal doubtless played an important role in the selection of the miracles and the construction of his text.

Ramos Gavilán's miracles offer an inventory of representative individuals and form a mosaic portraying seventeenth-century Andean society. This can be seen in the specificity with which each protagonist is represented. Every narrative specifies the protagonist's first and last name, age, race, place of origin, as well as, at times, his or her occupation and social status. In addition, the exact place and date of the miracle are noted. The Virgin of Copacabana saves, protects, forgives, or heals all these individuals, setting a broad, pluralistic example for the Church.

The characters in the different miracles are representatives of the entire social fabric as they fulfill various functions within each story. Some of the texts present the Spaniards as the agents for the appearance of the miracle. We see them as the ones who carry the wretched character to the church, or as the ones who place the *medida* of the Virgin on the sick or injured, or as the petitioners to the Virgin of Copacabana, who in turn intervenes miraculously. The protagonists, an equal number of Spanish and Indians, always benefit from the miracle.

Within the series, there is also a visible progression in the faith of the Indians. In the early miracles with Indian protagonists, the Virgin seems to perform the miracle *motu propio*, without invocation or petition for her service. Once reports of these miracles spread throughout the territory, the intermediate miracles show the Indians beginning to go to the church. They present offerings to the Virgin and invoke her name in cases of need. In the later miracles, the Indians appear as true devotees: the first thing they do in time of need is petition the Virgin, and they also make pilgrimages to her sanctuary. Progressively in the text, the Indians gradually appropriate the religion and finally claim full participation.

In the early miracles, the Indians do not invoke the Virgin, and sometimes even the protagonist does not know who she is. However, she appears and liberates the needy from their afflictions. An example of this happening is when in the village of Copacabana a stranger named Baltasar wanted to rid himself of his wife, so he hanged her. He carried her body to the top of the hill so that the condors would devour her remains. Although Baltasar had tried to erase his footprints leading to the scene of the crime, he still feared his crime would be discovered and returned to the hill to bury her remains. When he reached the top, he found his wife alive and sitting with her eyes raised toward heaven. She told him of a woman who appeared to her, untied the rope from around her neck, and told her that she was "the Mother of God who was in the church" (Ramos Gavilán 137).

In the early miracles, the Indians petition the Virgin only after learning about her other miracles. However, as the sequence progresses, the Indians are represented not only as believers but as practicing Catholics. In 1605 a blind Indian named Juan Aullo from Cayara made a pilgrimage to Copacabana. Before making his supplicatory offering to the Virgin so she might restore his sight, he "tried to settle his accounts with God through a confession, judging that was the true path to be followed when one wants to come near the divine Majesty" (Ramos Gavilán 203). Here we see an assimilated, completely internalized form of faith that is neither forced nor coerced. The offerings are freely given. Let us recall that in the earlier miracle of the possessed Indian, Domingo, the mass for the restoration of his health had been initiated by Father Montoro.

The last miracle in Ramos Gavilán's compilation recounts circumstances surrounding the festival of Corpus Christi in 1618. The Indian leaders in Copacabana petitioned the convent to join the procession as an Indian contingent, imitating the Spaniards, "carrying torches around the Lord's Image." The Indians did not receive an immediate answer, because the priests were not sure about the appropriateness of the request. But the next day, the candles of the Holy Sacrament appeared lit "como aprobando el Señor con este milagro lo que los Indios trataban" [as if the Lord were approving with this miracle what the Indians were requesting]. In light of these events, the Spaniards and the Indians emerged as one body during the *Octavario* procession, sharing solidarity in the faith.

It is therefore evident that Ramos Gavilán proposes in his series of miracles that the evangelizing mission would only succeed in Christianizing the Andean world by following the model of cooperation offered in Saint Augustine's *City of God*. His compilation illustrates the progress of the Indians' faith and how its acquisition was a slow process of internalization and appropriation.

Ramos Gavilán's miracles offer an exemplary history of the Christianization of the Titicaca region and present an alternative model for missionary work which differed significantly from the official policy of extirpation. Clearly, Ramos Gavilán realized that the destruction of idols and other punitive measures, in which he had earlier participated, were not the most efficacious ways to attract the Indians to Christianity. It was only possible to inspire the true faith within them once they had appropriated Christian discourse in a manner which connected with their Andean past. Instead of having to reject the forms of Christian piety, it was possible to make them their own once they could see that they were an evolution of their former beliefs.

CONTINUITY OF THE SACRED AT LAKE TITICACA: FROM VIRACOCHA TO THE VIRGIN OF COPACABANA

In the story of the Apostle, the Christian narrative cycle appropriates the myth of Viracocha and converts it into a Christian account. Yet the Apostle does not assume all the functions attributed to Viracocha by the different versions of the creation myth. At the cosmic level, Viracocha or Tunupa represent an organizing or creative deity in creation myths. The Apostle never possesses these attributes, because creative functions are reserved for the Christian God. In addition, the Apostle does not replace the protective, life-giving functions attributed to the solar divinity; these are represented by Christ on a spiritual level.

The Apostle's functions are in fact similar to those attributed in several versions to the Incas, whose efforts were destined to achieve social order. However, unlike the Incas, the Apostle is only a divine agent and does not exhibit the divinity that the Incas claimed by calling themselves the children of the Sun. The Apostle's functions partially overlap with those of Viracocha/Tunupa and those of the Incas, but the fact that the figure of the Apostle could not completely overshadow Tunupa explains why he survived in the oral local tradition.[125]

The case of the Virgin of Copacabana is analogous to the Apostle's in certain aspects and different in others. As discussed in Chapter 1, the Virgin of Copacabana partially shares attributes of the Pachamama. However, the oppositions between these two hierophanies made it impossible for the Virgin to assimilate all of the earth goddess's functions. As a result, Pachamama has maintained a place in Andean worship which the Virgin of Copacabana could not fill.

However, the Virgin did replace other deities in the Titicaca region and slowly appropriated their functions. The first miracles of the Virgin of Copacabana tell of her power to produce rain in order to water the fields. This was the primary function of the idol Copacati, whom Indians petitioned during times of drought (Ramos Gavilán 103). As the miracles of the Virgin of Copacabana took root in Andean culture, these other idols lost their relevance: the *huacas* were silenced forever. The only remaining testimonials of these *huacas* are carved in the stones that archeologists have discovered centuries later. As the discourse maintained its power as a reflection of the new social order, it also asserted itself in the divine order of the new hierophany—the Virgin of Copacabana.

Conclusion

The sacred history of Lake Titicaca incorporates myths and narratives from the various cultures that have thrived upon its shores from pre-Inca times until the enthronement of the Virgin of Copacabana at the end of the sixteenth century. The different versions of the Andean myths compiled by chroniclers during the sixteenth and seventeenth centuries may be perceived as a polyphonic chorus which apparently lacks an underlying harmony. In them, different voices are confused and intermingled. I have attempted here to confront the textual evidence and separate out the different voices in order to offer an explanation for this confusion.

Once a story is passed on, stasis is impossible. An analysis of the different versions of the creation myth demonstrates that each one offers a unique interpretation of the myths narrated to the chroniclers by their informants. These interpretations are shaped by different perspectives as well as by specific intentions. In certain cases the chroniclers superimpose European frames of reference; they try to adapt the narratives that they heard from indigenous sources to a Christian or, at least, European perspective in an effort to make them understandable. In other cases, certain local versions of the myth emphasize specific villages and regions as fundamental sites within the narrative to gain notoriety for the inhabitants, to support claims to their special status, or even to denigrate an ethnic group or polity in a given place. In my analysis, I have tried to identify all of these interpretations. In doing so, I have demonstrated that a concept of divine order, much more abstract than the chroniclers wanted to admit, lies below the surface of the pan-Andean myth of creation. Concepts and ideas that belong to Andean culture are transformed into characters and actions which mimic everyday life because the narrative itself demands it. The pan-Andean creation myth manifests a cosmic perspective. Mankind is an integral part of this vast picture and emerges without a specific ethnicity. The primordial site for the entire creation in the pan-Andean creation myth is Lake Titicaca. The creator's presence at the lake confers to it a sacred character that throughout time is maintained, revitalized, and resignified by the particular contents of each of the different creeds and beliefs brought to the region.

In contrast to the pan-Andean myth of creation, the Inca myth of origin associates one specific ethnic group with Lake Titicaca. As with the myth of creation, the different versions of the Inca origin myth are narrated from a European frame of reference foreign to the culture that is their source. There is also an attempt to authorize certain versions and delegitimize others. The Inca myth of origin focuses on one particular ethnic group which it connects with the sacred order. The link between the Incas and the divine order allowed the Incas to justify discursively the imposition of their hegemony throughout the entire area which had been influenced by the myth of creation. The particularization of the myth of origin with respect to the myth of creation occurs at another level—within the Inca ethnic group itself. The privileged family descends from the brothers Ayar, who originated the royal *panaca*. They are called upon to govern the other members of the Inca ethnic group and other ethnic groups as well.

Each one of these cycles refers to a different level of reality. However, these cycles are not consecutive, but rather simultaneous, showing varying levels of specificity. The mythic cycle of creation refers to the entire cosmos. Within that cosmos the Inca narrative cycle distinguishes and elevates the Inca ethnic group on the social level. This group, in turn, privileges the royal *panaca* of the brothers Ayar on a political level.

With the advent of Christianity new stories appear that associate Lake Titicaca with Christianity. This narrative cycle presents an appropriation and a recontextualization of discourses and attempts the substitution and replacement of Andean contents by Christian ones.

All of the narrative cycles refer to some type of chaos upon which a divinity or a divine representative must impose order. Viracocha or Tunupa impose order on a cosmic chaos, the Incas achieve a civilizing order, the brothers Ayar install a political order, and the Apostle and the Virgin of Copacabana seek to impose a Christian moral order.

Through appropriations and recontextualizations, the discourse of each one of these narratives is not only a polyphonic or multivoiced discourse; it also unveils an ambiguity that allows multiperspective interpretations from opposing points of view, which can often produce antithetical results. The narratives in the Kolla cycle speak of a cosmic chaos upon which their god, Viracocha or Tunupa, imposes a natural order; the Inca expansion interrupts this state of order. From the Kolla perspective, the narratives in the first cycle would speak of a golden age before the Incas. The discourse generated by these same narratives during the Inca hegemony would be discourses of both longing and resistance. The Inca narratives interpret the Kolla period as chaotic; they justify the subjection of the Kolla people and create a discourse of domination. At the same time, when the Inca and Kolla narratives confront the Spanish conquest and colonial occupation, they become discourses of resistance and of longing for the Inca empire.

The Christian narratives experience a similar phenomenon with regard to the earlier historical periods. By interpreting these cultures as morally chaotic, the Christian narrative justifies the imposition of a new order. The logic behind the Christian justification parallels that of the earlier narrative cycles. The Christian narrative transforms itself into a discourse of domination from the perspective of the earlier cycles. However, from the perspective of Christian doctrine, the future implied within these narratives presents an eschatology that generates a discourse of hope out of the promise of eternal salvation.

By recontextualizing the earlier narrative cycles, each cycle tries to erase the discontinuities and historical gaps that a new cultural age could produce. The new stories justify the coming of a new social order by directly linking it to a divine order. This is possible because each narrative cycle preserves the relationship among the natural, social, and divine orders, a relationship whose fundamental and unmoving center is Lake Titicaca.

The ambivalence and polysemy of these stories are the characteristics that distinguish the representation of the sacred in the Andes, which perhaps can be extended to all aspects of cultural production. Ramos Gavilán was one of the few who recognized the importance of establishing a continuity between the Christian present and the Andean past in order to achieve the goals of evangelization in the New World. His *Historia* constitutes a written cultural project that opposed the official policy of the extirpation of idolatry that dominated the final decades of the sixteenth century and the beginnings of the seventeenth century in the Andes and attempted to build on the past rather than destroy it.

Appendix: Tito Yupanqui's Letter

Tito Yupanqui's letter is written in a Spanish that perhaps has a Quechua syntactic substratum. That is, the Spanish text is composed within a Quechua syntactic structure. It is difficult to understand for most Spanish-speaking persons. Here the Spanish original was kept with all the errors in the manuscript, and an effort was made in translating his letter into English to keep it very close to the original, without any emendations beyond punctuation.

TEXT

El primer vez que lo impesabamos, don Felipe de Lion mi hermano con mego, on echora del vergen di barro, di on vara di grande, in timpo di on patre quelrrigo, llamado Antonio di Almeda, que mi lo dexo poneldo in altar, in dondi lo estaba mas que su año con medio, y despues lo vino otro patre llamado bachiller Montoro, que lo vendo esto me hichora que no ista mejor di bueno, que me lo saque mala para voz, y me lo sacaron in el sacristia y dispues disto nos afligivamos y lo hablavamos y yo con mi hirmano, Don Alonso di Viracocha Inca, in il oficio di intallado para que lo aprendiremos mucho ben, y dispoes di cuando que nos fuemos incontramos a don Alonso Viracocha Inca mi hirmano, se olgo di merarmi vendome, yo lo dije como lo fue di aque moynado del sorte que echava me obra el patre, y le conte el enojamento lo dixera me lo posiera al oficial di intallado mas que bueno milo inseñara para la intalladura, y me lo dixo que mucho in hora di bueno, y nos fuemos andando y melo llevo in la casa di on mastro que lo llamavan dego di ortez, y me lo dicaron para que lo aprindera de aprindes, dispoes di quando lo sabibamos on poco di algo di intalladura, me lo fui a ondi istava con el mi hirmano don Alonso Viracocha Inca, y dispoes disto lo dixe que lo es oficio facil, que yo lo entiendo que lo impesaria on hechora del Vergen, y lo dixo me hirmano que mucho in ora di bueno y que fueramos todos los Natorales a ver los hechoras del Vergen, para sacallo di alli pareciendo buena y lo

177

anduvimos meramdolo los Eclesias ono para ono, y dispues acirtabamos
en la Eclesia dil Santo Domenco, y con on hechora dista vergen dil propio sorte dil ropage, e dil neño, e dilo grandura con so candela y di la
mesma manera le traemos, y dispoes disto nos poncamos a hazer el
molde di barro todos tres, e don Felepe, e don Alonso nos ponemos a
hacer il molde, si lo acabamos como oy y a por il mañana estava que-
brado, e dispues lo tornamos a hacer otra vez y se tornava a quebrar, e
otra vez lo hazeamos, e assi se haze a mas de tres, o quatro vezes y assi
nos pessava mucho yo lo rogava a Dios, con el Vergen, y nos encome-
navamos para que este hechora se saliesse bueno, lo mande dezir un
missa di Santessema Trenedad, para que se saliesse bueno este hechora, e
dispoes disto lo trabajamos con lienzo y dispoes lo sacamos y lleve al
maestro Dego di Ortiz para que lo mirara si lo iba bueno o malo,
paraque me lo dexera si lo tenea falta, o mal hechora y me lo dezo bendo
el vulto que lo era bueno y me lo dexo que lo aprendia mocho di bien, no
me lo dexo mas, e yo lo lleve en casa de los pentores, para saber que me
lo dizen los pentores y loego me lo dexeron los pentores que esta mexo-
rada, e que era mal hecha y otros lo dexeron que era bien hecho, esto me
lo dexeron los pentores, e me lo queseron engañar, por que estava el Imagen acabado, e blanqueado que no lo faltava sino ponerlo con oro, logo
fui a Choquisaca a pedir el licencia de il Señor Obespo para cofradia di
nuestra Señora, e ser pentor e hazaer boltos, e lo leve un Imagen del Vergen pentada en tabla para presentarla a la Señora que lo presente, con un
peticion que lo dezia que quiero ser pentor, e hazer los hechores dil Vergen, e melo respondio que no lo quiero dar la licencia para que lo seays
pentor, ne que lo hayays las hechoras del Vergen, ni vultos, y si lo
quereys ser pentor pintaldo la mona con so mico, que no os lo quiero dar
el licencia para pentor e si vol lo pintays, y lo hazeys vultos di la Vergen
que yo os lo castigare muy bien, e lo sali dezendo JESUS Santa MARIA
valame Dios con el Vergen so matre, que me lo dexeron no estaba bien el
imagen, e que lo parece como hombre y lo esta con sus barbas quelo
parece barbas, e lo hecharon mocha falta que no es boena, e me lo dexeron que no lo haga no lo haga e dispoes di quando lo avia visto el Imagen
la Señoria, lo rieron mocho todos e los dimas echando el falta al pentor,
e lo meravan quando lo tenian con sus manos, e me lo tomava cada un
Español, o lo reya di merarlo, e me lo dexeron que los Natorales no se
poeden hazer el Imagenes del Vergen, ne voltos y luego estove medio des-
mayado, e lo fue espantado amohenado porque lo toxe el Imagen ante el
Obespo para que lo riera, e luego lo fue a la Ecclesia para pedir la
meserecordea di nostro Siñior para acertar el pintadura de la Emagen di
nostra Señiora y lo dimas, pedendo en me oracion licencia para alcanzar

este obra, e me lo disse mano para hazer voltos, e para ser buen pentor, e dispoes nos lo venimos todos a Chuquiabo e traemos el Vergen con dos Natorales, e passamos en todos los tambos e llegamos en el pueblo di hayoyaho al cabeldo de las casas, y lo queremos dormir in ellas, e vono el Corregidor, e me lo querian echar aporreado, para que lo traeys a esta esta casa este defundo, e dispoes que lo dexera, que era un echora del Vergen me lo dexaron dormir essa noche alli, por la mañana nos vamos yendo a Chuquiabo, e llegamos a nostracasa, e de ella vamos a boscar on mastro para que lo acabemos, e lo hagamos mas mejor di bueno el hechora dil Vergen y dispoes que fuemos al San Francesco lo topamos con on mastro que lo dezian Vargas, que me lo dexo, que lo ayude el retablo y me lo ayudara mucho di buena gana hazer el Vergen y todo lo demas si me lo comprays el oro para el Emagen, de alli lo llevamos al celda del padre predecador, llamado fray de Navarrete, y por el mandato del Corregidor llevamos a Copacabana la Vergen, aun que los Naturales no lo querian recebir el Santa Vergen, e lo dexeron que lo avian di traer otro Emagen bueno di Lima o Castilla, o estuvo en Tiquina el Emagen en el capilla de San Petro on poco di tempos, e despoes que llegado el Corregidor don Geronimo del Marañon lo queria entrar en la capilla y se lo alzaron sus cabellos, fue a Copacabana y lo dexo al cazique, que troxese diez hermagos para que lo trogessen al Vergen y los embio antes de oracion y lo llegaron antes di horas di dormer y lo aderezaron sos andas y salieron en cantando los gallos e tomaron a costas el Vergen y lo llegaron a este pueblo assi como el Sol queria yr saliendo, todos los gentes salemos a ver como venea el Vergen lo posimos el Vergen al pie dil cerro como lo baxabamos il baxada, lo acodian todos los gentes, y sos trompetas y traemos in la porcesion, y el patre lo istava aguardando foyra diste pueblo, visitado para dicir la misa, y con el josticia el corrigedor que lo llevo el pindon di la Vergen, y ansi lo intro in la Eclesia, y lo poso a onde istaba il Vergen, y ay lo poso en so dia, y lo dexo so mesa.

TRANSLATION

The first time that I and my brother, don Felipe de Lion, started to carve an image of the Virgin in clay, of about a vara in length, at the time when a priest by the name of Antonio de Almeda was there, and who told me to put it on the altar, where it was for over a year and a half. Later came another priest named bachiller Montoro who upon seeing my work said it was not as good, that I should take it out, and they took it out to the sacristy. After this we were very sad; and my brother and I talked [to] Alonso Viracocha Inca about the art of carving so that we would learn it very well, and after, when we left, we met Alonso Viracocha Inca my brother, who was very happy to see me, and I said to him how saddened I was because of the priest's evaluation of my work, and I told him about my distress and asked him to put me with the best carver so he could teach me the art, and he congratulated me, and we left and he took me to the house of a master carver by the name of Diego de Ortiz, and they spoke to him for me so that I could be his apprentice. Later when we knew something about carving, I went where he was with my brother Don Alonso Viracocha Inca, and told him that it was an easy art, and that I understood it, and that I would start an image of the Virgin, and he congratulated me and said that we, all the Natives should go to see the different statues of the Virgin, to copy one that seemed good and we went from church to church, until we finally got to Saint Domingo's, where we found an image similar to the one we finally made, with the same dress, with a baby Jesus, and with a candle of the same size, after that all three of us started to make a mold in clay, and Don Felipe and Don Alonso and I started doing the mold, and when we finished it during the day, the next morning it was broken, so we made it again and it broke again, and again we made it, so we made it three or four times, and we were so saddened. I was praying to God, with the Virgin, asking for their help so that this image would come out well, and I ordered a mass to the Holy Trinity, asking that this image would come out fine, and after this we painted it in a canvas and we took it to Master Diego de Ortiz for him to see if it was good or bad, so that he would tell me if it had faults, or was badly made, and he said, seeing the image, that it was good and that I had learned the art very well, and said no more. And I took it to the house of the painters and they told me that it had improved greatly, that it was badly made but some others said to me that it was well made. That is what the painters said, as they wanted to deceive me, because the Image was finished, and whitewashed, and the only thing left to do was to gild it. Later I went to Chuquisaca to ask the Bishop for permission to found a brotherhood of Our Lady, and to be a painter and sculptor of images, and I took an image of the Virgin painted in a wooden board to show him the image. And I showed it to him with a petition telling him that I wanted to be a painter, and to make images of the Virgin. And he answered that he did not want to give me license to become a painter, nor to carve images of the Virgin, nor other images, and if I wanted to be a painter I should paint monkeys with their babies, and if I made images of the Virgin he would punish me severely. I left crying JESUS [sic], Holy MARY [sic], God and his Mother have mercy on me. For they told me that the image was not well made, and that it looked like a man, bearded, or with what looked like a beard, and they found many faults in it. They said it was not good, that I should not make it, and after his lordship saw the image, they laughed a lot, he [the bishop] and all the rest, blaming the painter. Each of the Spaniards took it in his hands, and looked at it, laughing upon seeing it, and they said that the natives cannot make Images of the Virgin, nor sculpt them. I was then dismayed, shocked, and annoyed because I had brought the image to the bishop not for them to laugh at it. So I went to the Church to asked our Lord's mercy to help me paint the image of Our Lady and the rest, asking in my prayer license to be able to do this work. So we came to Chuquiabo and we brought the Virgin with two natives, and stopped in the inns, and arrived to the town of Ayoayo, and we wanted to sleep in the house of the *cabildo*, and the *Corregidor* came and wanted to kick us out, saying that we had brought to that house a dead body, and after I told him that it was an image of the Virgin he allowed me to spend the night there, in the morning we left for Chuquiabo and we arrived home, and from there we went to search for a master to help us finish it and to make it better. We went to Saint Francis and there we found a master named Vargas, who said to me that if I helped him in the work he was doing on the altar he would be glad to help me finish the image if I bought the gold for [gilding] the image. So we took the image to the cell of the father preacher, by the name of Navarrete, and following orders of the Corregidor we took the Virgin to Copacabana although the Natives did not want to receive the Holy Virgin, and they said that they were going to bring another good image from Lima or Castile. And the image was for some time in the chapel of Saint Peter in Tiquina, and after the *Corregidor*, Don Geronimo de Marañon, arrived and wanted to enter into the chapel, his hairs were raised, and he went to Copacabana and told the Cacique to bring ten brothers to bring the Virgin and he sent them before dawn and they arrived before the sleeping hour and we set the image over a pedestal and as soon as the cocks crowed we lifted the image and we came to the town when the sun was coming out; all the people came out to see how the Virgin was coming, and we put the Virgin at the skirt of a hill; as we were going down the hill people came, with their trumpets and we brought the image in a procession. And the priest was waiting outside the town, to say mass, and with the justices and the *corregidor* carrying the Banner of the Virgin and so we entered the Church, and we put the Virgin on Her day and left it on top of the table.

Notes

Chapter 1

1. For my own work on "sacred spaces" I am indebted to the works of Mircea Eliade and Gerardus Van der Leeuw.

2. For geological, archeological and ethnohistorical information on Lake Titicaca, see Bouysse Cassagne (1988) and Bandelier (1910). Bandelier's book remains an excellent source for geographical and archeological data on Lake Titicaca despite its biased and derogatory comments about the region's inhabitants.

3. All translations are my own unless otherwise noted.

4. Illimani is a peak in the Bolivian Andes which is 6,710 meters high. The city of La Paz lies at its base.

5. I discuss in more detail Ramos Gavilán's program of evangelization in Chapter 4.

6. For a complete study of the abolition of idolatry, see Duviols 1977.

7. In addition to my own field work on the worship of the Virgin of Copacabana, I have relied as well on Elías's useful research on this topic.

8. The Indian practice of celebrating a religious feast with traditional instruments and dances was prohibited during the colonial period because it was interpreted as a continuation of idolatrous rites.

9. For the political and historical implications of the division between the Anansaya and the Urinsaya, see Rostworowski (1988) and MacCormack (1984).

10. In Chapter 4 I discuss in more detail the dispute between the Urinsaya and the Anansaya.

11. The entire text of Tito Yupanqui's letter is transcribed and translated in the appendix.

12. That this dual religious system has continued to exist to the present day is attested to by the vast scholarship on the subject. Hans Van der Berg in *La tierra no da así nomás* examines exhaustively the pre-hispanic agricultural rituals in present-day Catholic Aymara communities. He postulates that the ancient religion and Catholicism coexist in an integrated religious system. In his chapter "Religión aymara" in *La cosmovisión aymara*, Van der Berg discusses the underlying autochthonous religiosity in today's Aymara Catholics and Protestants. Denise Y. Arnold, Domingo Jiménez, and Juan de Dios Yapita, in their *Hacia un*

orden andino de las cosas, have researched the Andean cosmic order in songs, legends, and textiles. Gabriel Martínez's *Una mesa ritual en Sucre* provides a semiotic analysis of hybrid rituals and is an excellent source for the study of the interweaving of Christian and Andean religious traditions. Eduardo López Rivas, *Cultura y religión en el Altiplano Andino,* traces to the pre-Hispanic past animal sacrifices (llamas and alpacas) performed presently. Juan van Kessel, *Cuando arde el tiempo sagrado,* discusses the cultural continuity of Aymara religious vision in the Tarapacá vision. Tomás Huanca's *El Yatiri en la comunidad aymara* is an invaluable source on the officiants of Aymara rituals: the Yatiri, who mediates between the Andean deities and the community, and the Riwutu who mediates between the world of the death and the living. Manuel M. Marzal, Xavier Albó, and Bartomeu Meliá, demonstrate that the Quechua, Aymara, and Guaraní religions are very much present in the Catholicism brought by the Spaniards five centuries ago.

13. *Mamapacha* is another name by which the Pachamama is known.

14. For studies of similar phenomena in Spain, see Christian.

15. On the cult of the Virgin Mary, see Warner.

16. I discuss this tension in some detail in Chapter 4.

Chapter 2

17. In one way or another, all of the narratives that I analyze deal with the representation of the sacred. In order to avoid unnecessary repetitions, I will refer to them simply as narratives.

18. This affirmation is valid for religious peoples. However, in cultures where religion lacks importance, it is not religious, but ideological.

19. Some colonial texts, as we shall see in due course, support my view.

20. On the archeology and the history of the Titicaca region along with their connection with the Inca empire, see Julien. For a broader study of the region, see Bouysse Cassagne 1988.

21. Bouysse Cassagne explains that during the colonial period the term could refer both to the inhabitants of the Kollasuyo without any differentiation between ethnic groups and to the pre-Inca ethnic polity whose capital, Hatuncolla, was located on the shores of Lake Titicaca. (1988, 54–69)

22. Bouysse Cassagne, who studies in great detail the different cultures that occupied Lake Titicaca, uses archeological and geological data to demonstrate the religious and political importance of the region. She also takes into account linguistic and ethnic factors that corroborate historical facts.

23. The different versions of the story about Viracocha that I consider come from the following authors:

1. Bartolomé de Las Casas (1550)
2. Juan de Betanzos (1551)
3. Pedro de Cieza de León (1553)
4. Pedro Sarmiento de Gamboa (1572). Two versions: Version I: 40–44; Version II: 44.

5. Cristóbal de Molina, el Cusqueño (1575)
6. Pedro Gutiérrez de Santa Clara (end of sixteenth century)
7. José de Acosta (1590). Two versions: Version I: 63–64; Version II: 219–220.
8. Joan de Santacruz Pachacuti Yamqui (1613)
9. Antonio de la Calancha (1637)
10. Bernabé Cobo (1653). Five versions: Version I: 149–150; Version II: 150; Version III: 151; Version IV: 151; Version V: 151.

24. José de Acosta refers to a "Viracocha" as if the name were a generic reference to a hero or a deity.
25. Eventually the word came to mean simply "señor." This is how it is currently used by the campesinos of the Bolivian highlands.
26. See Urbano 1981, xxxiii–xxiv.
27. Fernando Cervantes discusses the same pattern in Mesoamerican religion, where "negative and destructive forces were not the enemies of positive and constructive ones. Both were essential components of the Cosmos. Life came from death; creation from destruction." (Cervantes 41)
28. On this, see Pease (182).
29. This is how Betanzos (1551), Cristóbal de Molina (1575), and José de Acosta II (1590) identify him, and it is one of the names that Santa Cruz Pachacuti Yamqui (1613) attributes to the hero.
30. According to Cristóbal de Molina, el Cusqueño (1575), this is the name of one of the sons of Pachayachachi or Tecsi Viracocha.
31. In Cristóbal de Molina, el Cusqueño, this is Pachayachachic's younger son.
32. In Las Casas (1550), Taguapica Viracocha appears as the evil son of Condici Viracocha. However, Cieza states that Tuapaca was the name given to Ticiviracocha in the Kollao. Sarmiento de Gamboa (1572) assigns this name to one of the three men that Viracocha Pachayachachi saved from the flood; this man later blasphemed against Viracocha. One of the many names that Santa Cruz Pachacuti Yamqui gives to the hero is Tarapaca, which could also be Taguapaca, since the spellings differ greatly in the different texts.
33. On Andean sexual practices, see Cáceres who discusses sexuality from pre-Hispanic times to the present. See also Millones and Pratt.
34. See, for example, *Pequeño Larousse ilustrado*.
35. We will observe this process of "Christianization" during the third narrative cycle, in my discussion of the Christian stories associated with Lake Titicaca.
36. See Imbelloni, who has studied the different *pachacuti* which have been mentioned by the chroniclers. He studies them as different ages or "suns" in Andean culture. This temporal marker can also be used in the periodization that Guamán Poma proposed.
37. On the hierarchizing function of language in the area, see Bouysse Cassagne (1987).
38. I will have more to say about the association between Viracocha and fire when I discuss the versions by Santa Cruz Pachacuti and Sarmiento de Gamboa.

39. For example, in his rendering of the different places of worship in the Tawantinsuyo, Cobo states that on the road to the *Antisuyo*, along the first "ceque" (lines used by the Incas to divide spatially the empire) here was a "huaca" called *Turuca* which was dedicated to Ticciviracocha and on the road to the *Kollasuyo*, along the third "ceque," at the top of a hill called Llulpacturo, there was another (Cobo [1653] 1964, 174–176).

40. Interestingly enough, Molina recognizes the statues as man-made and attributes the myths about these large monolithic statues to a failure of memory and the lack of writing in the culture.

41. I use the term *chaos* not in its pejorative sense, but as denoting an absence of structure.

Chapter 3

42. Pärssinen provides the most comprehensive account of Inca expansion in the Kollasuyo, taking into consideration both historical and anthropological perspectives.

43. The Urus, who spoke Uruquilla, were a culturally and linguistically marginalized group.

44. The consequences of this pact, according to Millones (1987, 97), are mentioned in the hymn compiled by Santacruz Pachacuti. While it makes sense that Millones would cite this hymn to illustrate the alliance between Cari, the Lupaca chief, and Viracocha Inca, Santa Cruz Pachacuti transcribes it from another context: the words are delivered by the chief of the Hatuncolla during a visit to Cuzco (Santacruz Pachacuti 295–296).

45. According to Rowe, Inca Pachacuti was able to conquer only a small part of the Kollasuyu. Yet Pärsinnen, reconciling facts from an impressive amount of sources, proves convincingly that Pachacuti was able to conquer territory that extended much further south than Lake Titicaca (120ff).

46. I use the following versions:

1. Francisco López de Gómara (1552)
2. Agustín de Zárate (1555)
3. Pedro Pizarro (1571)
4. Cristóbal de Molina, "El Cusqueño" (1575)
5. Martín de Murúa (1590)
6. Garcilaso de la Vega (1609). Three different versions: Garcilaso I: 36–42; Garcilaso II: 42–43; Garcilaso III: 43–44.
7. Juan de Santacruz Pachacuti Yamqui (1613)
8. Felipe Guamán Poma de Ayala (1613)
9. Buenaventura de Salinas y Córdova (1630)
10. Antonio Vázquez de Espinosa (1630)
11. Bernabé Cobo (1653). Four different versions: Cobo I: 61–62; Cobo II: 62; Cobo III: 62–63; Cobo IV: 63.

47. The Incan solar cult can be traced to the ancient Tiawanacu celestial high god (Kolata 1993; Bouysse Cassagne 1988; Conrad and Demarest 1984). While

in the earlier Tiawanacu culture the sun might have been one of the elements of a more generalized deity, the Incas gave the Sun god a prominent and singular place in their religion (Conrad and Demarest 1984; Demarest 1981).

48. I quote the version provided by Teodoro Meneses, which Luis Millones considers to be the best translation from the Quechua.

49. For an excellent account of the relationship between some local ethnic cults and the Inca state religion, see MacCormack (1991, 149–159).

50. The *mascaipacha* was a headdress that the reigning Inca wore much like a crown.

51. In Inca temples, the *sanctum sanctorum* was dedicated to the Sun; smaller places of worship were dedicated to other, lesser divinities.

52. The following versions refer to the Incas as *hijos del sol:* Cristóbal Vaca de Castro, Juan de Betanzos, Cieza de León, Hernando de Santillán, Cristóbal de Molina, the version of the Indian lords who served Tupac Yupanqui, Cavello de Valboa, Garcilaso de la Vega I, Guamán Poma, Ramos Gavilán II, Salinas de Córdoba, Antonio Vázquez de Espinoza and Bernabé Cobo's four versions. Those who suggest a supernatural Inca origin without referring to the Sun god are Pedro Pizarro, Polo de Ondegardo, José de Acosta, Garcilaso de la Vega II, Santa Cruz Pachacuti and two versions by Bernabé Cobo.

53. Guamán Poma writes in the same vein.

54. MacCormack interprets the creation of the world and the origin of the Incas as two themes that were seen by Andeans as inseparable (1991, 100). Although it is certainly the way it was for the Inca ethnia, I believe that to ascribe this vision to all Andeans might be problematic, perhaps because the hegemonic power preceding the Spaniards was Inca, and because the state religion was omnipresent in the Tawantinsuyu that most of the compiled versions represent the myth of creation together with the Inca origins. But there is evidence that, as I discuss later, other ethnic myths also narrate their origins in conjunction with the myth of creation.

55. On Toledan policies, the delegitimization of the Incas, and the Lascasian and anti-Lascasian perspectives, see Arthur Franklin Zimmerman, Marcel Batallion, Isacio Pérez Fernández, and Gustavo Gutiérrez.

56. In all sixteen versions the Incas impose order on the other ethnic groups, but this order is not always considered just or legitimate.

57. One might interpret Guamán Poma's periodization of the history of the Indians as a superposition of the Judeo-Christian model. See Pease's introduction to his edition of Guamán Poma's text where he discusses how Guamán Poma's ages correlate with the classical western division of world history.

58. According to Santacruz Pachacuti, *hapiñuñus* were "los enemigos antiguos del género humano, que son los demonios y diablos" [the enemies of humankind, that is demons and devils].

59. Bouysse Cassagne comes to the same conclusion in her analysis of the elements that define the Aymara identity. She discovers a series of relationships between myths and ethnic and spatial divisions in the Aymara world. "Estas representaciones en las que el mundo cósmico y el mundo de los humanos viven en

estrecha dependencia constituyen probablemente uno de los fundamentos del pensamiento aymara. Esta correspondencia aclara muchos aspectos de la lógica del tiempo mítico y de la vida social" [These representations in which the cosmic world and the world of humans have a close interdependency probably constitute one of the foundations of Aymara thought] (1987, 183). The chapters titled "La palabra de los ancestros" and "Del espacio del grupo al espacio individual" in *La identidad Aymara* are particularly interesting.

60. Bouysse Cassagne explains: "El concepto de suyu, que es parte del término . . . [s]uele hacer referencia a una fracción sin tener en cuenta tamaño alguno: designa tanto la parte que le corresponde a un individuo en un trabajo colectivo como la porción de tierra en un reparto, o una de las cuatro divisiones del Imperio . . . Luis Capoche [ha recalcado] la presencia de dos *suyus* en el Collao: 'Y la parte del Collasuyu, . . . se dividía en dos bandos, que llamaron Urcosuyu y Umasuyu, que quiere decir (lo primero) gente que habita en los altos de los cerros, que tienen este nombre urco, y los umasuyu en lo bajo y llano, riberas de las aguas que en esta lengua llaman uma, otros dicen que significan los urcosuyus gente varonil y esforzada, porque por este nombre de urcu se entiende lo masculino, y los umasuyus (lo) femenino' (Luis Capoche, *Relación general de la villa imperial de Potosí.*)" [The concept of *suyu*, part of the term (urcosuyo) . . . usually denotes a fraction without reference to size: it designates the part of a collective task corresponding to an individual in a division of labor, or one of the four divisions of the Empire. . . . Luis Capote [has underscored] the presence of the two *suyus* in the Collao: "And the part of Collasuyu . . . was divided in two parts, called Urcosuyu and Umasuyu, the first meaning people who inhabit the high mountains, called *urco*, and the umasuyu in the lowlands, shores which in this language they call *uma*, others say that urcosuyus means manly and brave people, because the term urcu means 'masculine' and the umasuyus what is feminine"] (1987, 208).

61. This second stage of the journey occurs in almost every variant of the Inca myth of origins, even those versions not considered in this study.

62. Zuidema (1993) discusses the figure of Mama Huaco as a goddess of corn to whom many agricultural festivals were dedicated. These ceremonies survived in a syncretic manner during the colonial period.

63. Urton goes even further. Because of the lack of writing in the Inca empire, the preservation of "their" stories was left to foreigners, and, thus, "one of the more general consequences is that we have, in fact, no true "Inka" myths. All myths and histories purporting to be Incaic were in fact recorded by European (or European-trained) soldiers, chroniclers, and bureaucrats following the entry of the Spaniards into Peru in the early 1530's" (5).

64. This custom continues today as part of the ceremony of the *challa*, to which I have referred earlier.

65. This excellent work studies the different styles, symbolism, and production of precolonial and postcolonial textiles in the Andean region. On the aesthetics and representation of Andean concepts in woven fabrics, also see Cereceda.

66. Cristóbal de Molina and Cristóbal Albornoz compiled an enormous amount of information about the myths and rituals of the Indians, where the role

of agriculture becomes evident. A recent edition prepared by Henrique Urbano and published by Historia 16 in Madrid makes this material readily available to the reader for the first time. For the religious aspects in agriculture or rural farming communities today, see van den Berg.

67. See Platt 1976.

68. This Quechua division of *hanan* and *hurin* corresponds to the Aymara *uma* and *urco*.

69. The names of these characters do not always coincide in the various versions. Sometimes there are just simple spelling differences, but in other cases the names are completely different. For example, Guamán Poma gives the following names for the males: Huana Cauri Ynga, Cuzco Uanca Ynga, Apomancocapac, and Tupa Ayarcochi Ynga. When referring to the story of the Ayar brothers, I follow Murúa and Garcilaso, who seem to use the more standard names.

70. Although *mediodía* in the southern hemisphere refers to the North, Garcilaso says that Pacaritambo is eight leagues to the *mediodía* from Cuzco. Garcilaso, who is using incorrectly the term *mediodía*, is obviously referring to the south, taking the northern hemisphere as his reference point.

71. The different versions do not consistently associate the same hero with the same event. Cieza de León attributes to Ayar Cachi what Murúa says happened to Ayar Auca. Bernabé Cobo "solves" this problem in his second version by not specifying the names; he simply says "one of the brothers." I will follow Murúa.

72. MacCormack (1988) discusses the symbolic meaning of the rainbow in the iconography of colonial Peru from the perspective of both Andean and European culture.

73. According to Guamán Poma, two brothers were captured by the *huaca* and turned into stone.

74. A ceque was a sacred line radiating out ot the center of Cuzco. For a complete discussion of the ceque system, see Zuidema (1964).

75. For a discussion and description of the *capac cocha*, see Sallnow (39 ff.) and MacCormack 1991.

76. It is interesting to note that polygamy began for the Inca in the myth of origin. Only the Inca and those who represented him were allowed to participate in polygamy.

77. Murra discusses the role of corn as a means of social differentiation.

78. On land-related issues among the Incas, see Rostworowski (238–251).

79. For a fine discussion of the means by which the Incas carried out their conquest, see Rostworowski.

80. These ritual practices have survived in the present south-Andean ritual of the *tinku*: a ritual battle performed by rival *ayllus* to ease interethnic tensions. For a detailed analysis of this ritual and its precolonial and colonial roots, see Platt (1987, 61–122).

81. There is a lot of information in the chronicles regarding temples and *huacas* dedicated to Viracocha. Illapa, the thunder god, is closely linked to Viracocha and the Sun, and its cult was extended in the entire Andean region. In the present study Illapa was not discussed since it is not specifically mentioned in the myths.

For Illapa's relation to Viracocha, see Conrad and Demarest (1984), Bouysse Cassagne (1993, 163–180), and Gisbert (1993, 181–202).

82. Urton discusses the Pacaritambo myth from a mythohistorical approach (1–40). He also proves very convincingly how each *ayllu* tries to construct its own legitimizing version of a myth of origin in order to represent continuity with a remote past and gain especial status with the colonial order.

83. For instance, Antonio de la Calancha, in his *Crónica moralizada*, says: "De más de las estatuas de piedra i oro que digimos, en que se davan a entender tenían noticia del misterio inefable de la santísima Trinidad . . ." (769). Other authors, such as Pedro Mártir, Fernández de Oviedo, Gómara, Cieza de León, and Zárate, propose that the similarity between certain Andean beliefs and the Holy Trinity was the work of the Devil.

Chapter 4

84. The Indian warriors who resisted the Spanish belonged to seven different Aymara ethnic groups: the Carangas, Caracaras, Charcas, Chichas, Chuis, Quillacas, Soras, and Yamparaes. See Bouysse Cassagne (1987).

85. In her text *La identidad*, Bouysse Cassagne presents a detailed analysis of the partitioning of land into encomiendas that occurred after the conquest of the Kollao.

86. For example, the Spaniards required the Lupacas to send 2200 men annually to the mines at Potosí. We can see that this number is extremely high if we consider that the total population of Chucuito around 1550 was 14,176. This information is presented in "Relación de algunos repartimientos de los Reinos del Perú de la cantidad de indios que tienen y tributos que han sacado de la visita y tasas primeras que se hizo por mandato del presidente La Gasca" (quoted in Bouysse Cassagne 1987, 94).

87. An *encomendero* was a person who received a royal grant for his service to the Crown. It consisted of the privilege to enjoy some of the Indians' tributes in exchange for protecting them and instructing them in the Catholic faith. For a discussion of the implications and importance of the *encomienda*, see Lockhart.

88. I mentioned these two priests in the first chapter for their role in the creation of the Image of the Virgin of Copacabana.

89. The First Council of Lima took place in 1551. It attempted to unify the methods of evangelization. It required the construction of churches, the celebration of the rites, and the administration of the sacraments. The council also directed the destruction of idolatry—destruction of temples, idols, punishments against Indians who practice idolatry, etc. (Duviols 1977, 97–100).

The Second Council of Lima took place in 1567. At this point, the Church had obtained a great deal of information about the religious practices of the Indians. The reports that the Church received indicated that the Indians continued to practice their ancient rituals, either clandestinely or behind the mask of Christian ritual. The Second Council continued its support of the destruction of temples and idols; however, it modified its position with regard to the treatment shown to the Indians: "se preconiza un método suave" (ibid., 131–132). The Third Council of Lima (1582–1583) ratified the statutes proposed in the Second Council. It also focused on the production of multilingual, didactic materials to aid in the teaching of doctrine (catechisms, books of sermons, and confessors' manuals).

90. The circumstances are unclear surrounding Ávila's discovery of rampant idolatry in Huarochirí, which eventually unleashed the furious campaigns and *Visitas de idolatría*. The Indians of his parish accused him of tremendous abuses and initiated a legal proceeding against him. See Duviols 1977, 177–187.

91. For a complete study of the evangelizing campaigns and the extirpation of idolatry during the viceregal period in Peru, see Duviols (1977).

92. The mummified bodies of the Indians' ancestors.

93. This report is the "Parecer y Arbitrio" by Francisco de Ávila (1616) (Duviols 1977, 190).

94. An example appears during the archbishopric of Hernando Arias Ugarte (1630–1638). This prelate thought that the "idolatries" were more imagined than real. He considered some accusations, like the use of alcohol, to be social problems and not a manifestation of idolatry.

95. In their letters, the Augustinians stated that "deja[ban] constancia que los pueblos que se enc[ontraban] a su cargo esta[ban] extentos de sus vicios, a tal punto que no es posible notar el menor trazo de ellos, a pesar de que las encuestas han sido minuciosamente realizadas" [evidence proved that the towns under their jurisdiction were free of vices, to such an extent that it [was] difficult to find a trace in them, in spite of having punctiliously conducted the surveys] (Duviols 1977, 206).

96. By *criollo* I refer to Europeans born in the New World.

97. Satan as God's imitator was one of the most common tenets of medieval and renaissance demonology. See Ciruelo (1530), Sprenger and Kramer (1486), Michelet (1939), and Caro Baroja (1985). For an excellent account of Acosta's demonology, see Cervantes (25–33).

98. According to Calancha, the clearest case of a change in the pronunciation is in Paraguay, where Tomé is transformed into Zumé. Regarding the name's change of meaning, Calancha follows the biblical model of changing names and meanings—Abraham, Sarah, and Peter are examples. The names by which the Apostle and his disciple are known in the Titicaca region are Tunupa and Taapac, which mean "Maestro Sabio" [wise master] and "hijo del Criador" [son of the creator], respectively.

99. *Newen Zeytung auss Breisillg Landt*, 1508, quoted in Pierre Duviols 1977, 56.

100. Solórzano writes that "all of the Indians discovered so far in this New World, were infidels, and idolaters, . . . they had no knowledge of our true God and Creator, and even less of his precious Son, our Savior and Redemptor Jesus Christ, nor of the evangelical law, nor of Grace, who came to preach to the World, and *this is enough a cause, even if there weren't any other, to wage war on them and deprive and dispossess them of their land and their belongings, taking under the dominium and superior government of the Catholic princes* . . . (91, emphasis added). Sepúlveda was also one of the most important defenders

of Christianization as the justification for waging war against the Indians (Hernández 47). Vitoria, although he defended the natives and found almost no justification in the use of violence to Christianize them, declares that anthropagia and human sacrifices are reasons that would justify a war against those who perpetrate these crimes against innocent people (Vitoria 110).

101. For example, the Dominican friar Francisco de la Cruz was accused of heresy and sent to be burned at the stake in 1578 (Duviols 1977, 270).

102. Bartolomé de Las Casas, *Del único modo de atraer a todos los pueblos a la verdadera religión* (written in 1617, but not published for more than three and a half centuries).

103. For a thorough discussion of Garcilaso's portrayal of Pachacámac, see MacCormack (1991, 342–352).

104. This is a similar stance to the ones displayed by Inca Garcilaso or Guamán Poma, who attempt to fix or fill the void of historical writing through their own texts. On Garcilaso's self-assigned role as scribe and translator of the Incas' version of history, see Zamora. On Guamán Poma's attempt to reconstruct pre-Conquest Andean history, see Adorno (1986).

105. Parts of this section appeared in my 1992 article "The Apostle's Footprints in Ancient Perú: Christian Appropriation of Andean Myths," *Journal of Hispanic Philology*, 16:2.

106. A Castilian *vara* was 0.835 meters.

107. For a discussion on Calancha's historical perspective, see MacCormack (1982).

108. See Chapter 2.

109. It is interesting that Guamán Poma gives the name of Anti Vira Cocha to this first Christian because, like most *mestizo* cultural manifestations in the Andes, the name has two possible readings: In Quechua it would mean "Lord of the Andes," but in Spanish "against Viracocha." In the context of Guamán Poma's work, both are possible. Throughout his text he demands autonomy and perhaps this could hint at the same in the realm of the religious. But he also condemns idolatry, and if Viracocha is taken to represent one of the divinities of the Andean pantheon, his new name in Spanish would mean the debunking of this God.

110. See Adorno's "Icons in Space: The Silent Orator," for the best analysis of Guamán Poma's drawings (80–119). López-Baralt discusses how Guamán Pomas manipulates traditional European *topoi*, especially in his drawings, to "create the first cultural typology purely American" (1983); she also demonstrates how Guamán Poma uses the "strident silence" in his drawings to underscore what at times words cannot convey (1989).

111. *The Golden Legend* or *Legenda Sanctorum* has been the primary hagiographic source since the Middle Ages; see Jacobus de Voragine (1228–1298).

112. Swinton Bland, in his introduction to the English edition of Herolt, narrates a brief history of the tradition of miracles of the Virgin from the eleventh century.

113. For a thorough history of the cult of the Virgin Mary, see Warner.

114. This affirmation is based on the collections of miracles of the Virgin of Guadalupe which were published at the same time as Ramos Gavilán's text; see Diego de Montalvo. It is also based on those miracles cited in the analyses by Alban Forcione and William Christian.

115. During the seventeenth century at least four different authors published collections of miracles of the Virgin of Copacabana: Ramos Gavilán, Calancha (who narrates the miracles as part of his Augustinian chronicle), Gabriel de León, and Andrés de San Nicolás.

116. Borges traces the Christianization efforts from their beginnings. He examines the different stages of the evangelization process and discusses the missionary methods employed in the Christianization of America.

117. The *medida* of the Virgin is a ribbon of the same length as the image. It is believed to have the same miraculous powers as the image itself.

118. From 1570 on, Viceroy Francisco de Toledo made important political reforms which had enormous impact on the lives of many Indians. He ordered a *Visita General* of all the territory with the purpose of taking a census of the territory that had been the Tahuantinsuyo. All males between the ages of 18 and 50, with the exception of the *caciques* and nobles, were subject to taxation. The amount depended on the region's productive capabilities. The *mita* was also part of his reforms. The Potosí mines had been discovered in 1545, but after 1570, with the introduction of quicksilver for the extraction of silver, the demands for labor increased greatly. All males susceptible to taxation from the surrounding region, including the Lake Titicaca area, were obliged to serve periodically in the mines (on the average once every seven years). For instance, Chucuito (the Lake province) had to provide 16 percent of the labor force (López Beltrán 191–225).

119. The myth of Incarrí can be viewed as a representation of the feeling of divestiture that the Indians experienced. The myth of Incarrí tells that "la conquista habría cercenado la cabeza del Inca que desde entonces estaría separada de su cuerpo; cuando ambos se encuentren, terminará ese período de desorden, confusión y oscuridad que iniciaron los europeos y los hombres andinos (los runas) recuperarán su historia" [the conquest had decapitated the Inca and since then the head was separated from his body; when both of them meet, the period of disorder, confusion, and obscurity initiated by the Europeans would end and the Andeans will recover their history] (Flores Galindo 18). Pease points out that the myth of Incarrí circulated during the first several years of the seventeenth century.

120. The title of this section is taken from Sabine MacCormack's excellent article, and in recognition of her enormous contribution to Andean studies, I use it as a tribute to her.

121. The *mitimaes* were state-organized colonizers who were sent by the Incas to settle the conquered territories.

122. I have discussed and summarized this miracle in Chapter 1.

123. Until the image was finally moved to Copacabana, the Urinsaya opposition fought to prevent it from being transported. Gregorio Marañón arbitrated the dispute and convinced the Urinsaya to finally accept the Image.

124. Upon comparing the two images in Figure 3 (appearing in Chapter 1), it is apparent that one Virgin is holding the Child and the other is not. It appears that the figure of the Virgin is composed of two separate parts—the body of the Virgin and the body of the Child. Correcting the error found by Montoro would not have been difficult; however, Ramos Gavilán represents its rectification as a miraculous event.

125. The figure of Tunupa would also inspire a beautiful poetic rendition by Fernando Diez de Medina, who as founder of an "Aesthetic Indigenism" movement elevates the Indian themes and traditions to new philosophical and artistic heights.

Works Cited

Acosta, José de. [1590] 1952. *De Procuranda Indorum Salute*. Ed. Francisco Mateos. Madrid: I. G. Magerit.

———. [1590] 1985. *Historia natural y moral de las Indias*. Ed. Edmundo O'Gorman. México: FCE.

Adorno, Rolena. 1986. *Guamán Poma: Writing and Resistance in Colonial Peru*. Austin: University of Texas Press.

Albornoz, Cristóbal. 1989. *Instrucción para descubrir todas las guacas del Piru y sus camayos y haziendas*. In *Fábulas y mitos de los incas,* ed. Henrique Urbano and Pierre Duviols. Madrid: Historia 16.

Anónima. [1615] 1968. *Relación de las costumbres antiguas de los Naturales del Pirú,* ed. Francisco Esteve Barba. Madrid: Atlas.

Arguedas, José Maria. 1976. *Señores e Indios: acerca de la cultura quechua*. Lima: Arca.

Arnold, Denise Y., Domingo Jiménez, and Juan de Dios Yapita. 1992. *Hacia un orden andino de las cosas*. La Paz: Hisbol.

Arriaga, Pablo Joseph de. [1621] 1920. *La extirpación de la idolatría en el Perú*. Ed. Horacio H. Urteaga. Lima: Sanmartí y Cía.

Bandelier, Adolph F. 1910. *The Islands of Titicaca and Koati*. New York: Hispanic Society of America.

Batallion, Marcel. 1965. *Etudes sur Bartolomé de Las Casas*. Paris: Centre de Recherches de l'Institut d'Etudes Hispaniques.

Bertonio, Ludovico. [1612] 1984. *Vocabulario de la lengua Aymara*. Facsimile edition. Cochabamba: Ediciones Ceres.

Betanzos, Juan de. [1551] 1987. *Suma y narración de los Incas*. Madrid: Atlas.

Bland, C. C. Swinton. 1928. "Translator's Preface." In Herolt, 1–8.

Borges, Pedro. 1960. *Métodos misionales de la cristianización de América, siglo XVI*. Madrid: CSIC.

Bouysse Cassagne, Thérése. 1987. *La identidad aymara: Aproximación histórica (siglo XV, siglo XVI)*. La Paz: Hisbol.

———. *Lluvias y cenizas: Dos Pachacuti en la Historia*. 1988. La Paz: Hisbol.

———. 1993. "*El rayo que no cesa*: d'un Dieu Pukina à un Dieu Inca." In Duviols, *Religions des Andes*, 163–180.

Bouysse Cassagne, Thérése, and Olivia Harris. 1987. "Pacha: En torno al pensamiento aymara." In Bouysse Cassagne et al., 11–59.

Bouysse Cassagne, Thérése, Olivia Harris, Tristan Platt, and Verónica Cereceda. 1987. *Tres reflexiones sobre el pensamiento andino.* La Paz: Hisbol.

Cáceres Velásquez, Artidoro. 1992. *La sexualidad en el Perú pre-Colombino.* Lima: Concytec.

Caillois, Roger. 1959. *Man and the Sacred.* Trans. Meyer Barash. Glencoe, Illinois: The Free Press.

Calancha, Antonio de la. 1974. *Crónica moralizada.* Ed. Ignacio Prado Pastor. Lima: Universidad Mayor de San Marcos.

Caro Baroja, Julio. 1985. *Las formas complejas de la vida religiosa (siglos XVI– XVII).* Madrid: Sarpe.

Cereceda, Verónica. 1987. "Aproximaciones a una estética andina: de la belleza al *tinku.*" In Bouysse Cassagne et al., 133–231.

Cervantes, Fernando. 1994. *The Devil in the New World: The Impact of Diabolism in New Spain.* New Haven: Yale University Press.

Christian, William. 1981. *Apparitions in Late Medieval and Renaissance Spain.* Princeton, N.J.: Princeton University Press.

Cieza de León, Pedro. [1553] 1967. *El señorío de los Incas.* Ed. C. Aranibar. Lima: Instituto de Estudios Peruanos.

———. 1979. *History of the Inca Empire.* Austin: University of Texas Press.

Cirlot, Juan Eduardo. 1982. *Diccionario de símbolos.* Barcelona: Labor.

Ciruelo, Pedro. 1978. *Reprouacion de las supersticiones y hechizerias.* Ed. Alva v. Ebersole. Madrid: Albatrós Hispanófila.

Cobo, Bernabé. [1653] 1964. *Historia del Nuevo Mundo.* Madrid: Atlas.

———. 1979. *History of the Inca Empire.* Trans. Roland Hamilton. Austin: University of Texas Press.

Colón, Cristóbal. 1984. *Textos y documentos completos.* Ed. Consuelo Varela. Madrid: Alianza Universidad.

Concilios Limenses (1551–1772). 1952. Ed. Ruben Vargas Ugarte. 3 vols. Lima: n.p.

Conrad, Geoffrey W., and Arthur A. Demarest. 1984. *Religion and Empire: The Dynamic of Aztec and Inca Expansionism.* London: Cambridge University Press.

Covarrubias, Sebastián de. [1611] 1987. *Tesoro de la Lengua Castellana o Española.* Ed. Martín de Riquer. Barcelona: Sirven Gráfic.

Demarest, Arthur A. 1981. *Viracocha, the Nature and Antiquity of the Andean High God.* Monographs of the Peabody Museum, no. 6. Cambridge, Mass.: Peabody Museum Press.

Diamond, Stanley. 1960. *Culture in History: Essays in Honor of Paul Radin.* New York: Columbia University Press.

Diez de Medina, Fernando. 1990. *Thunupa.* La Paz: Juventud.

Duviols, Pierre. 1977. *La destrucción de las religiones andinas (Conquista y colonia).* Mexico: UNAM.

———. 1986. *Cultura andina y represión.* Cusco: Centro de Estudios Rurales Andinos "Bartolomé de Las Casas."

———. 1993. *Religions des Andes et Langues Indigénes: Equateur—Pérou—Bolivie avant et aprés la Conquete Espagnole.* Aix-en-Provance: Publications del'Université de Provence.

Eliade, Mircea. 1959. *The Sacred and the Profane: The Nature of Religion.* New York: Harcourt, Brace & World.

———. 1963. *Patterns in Comparative Religion: A Study of the Element of the Sacred in the History of Religious Phenomena.* Trans. Rosemary Sheed. New York: The World Publishing Co.

———. 1964. *Tratado de historia de las religiones.* México: Era.

Elías, Julio María. 1981. *Copacauana—Copacabana.* Tarija, Bolivia: Editorial Franciscana.

Espinoza Soriano, Waldemar. 1987. *Los Incas: Economía, sociedad y estado en la era del Tahuantinsuyu.* Lima: Amaru Editores.

Fernández, Isacio Pérez. 1988. *Bartolomé de Las Casas en el Perú.* Cuzco: Centro de Estudios Rurales Andinos "Bartolomé de Las Casas."

Flores Galindo, Alberto. 1985. *Buscando un Inca: Identidad y Utopia en los Andes.* La Habana: Casa de las Américas.

Forcione, Alban K. 1982. *Cervantes and the Humanist Vision: A Study of Four Exemplary Novels.* Princeton, N.J.: Princeton University Press.

Garcilaso de la Vega, Inca. [1609] 1976. *Comentarios reales.* Ed. Aurelio Miró Quesada. Lima: Biblioteca Ayacucho.

———. 1966. *Royal Commentaries of the Incas.* Trans. Harold V. Livermore. Austin: University of Texas Press.

Gisbert, Teresa. 1980. *Iconografía y mitos indígenas en el arte.* La Paz: Gisbert y Cía.

———. 1993. "Pachacamac y los dioses del collao." In Duviols, *Religions des Andes.* 181–202.

Gisbert, Teresa, Silvia Arze, and Martha Cajías. 1987. *Arte textil y mundo andino.* La Paz: Gisbert y Cía.

Gómara, Francisco López de. [1552] 1954. *Historia general de las Indias. Historiadores primitivos de Indias.* Vol. 1. Madrid: Atlas.

Guamán Poma de Ayala, Felipe. 1980. *El primer nueva corónica y buen gobierno.* Ed. John V. Murra and Rolena Adorno. Mexico City: Siglo Veintiuno.

Guardia Mayorga, C. "El enigma del dios Wiracocha." Congreso Nacional de Historia del Perú, Vol. 2, 133–155. Lima: El Centro.

Gutiérres de Santa Clara, Pedro. *Quinquenarios o Historias de las guerras civiles del Perú.* [end of 16th century] 1963. Madrid: Atlas.

Gutiérrez, Gustavo. 1982. "Una teología política en el Perú del siglo XVI," *Allpanchis* 19: 7–29.

Hemming, John. 1970. *The Conquest of the Incas.* New York: Harcourt, Brace, Jovanovich.

Hernández, Ramón. 1993. "Francisco de Vitoria y Bartolomé de Las Casas," *Las Casas entre dos mundos,* 47–74. Cusco: Instituto Bartolomé de Las Casas.

Herolt, Johannes Herolt. 1928. *Miracles of the Blessed Virgin Mary (1435– 1440).* Trans. C. C. Swinton Bland. London: George Routledge & Sons.

Holguín, D.G. [1592]. *Vocabulario.*

Huanca, Tomás. 1989. *El Yatiri en la comunidad aymara.* La Paz: Hisbol.

Hyslop, John. 1976. "Archaeological Investigation of the Lupaca Kingdom and Its Origins." Doctoral dissertation, Department of Anthropology, Columbia University, New York.

Imbelloni, José. 1979. *Religiosidad indígena americana.* Buenos Aires: Castañeda.

Julien, Catherine J. 1983. *Hatunqolla: A View of Inca Rule from the Lake Titicaca Region.* Berkeley: University of California Press.

Kessel, Juan van. 1992. *Cuando arde el tiempo sagrado.* La Paz: Hisbol.

Kolata, Alan. 1993. *The Tiwanaku: Portrait of an Andean Civilization.* Cambridge, Mass.: Blackwell.

Lara, Jesus. 1976. *La cultura de los Inkas.* 2nd ed. La Paz: Los Amigos del Libro.

Las Casas, Bartolomé de. *Apologética historia* [1550] 1909. Madrid: Bailly Balliére e hijos.

———. 1975. *Del único modo de atraer a todos los pueblos a la verdadera religión.* México: FCE.

———. 1992. *The Only Way.* Ed. Helen Rand Parish. Trans. Francis Patrick Sullivan. New York: Paulist Press.

León, Gabriel de. 1663. *Compendio del origen de la Esclarecida y Milagrosa Imagen de N.S. de Copacabana, Patrona del Perú.* Madrid: María de Aragón.

Lockhart, James. 1994. *Spanish Peru: 1532–1560. A Social History.* 2nd ed. Madison: University of Wisconsin Press.

López-Baralt, Mercedes. 1989. "La estridencia silente: oralidad, escritura e iconografía en la Nueva Coronica de Guamán Poma," *La Torre* 3(2): 609–649.

———. 1983. "La iconografía de vicios y virtudes en el arte de reinar de Guaman Poma de Ayala: Emblemática política al servicio de una tipologia cultural americana." *Dispositio* 8(22–23): 101–122.

López Beltran, Clara. 1988. *Estructura económica de una sociedad colonial: Charcas en el siglo XVII.* La Paz: Ceres.

López Rivas, Eduardo. 1976. *Cultura y religión en el Altiplano andino.* La Paz: Editorial Los Amigos del Libro.

MacCormack, Sabine. 1982. "Antonio de la Calancha: Un agustino del siglo XVII en el Nuevo Mundo." *Bulletin Hispanique* 84: 60–94.

———. 1984. "From the Sun of the Incas to the Virgin of Copacabana." *Representations* 8: 30–59.

———. 1988. "Miracles, Punishments, and Last Judgement: Visionary Past and Prophetic Future in Early Colonial Perú," *American Historical Review* 93: 960–1006.

———. 1991. *Religion in the Andes: Vision and Imagination in Early Colonial Peru.* Princeton, N.J.: Princeton University Press.

Martínez, Gabriel. 1987. *Una mesa ritual en Sucre: Aproximaciones semióticas al ritual andino.* La Paz: Hisbol-Asur.

Marzal, Manuel M., Xavier Albó, and Bartomeu Meliá. 1992. *Rostros Indios de Dios.* La Paz: Hisbol.

Meiklejohn, Norman. 1988. *La iglesia y los Lupaqas durante la colonia.* Cusco: Centro de Estudios Rurales Andinos "Bartolomé de Las Casas."

Meneses, Teodoro. 1982. "Himnos quechuas del cronista indio colla Santa Cruz Pachacuti Yamqui Salcamayhua." *Lienzo* (Lima) 3/4: 113–131.

Michelet, Jules. 1939. *Satanism and Witchcraft: A Study of Medieval Superstition.* Trans. A. R. Allison. New York: The Citadel Press.

Millones, Luis. 1987. *Historia y poder en los Andes centrales.* Madrid: Alianza Editorial.

Millones, Luis, and Mary Louise Pratt. 1990. *Amor Brujo: Images and Culture of Love in the Andes.* Syracuse, N.Y.: Syracuse University Press.

Molina, Cristóbal de. [1575] 1988. *Relación de la fabulas i ritos de los ingas.* Ed. Henrique Urbano and Pierre Duviols. Madrid: Historia 16.

Montalvo, Diego de. 1631. *Venida de la Soberana Virgen de Guadalupe a España.* Lisbon: Pedro Craesbeeck.

Montoya Martínez, Jesús. 1981. *Las colecciones de milagros de la Virgen en la Edad Media (El milagro literario).* Granada, Spain: Universidad de Granada.

Murra, John V. 1960. "Rite and Crop in the Inca State." In Diamond, 393–407.

Murúa, Martín de. [1590] 1962. *Historia del origen y genealogía de los reyes incas.* Ed. M. Ballesteros-Gaibrois. Madrid: Biblioteca Americana Vetus.

Otto, Rudolf. 1950. *The Idea of the Holy: An Inquiry into the Non-Rational Factor in the Idea of the Divine and Its Relation to the Rational.* 2nd ed. Trans. John W. Harvey. New York: Oxford University Press.

Paredes, Rigoberto. 1920. *Mitos, supersticiones y supervivencias populares de Boliva.* La Paz: Arno Hermanos.

Pärssinen, Martii. 1992. *Tawantinsuyu: The Inca State and Its Political Organization.* Helsinki: Tiedekirja.

Pease, Franklin. 1973. *El Dios creador andino.* Lima: Mosca Azul.

Pizarro, Pedro. [1570] 1978. *Relación del descubrimiento y conquista de los reinos del Perú.* Ed. G. Lohman Villena. Lima: Fondo Editorial.

Platt, Tristán. 1976. *Espejos y maiz: Temas de la estructura simbólica andina.* La Paz: CIPCA.

———. 1987. "Entre *ch'axwa* y *muxsa*: Para una historia del pensamiento político Aymara." In Bouysse Cassagne et. al., 61–132.

Ponce Sanjinés, Carlos. 1982. *Tunupa y Ekako.* La Paz: Juventud.

Porras Barrenechea, Raúl. 1986. *Los cronistas del Perú (1528–1650).* Lima: DESA.

Ramos Gavilán, Alonso. [1621] 1979. *Historia del celebre santuario de Nuestra Señora de Copacabana, y sus Milagros, è Inuencion de la Cruz de Carabuco.* Lima: Geronimo de Contreras.

Ricardo, Antonio. [1636] 1951. *Vocabulario y phrasis en la lengua general de los indios del Perú, llamada quichua: El más copioso y elegante que hasta agora se ha impreso.* Lima: Universidad Nacional Mayor de San Marcos, Instituto de Historia de la Facultad de Letras.

Rostworowski de Diez Canseco, María. 1988. *Historia del Tahuantinsuyo.* Lima: Instituto de Estudios Peruanos.

Rowe, John H. 1945. "Absolute Chronology in the Andean Area." *American Antiquity* 10(3): 265–284.

———. 1946. "Inca Culture at the Time of Spanish Conquest." In *Handbook of South American Indians.* Ed. J. H. Steward. Vol. 2, The Andean Civilization. Washington, D.C.

Sahagún, Bernardino de. 1988. *Historia general de las cosas de Nueva España.* Madrid: Alianza Universidad.

Salinas y Córdova, Buenaventura de. [1630] 1957. *Memorial de las historias del Nuevo Mundo, Pirú.* Ed. Luis E. Valcarcel. Lima: Clásicos Peruanos.

Sallnow, Michael J. 1987. *Pilgrims of the Andes: Regional Cults in Cusco.* Washington, D.C.: Smithsonian Institution Press.

San Nicolás, Andres de. 1663. *Imagen de N. S. de Copacavana: Portento del Nuevo Mundo.* Madrid: Andrés Garcia de la Iglesia.

Santacruz Pachacuti Yamqui Salcamaygua, Joan de. [1613] 1968. *Relación de antigüedades deste reyno del Perú.* Madrid: Atlas.

Sarmiento de Gamboa, Pedro. [1572] 1943. *Historia de los Incas.* Buenos Aires: Emecé Editores.

Solorzano y Pereyra, Juan de. [1629] 1972. *Política Indiana.* Madrid: Ediciones Atlas.

Sprenger, Jacobus, and Heinrich Kramer. 1968. *Malleus Maleficarum.* Trans. Mantague Summers. London: The Chaucer Press.

Toledo, Francisco de. [1572–1575] 1920. "Informaciones al Virrey Toledo." In *Informaciones sobre el antiguo Perú.* Lima: Col. Lib. Doc. Ref. Historia del Perú, series 2, vol. 3.

Urbano, Henrique. 1981. *Wiracocha y Ayar: Héroes y funciones en las sociedades andinas.* Cusco: Centro de Estudios Rurales Andinos "Bartolomé de Las Casas."

———. 1988. Introduction. *Fábulas y mitos de los incas,* by Cristóbal de Molina and C. de Albornoz. Madrid: Historia 16.

Urton, Gary. 1990. *The History of a Myth: Pacariqtambo and the Origin of the Inkas.* Austin: University of Texas Press.

Van den Berg, Hans. 1990. *La tierra no da así nomás: los ritos agrícolas en la religión de los aymara-cristianos.* La Paz: Hisbol.

Van den Berg, Hans, and Norbert Schiffers. 1992. *La cosmovisión Aymara.* La Paz: Hisbol.

Van der Leeuw, Gerardus. 1938. *Religion in Essence and Manifestation: A Study in Phenomenology.* Trans J. E. Turner. London: George Allen & Unwin.

Vázquez de Espinosa, Antonio. [1630] 1969. *Compendio y descripción de Indias Occidentales.* Madrid: Atlas.

Villanueva Urteaga, Horacio. [1551] 1987. "Juan Diez de Betanzos y el Cuzco." In Betanzos, xxxi–xxxvii.

Villarejo, Avencio. 1965. *Los Agustinos en el Perú y Bolivia.* Lima: Edición Ausonia.

Vitoria, Francisco de. [1539] 1967. *Relectio de Indis.* Ed. L. Pereña and J. M. Pérez Préndes. Madrid: Consejo Superior de Investigaciones Científicas.

Voragine, Jacobus de. 1987. *The Golden Legend.* Trans. Granger Ryan and Helmut Ripperger. Salem, New Hampshire: Longmans, Green.

Walker, Williston, et al. 1985. *A History of the Christian Church.* 4th ed. New York: Scribner.

Warner, Marina. 1983. *Alone of All Her Sex: The Myth and the Cult of the Virgin Mary.* New York: Random House.

Zamora, Margarita. 1988. *Language, Authority, and Indigenous History in the* Comentarios reales de los incas. Cambridge, England: Cambridge University Press.

Zárate, Agustín de. [1555] 1913. *Historia del descubrimiento y conquista del Perú. Historiadores Primitivos de Indias,* vol. 2. Madrid: Atlas.

Zimmerman, Arthur Franklin. 1938. *Francisco de Toledo.* Caldwell, England: The Caxton Printers.

Zuidema, R. T. 1964. *The Ceque System of Cuzco: The Social Organization of the Capital of the Inca.* Leiden, The Netherlands: E. J. Brill.

———. 1993. "De la Tarasca a Mama Huaco: La historia de un mito y rito cuzqueño." In Duviols, *Religions des Andes,* 331–381.

Index